Downers Grove Public Library
1050 Curtiss St.
Downers Grove, IL 60515
(630) 960-1200
www.downersgrovelibrary.org

GAYLORD

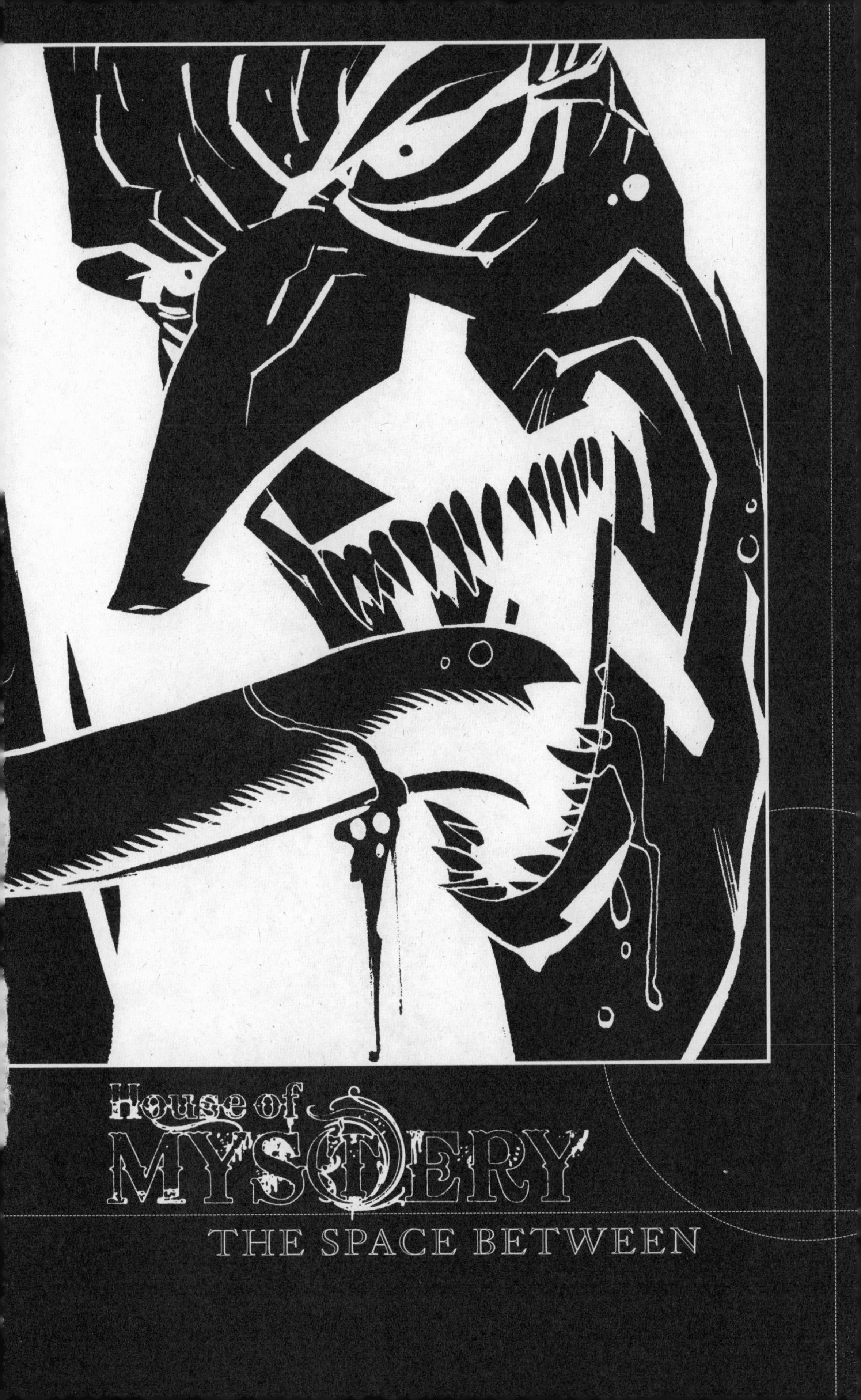

House of MYSTERY

THE SPACE BETWEEN

KAREN BERGER   SVP – EXECUTIVE EDITOR
ANGELA RUFINO
SHELLY BOND   EDITORS – ORIGINAL SERIES
GEORG BREWER   VP – DESIGN & DC DIRECT CREATIVE
BOB HARRAS   GROUP EDITOR – COLLECTED EDITIONS
SCOTT NYBAKKEN   EDITOR
ROBBIN BROSTERMAN   DESIGN DIRECTOR – BOOKS

DC COMICS

PAUL LEVITZ   PRESIDENT & PUBLISHER
RICHARD BRUNING   SVP – CREATIVE DIRECTOR
PATRICK CALDON   EVP – FINANCE & OPERATIONS
AMY GENKINS   SVP – BUSINESS & LEGAL AFFAIRS
JIM LEE   EDITORIAL DIRECTOR – WILDSTORM
GREGORY NOVECK   SVP – CREATIVE AFFAIRS
STEVE ROTTERDAM   SVP – SALES & MARKETING
CHERYL RUBIN   SVP – BRAND MANAGEMENT

COVER ILLUSTRATION BY ESAO ANDREWS.

HOUSE OF MYSTERY: THE SPACE BETWEEN
PUBLISHED BY DC COMICS. COVER, SKETCHES AND COMPILATION
COPYRIGHT © 2010 DC COMICS. ALL RIGHTS RESERVED. ORIGINALLY
PUBLISHED IN SINGLE MAGAZINE FORM AS HOUSE OF MYSTERY
11-15. COPYRIGHT © 2009 DC COMICS. ALL RIGHTS RESERVED.
ALL CHARACTERS, THEIR DISTINCTIVE LIKENESSES AND RELATED
ELEMENTS FEATURED IN THIS PUBLICATION ARE TRADEMARKS OF
DC COMICS. THE STORIES, CHARACTERS AND INCIDENTS FEATURED
IN THIS PUBLICATION ARE ENTIRELY FICTIONAL. DC COMICS DOES
NOT READ OR ACCEPT UNSOLICITED SUBMISSIONS OF IDEAS,
STORIES OR ARTWORK. DC COMICS. 1700 BROADWAY, NEW YORK, NY
10019. A WARNER BROS. ENTERTAINMENT COMPANY. PRINTED BY
WORLD COLOR PRESS, INC., ST-ROMUALD, QC, CANADA 12/30/09.
FIRST PRINTING. ISBN: 978-1-4012-2581-0

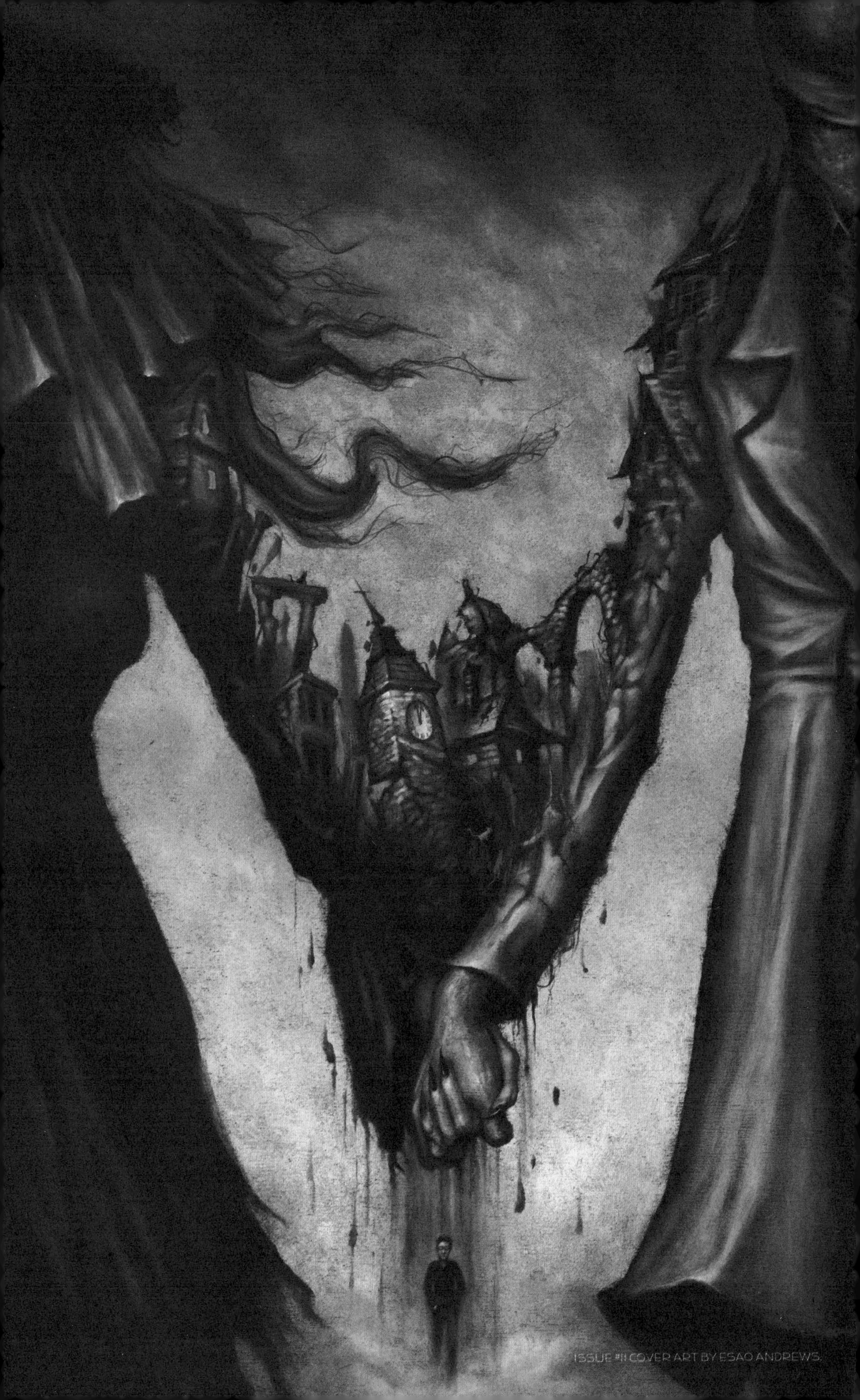
ISSUE #11 COVER ART BY ESAO ANDREWS.

House of MYSTERY
THE SPACE BETWEEN

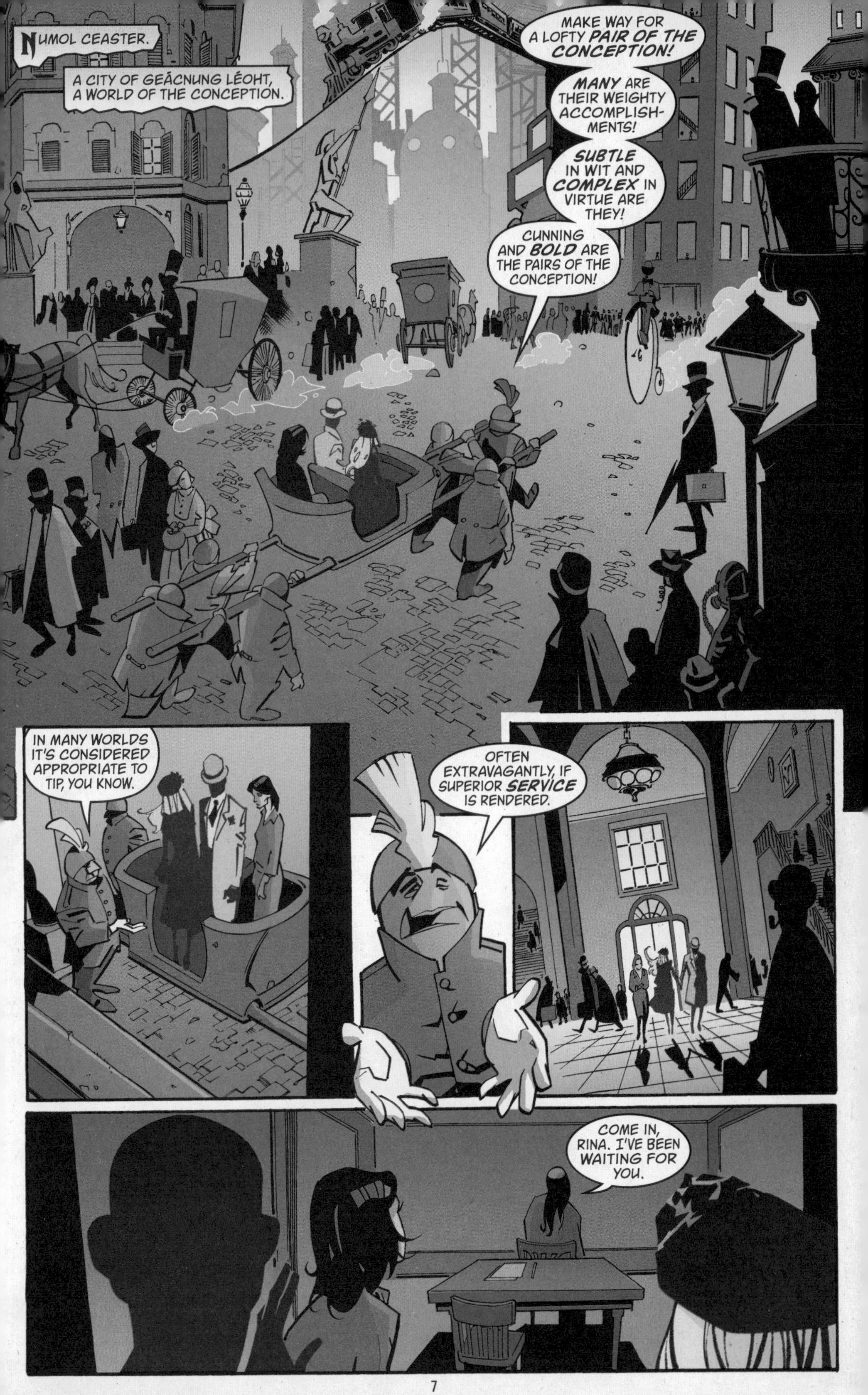
NUMOL CEASTER.
A CITY OF GEÁCNUNG LÉOHT, A WORLD OF THE CONCEPTION.
MAKE WAY FOR A LOFTY PAIR OF THE CONCEPTION!
MANY ARE THEIR WEIGHTY ACCOMPLISHMENTS!
SUBTLE IN WIT AND COMPLEX IN VIRTUE ARE THEY!
CUNNING AND BOLD ARE THE PAIRS OF THE CONCEPTION!
IN MANY WORLDS IT'S CONSIDERED APPROPRIATE TO TIP, YOU KNOW.
OFTEN EXTRAVAGANTLY, IF SUPERIOR SERVICE IS RENDERED.
COME IN, RINA. I'VE BEEN WAITING FOR YOU.

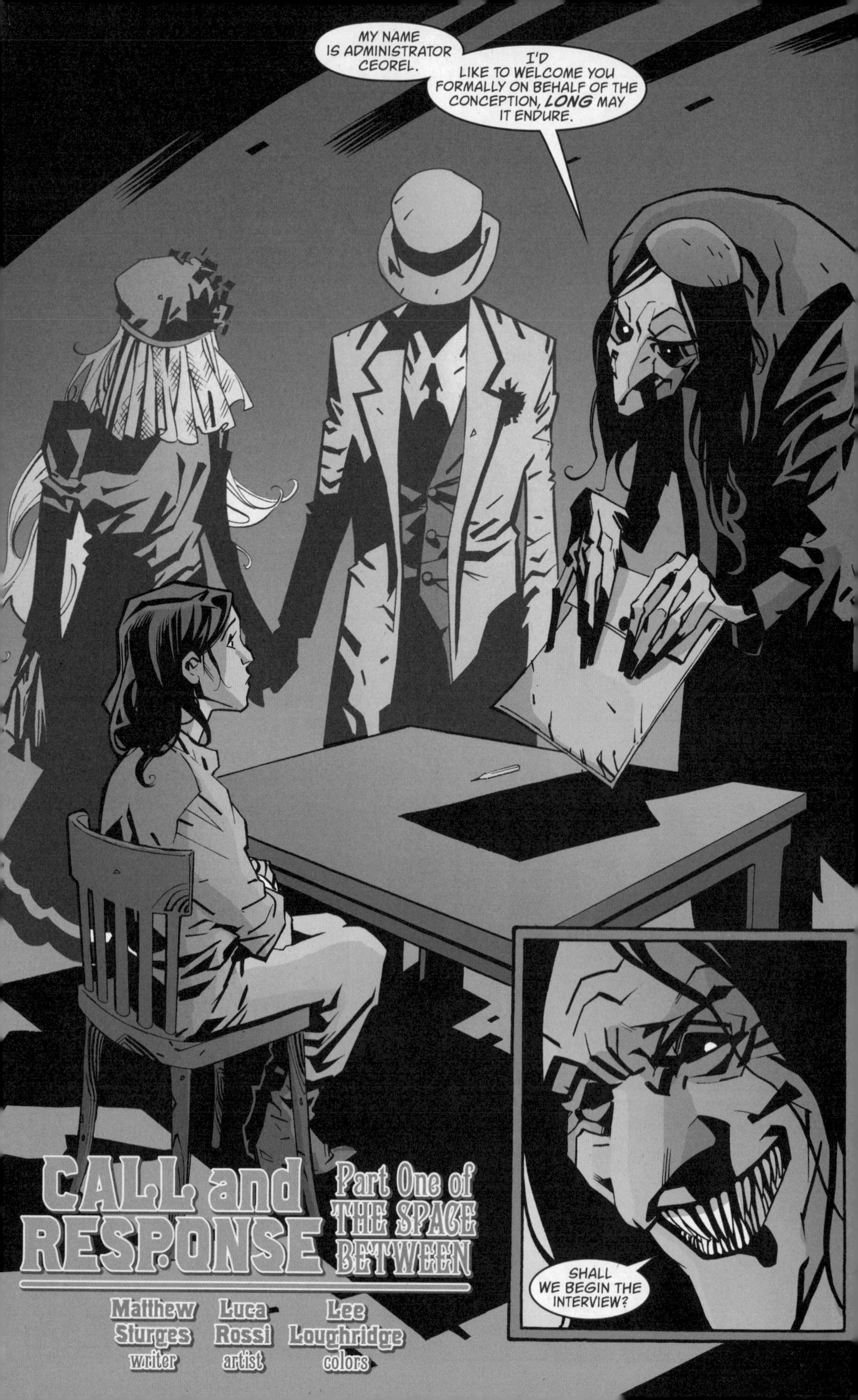
MY NAME IS ADMINISTRATOR CEOREL.
I'D LIKE TO WELCOME YOU FORMALLY ON BEHALF OF THE CONCEPTION, LONG MAY IT ENDURE.
SHALL WE BEGIN THE INTERVIEW?
CALL and RESPONSE
Part One of THE SPACE BETWEEN
Matthew Sturges writer
Luca Rossi artist
Lee Loughridge colors

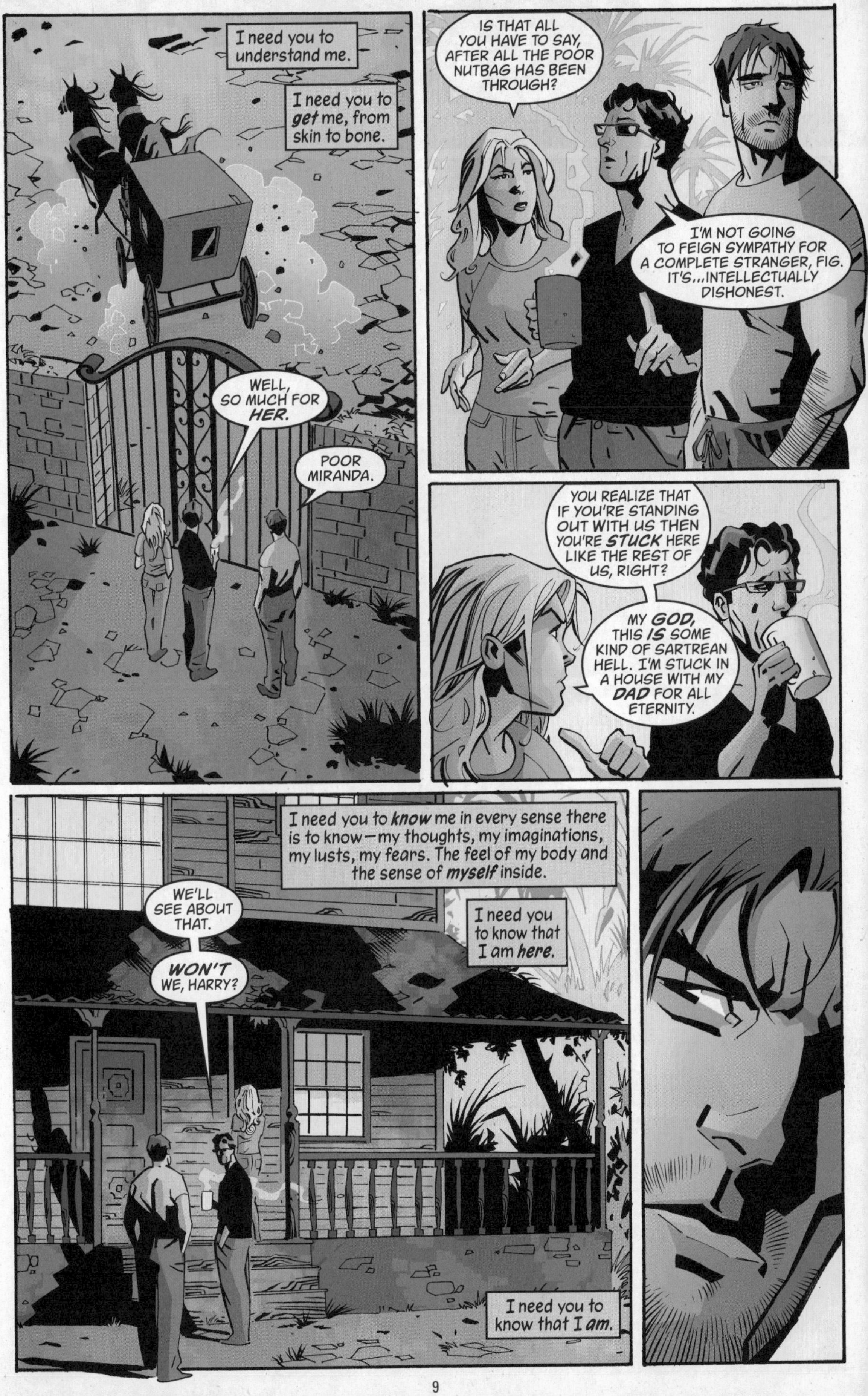
I need you to understand me.
I need you to *get* me, from skin to bone.
WELL, SO MUCH FOR *HER.*
POOR MIRANDA.
IS THAT ALL YOU HAVE TO SAY, AFTER ALL THE POOR NUTBAG HAS BEEN THROUGH?
I'M NOT GOING TO FEIGN SYMPATHY FOR A COMPLETE STRANGER, FIG. IT'S...INTELLECTUALLY DISHONEST.
YOU REALIZE THAT IF YOU'RE STANDING OUT WITH US THEN YOU'RE *STUCK* HERE LIKE THE REST OF US, RIGHT?
MY *GOD,* THIS *IS* SOME KIND OF SARTREAN HELL. I'M STUCK IN A HOUSE WITH MY *DAD* FOR ALL ETERNITY.
I need you to *know* me in every sense there is to know—my thoughts, my imaginations, my lusts, my fears. The feel of my body and the sense of *myself* inside.
WE'LL SEE ABOUT THAT.
WON'T WE, HARRY?
I need you to know that I am *here.*
I need you to know that I *am.*

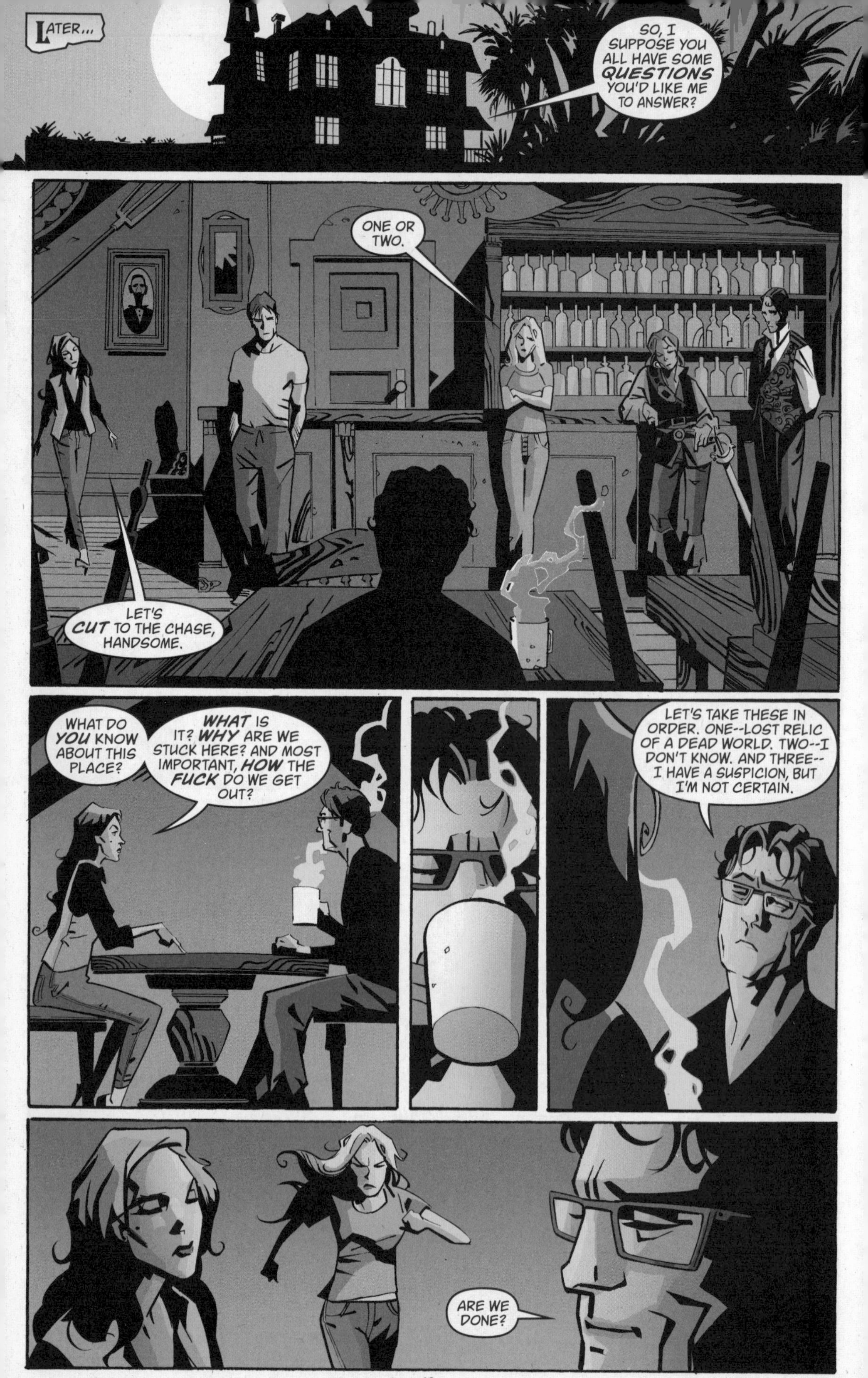
LATER...
SO, I SUPPOSE YOU ALL HAVE SOME QUESTIONS YOU'D LIKE ME TO ANSWER?
ONE OR TWO.
LET'S CUT TO THE CHASE, HANDSOME.
WHAT DO YOU KNOW ABOUT THIS PLACE?
WHAT IS IT? WHY ARE WE STUCK HERE? AND MOST IMPORTANT, HOW THE FUCK DO WE GET OUT?
LET'S TAKE THESE IN ORDER. ONE--LOST RELIC OF A DEAD WORLD. TWO--I DON'T KNOW. AND THREE--I HAVE A SUSPICION, BUT I'M NOT CERTAIN.
ARE WE DONE?

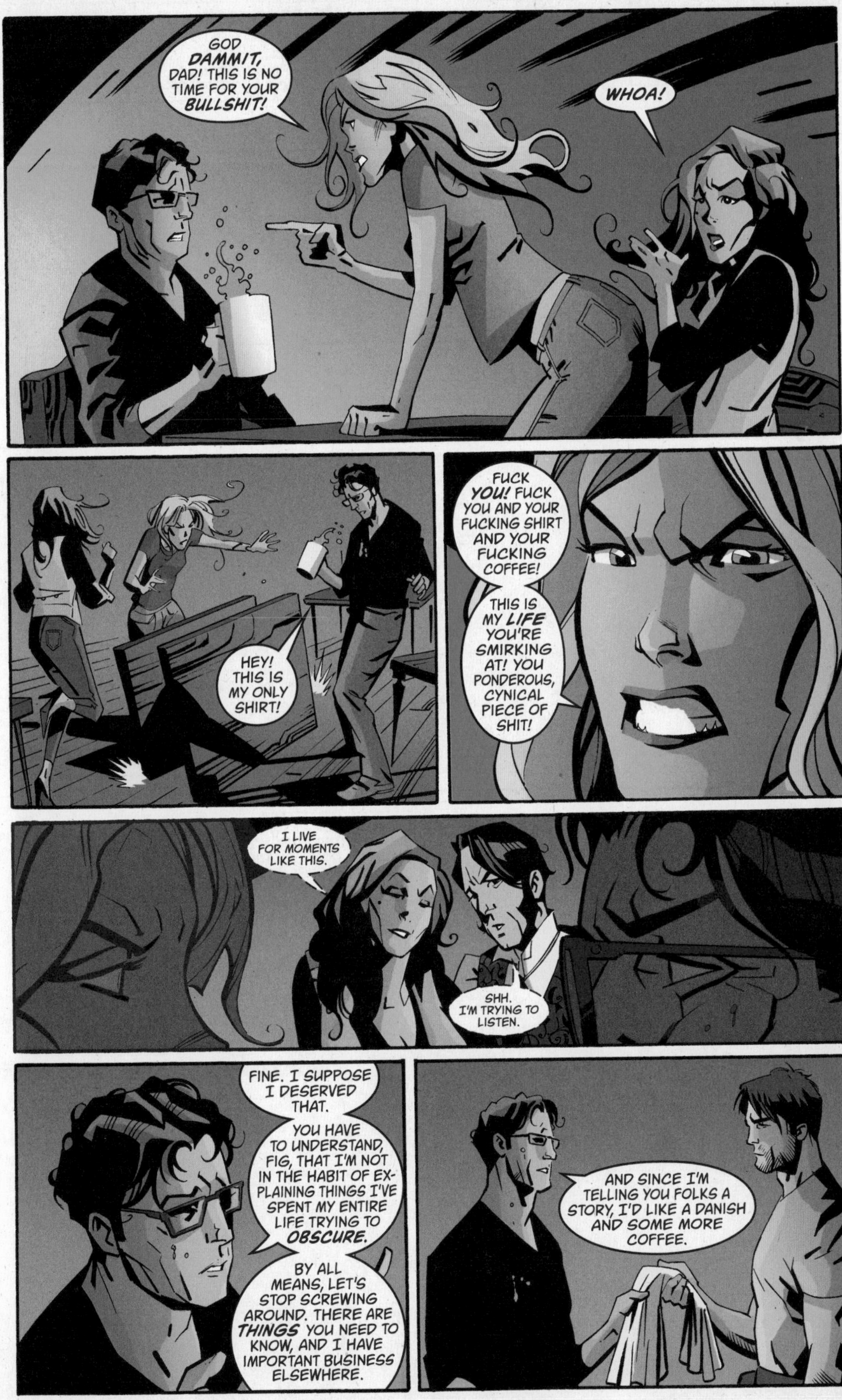
GOD DAMMIT, DAD! THIS IS NO TIME FOR YOUR BULLSHIT!
WHOA!
HEY! THIS IS MY ONLY SHIRT!
FUCK YOU! FUCK YOU AND YOUR FUCKING SHIRT AND YOUR FUCKING COFFEE!
THIS IS MY LIFE YOU'RE SMIRKING AT! YOU PONDEROUS, CYNICAL PIECE OF SHIT!
I LIVE FOR MOMENTS LIKE THIS.
SHH. I'M TRYING TO LISTEN.
FINE. I SUPPOSE I DESERVED THAT.
YOU HAVE TO UNDERSTAND, FIG, THAT I'M NOT IN THE HABIT OF EX-PLAINING THINGS I'VE SPENT MY ENTIRE LIFE TRYING TO OBSCURE.
BY ALL MEANS, LET'S STOP SCREWING AROUND. THERE ARE THINGS YOU NEED TO KNOW, AND I HAVE IMPORTANT BUSINESS ELSEWHERE.
AND SINCE I'M TELLING YOU FOLKS A STORY, I'D LIKE A DANISH AND SOME MORE COFFEE.

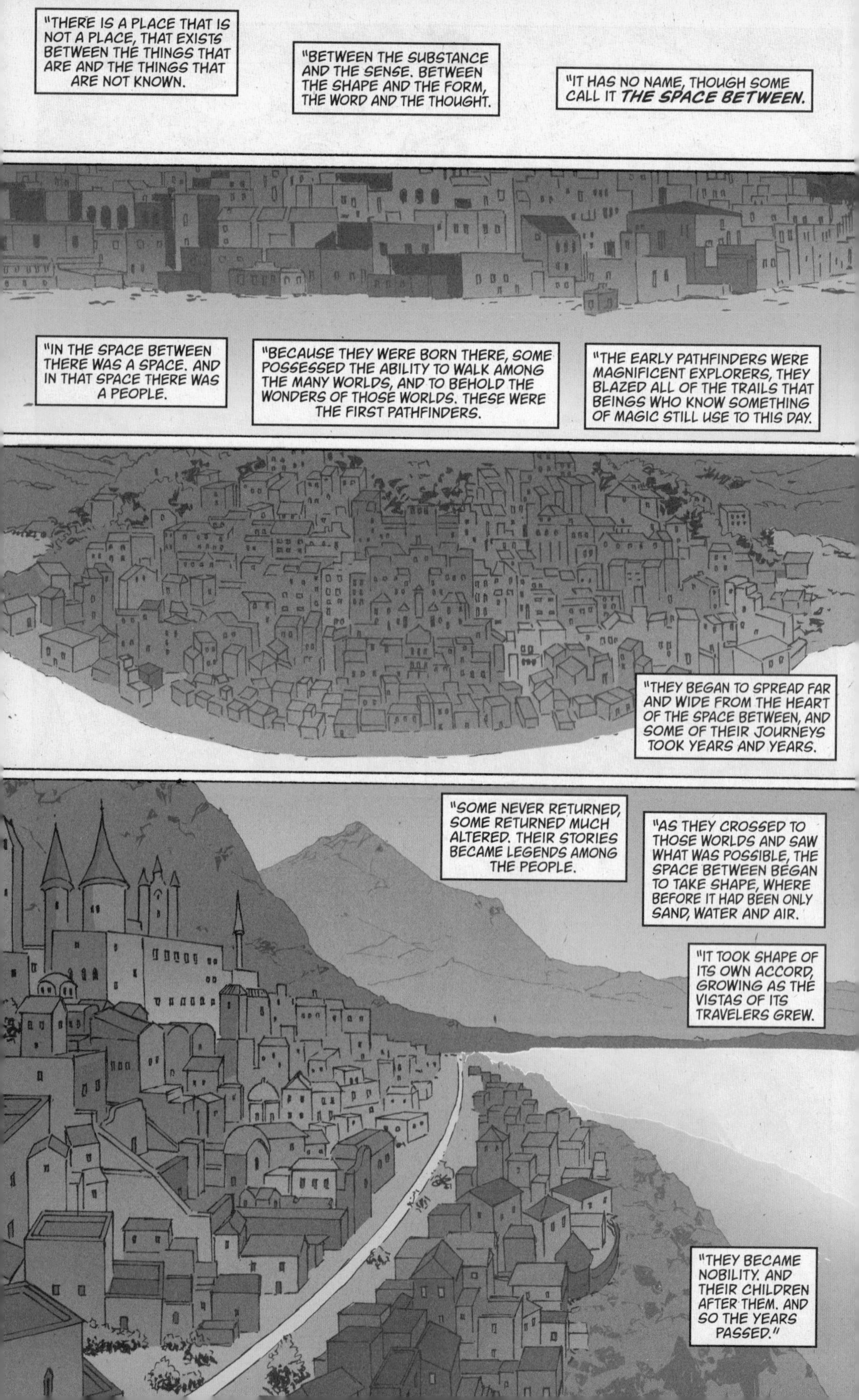
"THERE IS A PLACE THAT IS NOT A PLACE, THAT EXISTS BETWEEN THE THINGS THAT ARE AND THE THINGS THAT ARE NOT KNOWN.
"BETWEEN THE SUBSTANCE AND THE SENSE. BETWEEN THE SHAPE AND THE FORM, THE WORD AND THE THOUGHT.
"IT HAS NO NAME, THOUGH SOME CALL IT ***THE SPACE BETWEEN.***
"IN THE SPACE BETWEEN THERE WAS A SPACE. AND IN THAT SPACE THERE WAS A PEOPLE.
"BECAUSE THEY WERE BORN THERE, SOME POSSESSED THE ABILITY TO WALK AMONG THE MANY WORLDS, AND TO BEHOLD THE WONDERS OF THOSE WORLDS. THESE WERE THE FIRST PATHFINDERS.
"THE EARLY PATHFINDERS WERE MAGNIFICENT EXPLORERS, THEY BLAZED ALL OF THE TRAILS THAT BEINGS WHO KNOW SOMETHING OF MAGIC STILL USE TO THIS DAY.
"THEY BEGAN TO SPREAD FAR AND WIDE FROM THE HEART OF THE SPACE BETWEEN, AND SOME OF THEIR JOURNEYS TOOK YEARS AND YEARS.
"SOME NEVER RETURNED, SOME RETURNED MUCH ALTERED. THEIR STORIES BECAME LEGENDS AMONG THE PEOPLE.
"AS THEY CROSSED TO THOSE WORLDS AND SAW WHAT WAS POSSIBLE, THE SPACE BETWEEN BEGAN TO TAKE SHAPE, WHERE BEFORE IT HAD BEEN ONLY SAND, WATER AND AIR.
"IT TOOK SHAPE OF ITS OWN ACCORD, GROWING AS THE VISTAS OF ITS TRAVELERS GREW.
"THEY BECAME NOBILITY. AND THEIR CHILDREN AFTER THEM. AND SO THE YEARS PASSED."

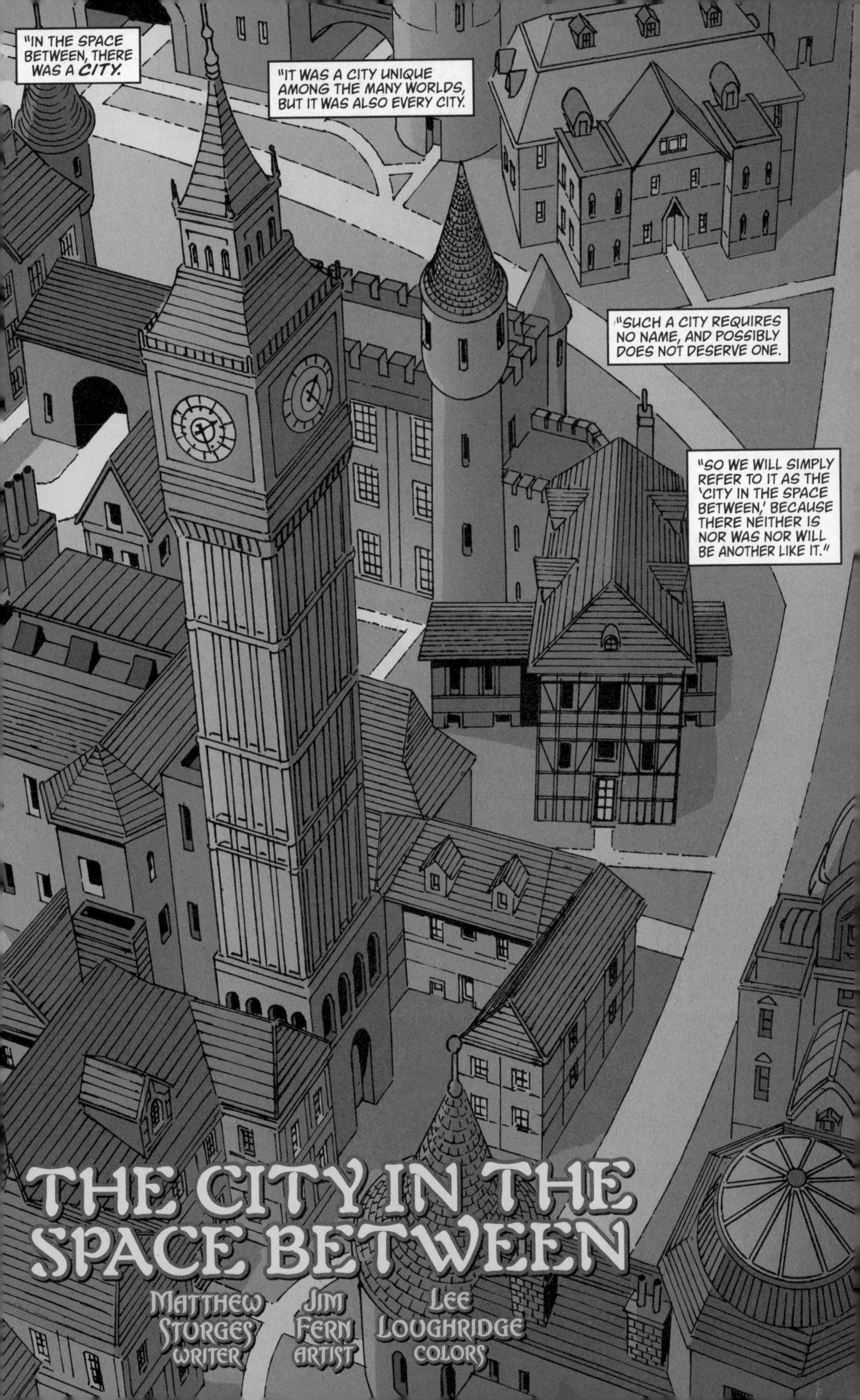

"IN THE SPACE BETWEEN, THERE WAS A *CITY.*
"IT WAS A CITY UNIQUE AMONG THE MANY WORLDS, BUT IT WAS ALSO EVERY CITY.
"SUCH A CITY REQUIRES NO NAME, AND POSSIBLY DOES NOT DESERVE ONE.
"SO WE WILL SIMPLY REFER TO IT AS THE 'CITY IN THE SPACE BETWEEN,' BECAUSE THERE NEITHER IS NOR WAS NOR WILL BE ANOTHER LIKE IT."
THE CITY IN THE SPACE BETWEEN
MATTHEW STURGES WRITER
JIM FERN ARTIST
LEE LOUGHRIDGE COLORS

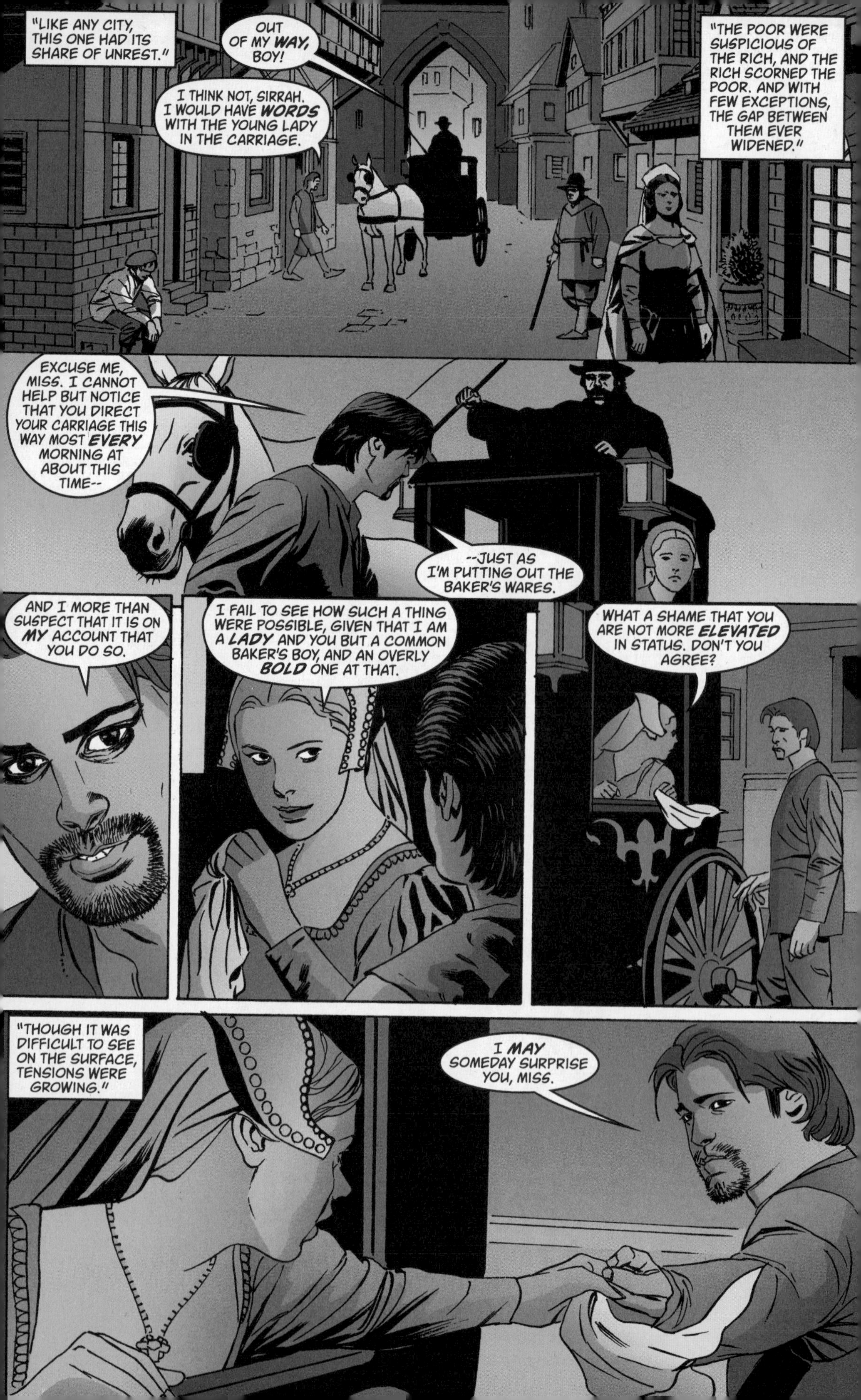
"LIKE ANY CITY, THIS ONE HAD ITS SHARE OF UNREST."
OUT OF MY *WAY,* BOY!
I THINK NOT, SIRRAH. I WOULD HAVE *WORDS* WITH THE YOUNG LADY IN THE CARRIAGE.
"THE POOR WERE SUSPICIOUS OF THE RICH, AND THE RICH SCORNED THE POOR. AND WITH FEW EXCEPTIONS, THE GAP BETWEEN THEM EVER WIDENED."
EXCUSE ME, MISS. I CANNOT HELP BUT NOTICE THAT YOU DIRECT YOUR CARRIAGE THIS WAY MOST *EVERY* MORNING AT ABOUT THIS TIME--
--JUST AS I'M PUTTING OUT THE BAKER'S WARES.
AND I MORE THAN SUSPECT THAT IT IS ON *MY* ACCOUNT THAT YOU DO SO.
I FAIL TO SEE HOW SUCH A THING WERE POSSIBLE, GIVEN THAT I AM A *LADY* AND YOU BUT A COMMON BAKER'S BOY, AND AN OVERLY *BOLD* ONE AT THAT.
WHAT A SHAME THAT YOU ARE NOT MORE *ELEVATED* IN STATUS. DON'T YOU AGREE?
"THOUGH IT WAS DIFFICULT TO SEE ON THE SURFACE, TENSIONS WERE GROWING."
I *MAY* SOMEDAY SURPRISE YOU, MISS.

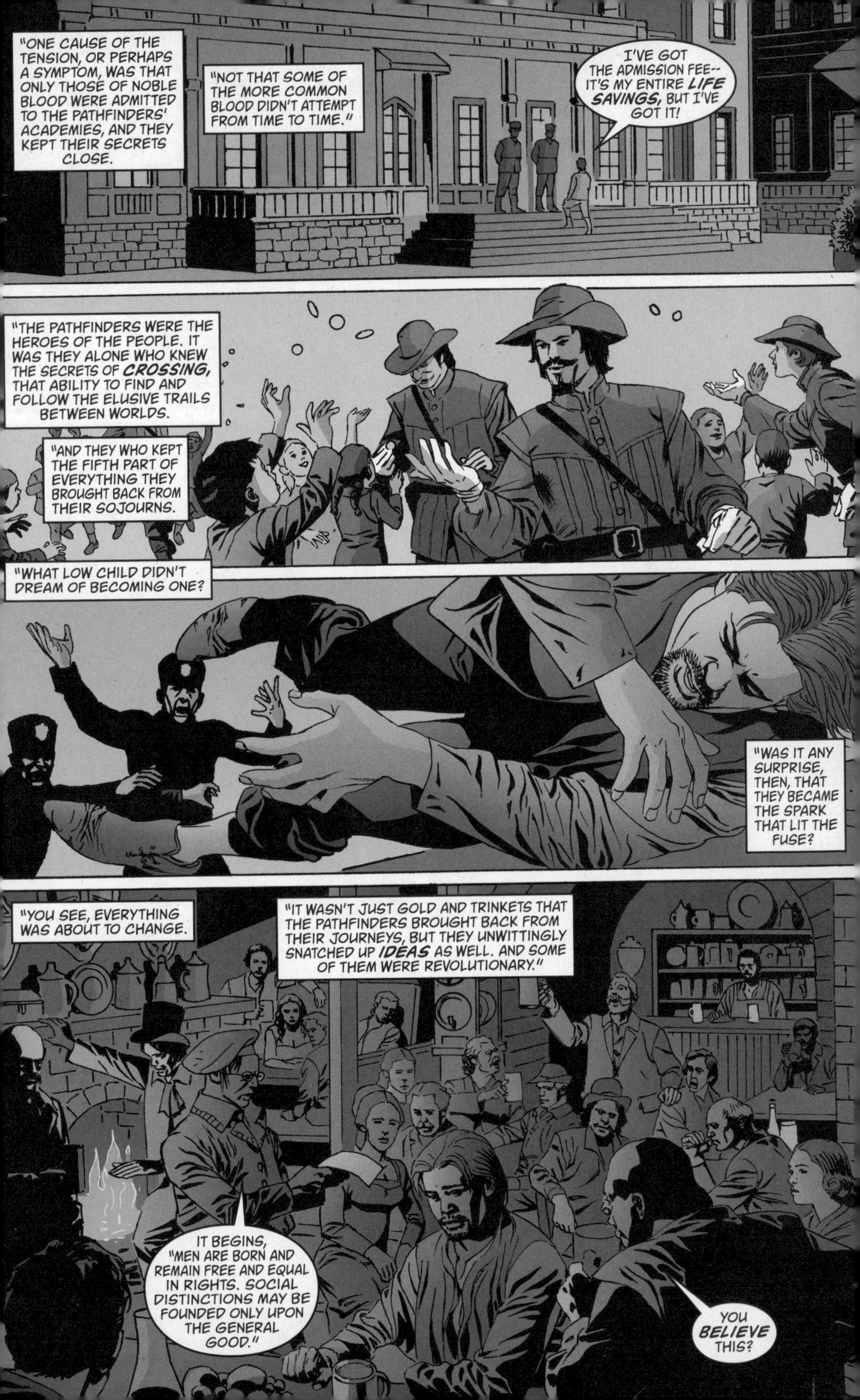
"ONE CAUSE OF THE TENSION, OR PERHAPS A SYMPTOM, WAS THAT ONLY THOSE OF NOBLE BLOOD WERE ADMITTED TO THE PATHFINDERS' ACADEMIES, AND THEY KEPT THEIR SECRETS CLOSE.
"NOT THAT SOME OF THE MORE COMMON BLOOD DIDN'T ATTEMPT FROM TIME TO TIME."
I'VE GOT THE ADMISSION FEE-- IT'S MY ENTIRE LIFE SAVINGS, BUT I'VE GOT IT!
"THE PATHFINDERS WERE THE HEROES OF THE PEOPLE. IT WAS THEY ALONE WHO KNEW THE SECRETS OF CROSSING, THAT ABILITY TO FIND AND FOLLOW THE ELUSIVE TRAILS BETWEEN WORLDS.
"AND THEY WHO KEPT THE FIFTH PART OF EVERYTHING THEY BROUGHT BACK FROM THEIR SOJOURNS.
"WHAT LOW CHILD DIDN'T DREAM OF BECOMING ONE?
"WAS IT ANY SURPRISE, THEN, THAT THEY BECAME THE SPARK THAT LIT THE FUSE?
"YOU SEE, EVERYTHING WAS ABOUT TO CHANGE.
"IT WASN'T JUST GOLD AND TRINKETS THAT THE PATHFINDERS BROUGHT BACK FROM THEIR JOURNEYS, BUT THEY UNWITTINGLY SNATCHED UP IDEAS AS WELL. AND SOME OF THEM WERE REVOLUTIONARY."
IT BEGINS, "MEN ARE BORN AND REMAIN FREE AND EQUAL IN RIGHTS. SOCIAL DISTINCTIONS MAY BE FOUNDED ONLY UPON THE GENERAL GOOD."
YOU BELIEVE THIS?

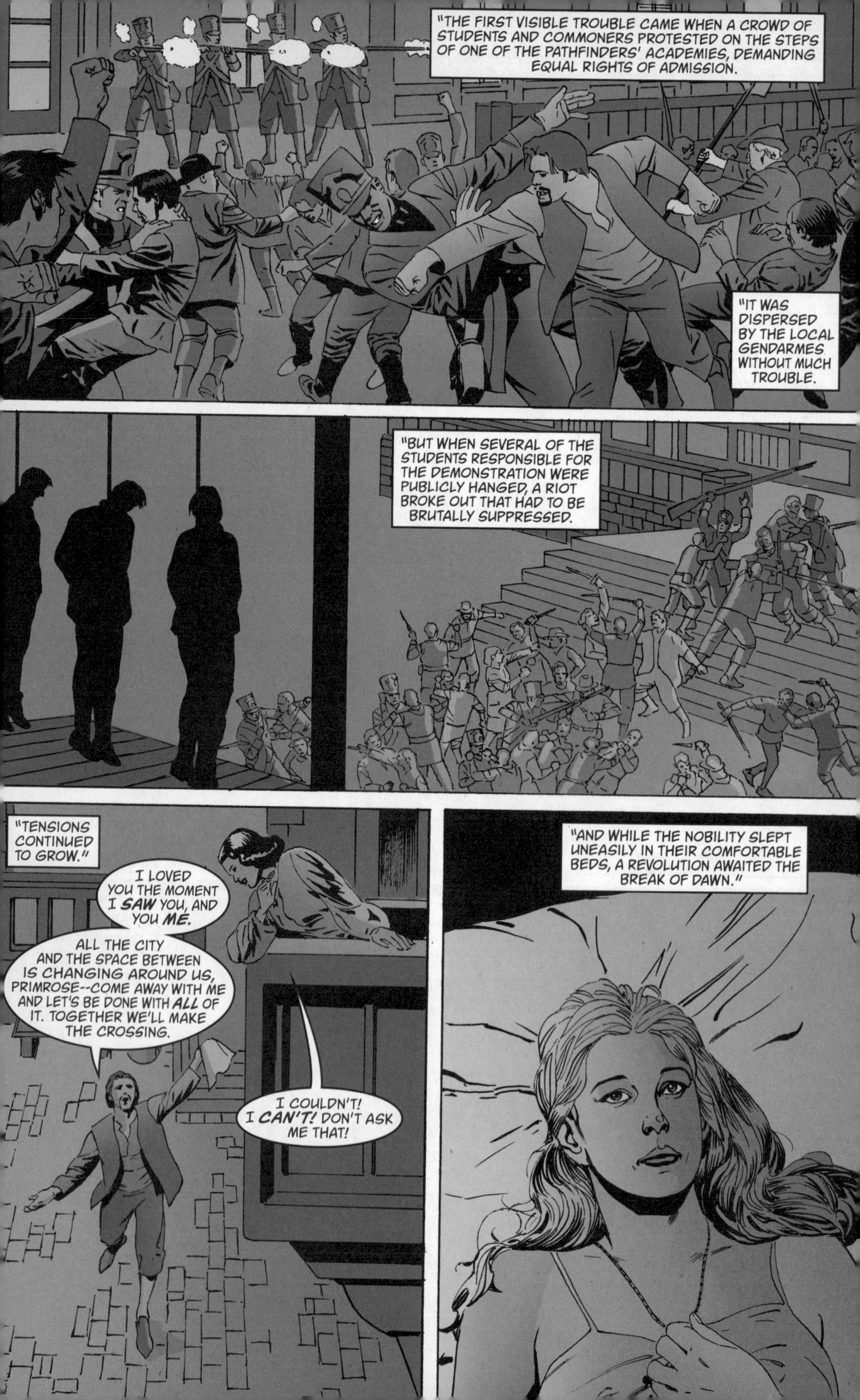
"THE FIRST VISIBLE TROUBLE CAME WHEN A CROWD OF STUDENTS AND COMMONERS PROTESTED ON THE STEPS OF ONE OF THE PATHFINDERS' ACADEMIES, DEMANDING EQUAL RIGHTS OF ADMISSION.
"IT WAS DISPERSED BY THE LOCAL GENDARMES WITHOUT MUCH TROUBLE.
"BUT WHEN SEVERAL OF THE STUDENTS RESPONSIBLE FOR THE DEMONSTRATION WERE PUBLICLY HANGED, A RIOT BROKE OUT THAT HAD TO BE BRUTALLY SUPPRESSED.
"TENSIONS CONTINUED TO GROW."
I LOVED YOU THE MOMENT I SAW YOU, AND YOU ME.
ALL THE CITY AND THE SPACE BETWEEN IS CHANGING AROUND US, PRIMROSE--COME AWAY WITH ME AND LET'S BE DONE WITH ALL OF IT. TOGETHER WE'LL MAKE THE CROSSING.
I COULDN'T! I CAN'T! DON'T ASK ME THAT!
"AND WHILE THE NOBILITY SLEPT UNEASILY IN THEIR COMFORTABLE BEDS, A REVOLUTION AWAITED THE BREAK OF DAWN."

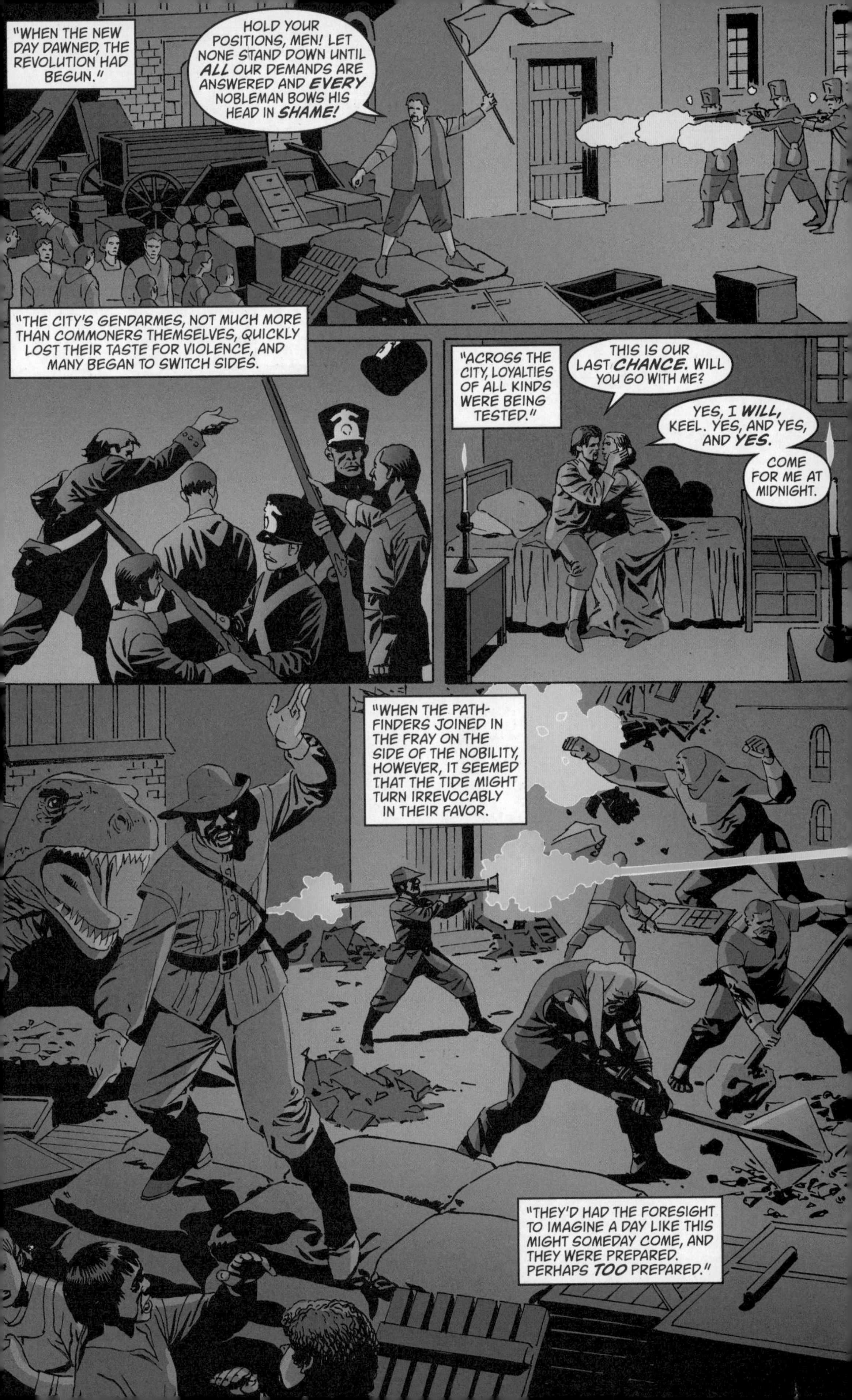

"WHEN THE NEW DAY DAWNED, THE REVOLUTION HAD BEGUN."
HOLD YOUR POSITIONS, MEN! LET NONE STAND DOWN UNTIL ALL OUR DEMANDS ARE ANSWERED AND EVERY NOBLEMAN BOWS HIS HEAD IN SHAME!
"THE CITY'S GENDARMES, NOT MUCH MORE THAN COMMONERS THEMSELVES, QUICKLY LOST THEIR TASTE FOR VIOLENCE, AND MANY BEGAN TO SWITCH SIDES.
"ACROSS THE CITY, LOYALTIES OF ALL KINDS WERE BEING TESTED."
THIS IS OUR LAST CHANCE. WILL YOU GO WITH ME?
YES, I WILL, KEEL. YES, AND YES, AND YES.
COME FOR ME AT MIDNIGHT.
"WHEN THE PATH-FINDERS JOINED IN THE FRAY ON THE SIDE OF THE NOBILITY, HOWEVER, IT SEEMED THAT THE TIDE MIGHT TURN IRREVOCABLY IN THEIR FAVOR.
"THEY'D HAD THE FORESIGHT TO IMAGINE A DAY LIKE THIS MIGHT SOMEDAY COME, AND THEY WERE PREPARED. PERHAPS TOO PREPARED."

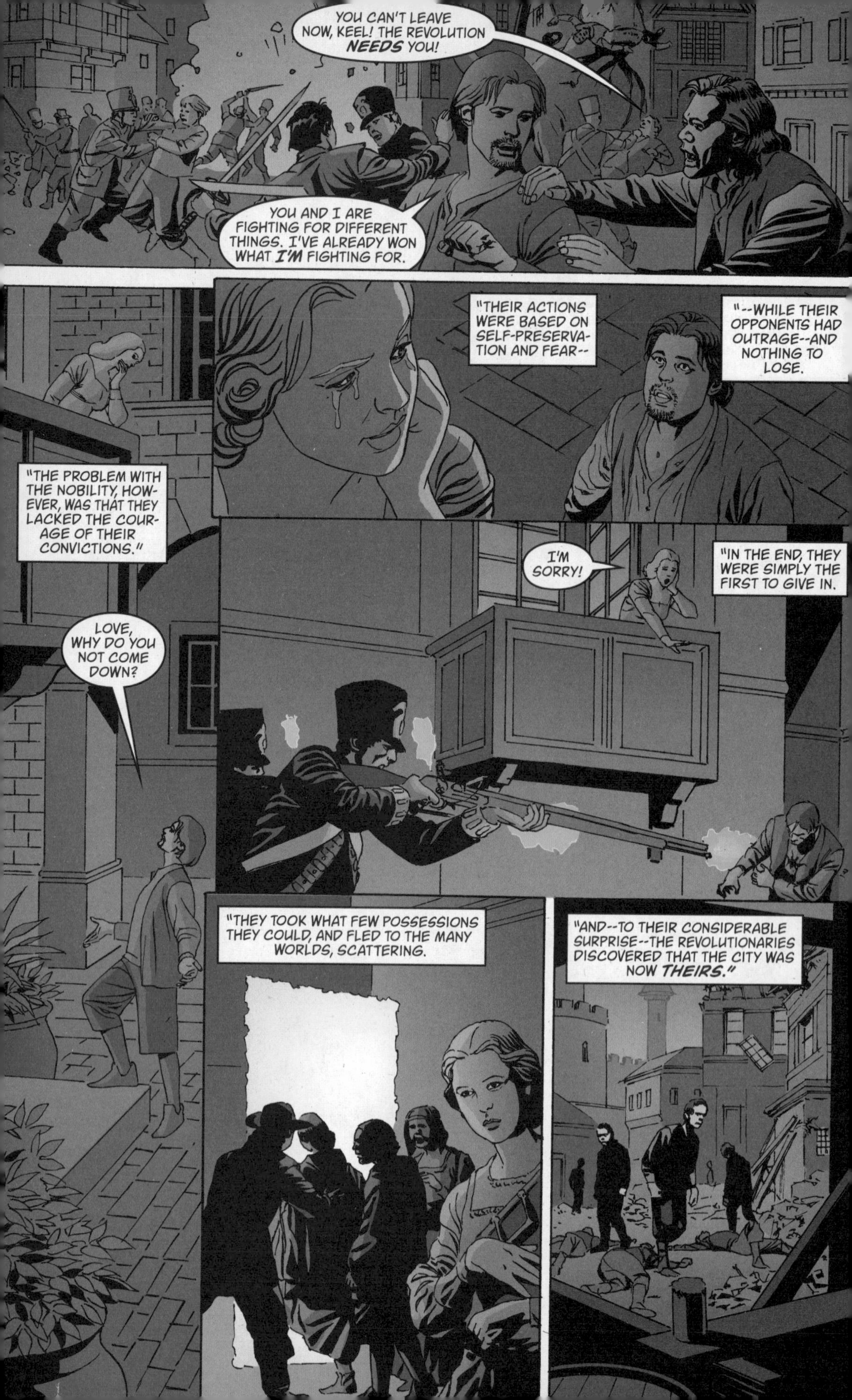

YOU CAN'T LEAVE NOW, KEEL! THE REVOLUTION NEEDS YOU!
YOU AND I ARE FIGHTING FOR DIFFERENT THINGS. I'VE ALREADY WON WHAT I'M FIGHTING FOR.
"THEIR ACTIONS WERE BASED ON SELF-PRESERVATION AND FEAR--
"--WHILE THEIR OPPONENTS HAD OUTRAGE--AND NOTHING TO LOSE.
"THE PROBLEM WITH THE NOBILITY, HOWEVER, WAS THAT THEY LACKED THE COURAGE OF THEIR CONVICTIONS."
LOVE, WHY DO YOU NOT COME DOWN?
I'M SORRY!
"IN THE END, THEY WERE SIMPLY THE FIRST TO GIVE IN.
"THEY TOOK WHAT FEW POSSESSIONS THEY COULD, AND FLED TO THE MANY WORLDS, SCATTERING.
"AND--TO THEIR CONSIDERABLE SURPRISE--THE REVOLUTIONARIES DISCOVERED THAT THE CITY WAS NOW THEIRS."

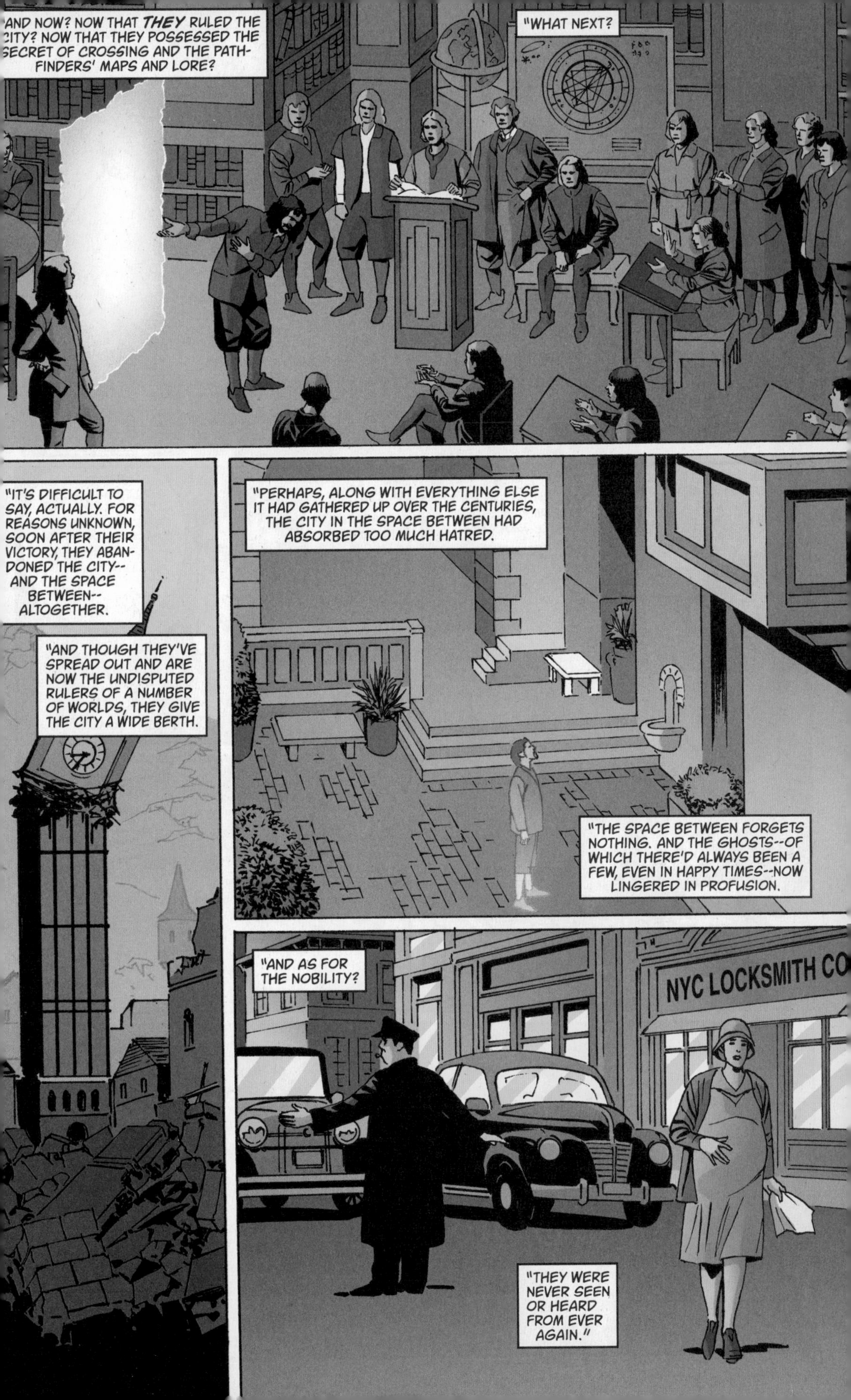
AND NOW? NOW THAT THEY RULED THE CITY? NOW THAT THEY POSSESSED THE SECRET OF CROSSING AND THE PATHFINDERS' MAPS AND LORE?
"WHAT NEXT?
"IT'S DIFFICULT TO SAY, ACTUALLY. FOR REASONS UNKNOWN, SOON AFTER THEIR VICTORY, THEY ABANDONED THE CITY-- AND THE SPACE BETWEEN-- ALTOGETHER.
"AND THOUGH THEY'VE SPREAD OUT AND ARE NOW THE UNDISPUTED RULERS OF A NUMBER OF WORLDS, THEY GIVE THE CITY A WIDE BERTH.
"PERHAPS, ALONG WITH EVERYTHING ELSE IT HAD GATHERED UP OVER THE CENTURIES, THE CITY IN THE SPACE BETWEEN HAD ABSORBED TOO MUCH HATRED.
"THE SPACE BETWEEN FORGETS NOTHING. AND THE GHOSTS--OF WHICH THERE'D ALWAYS BEEN A FEW, EVEN IN HAPPY TIMES--NOW LINGERED IN PROFUSION.
"AND AS FOR THE NOBILITY?
NYC LOCKSMITH CO
"THEY WERE NEVER SEEN OR HEARD FROM EVER AGAIN."

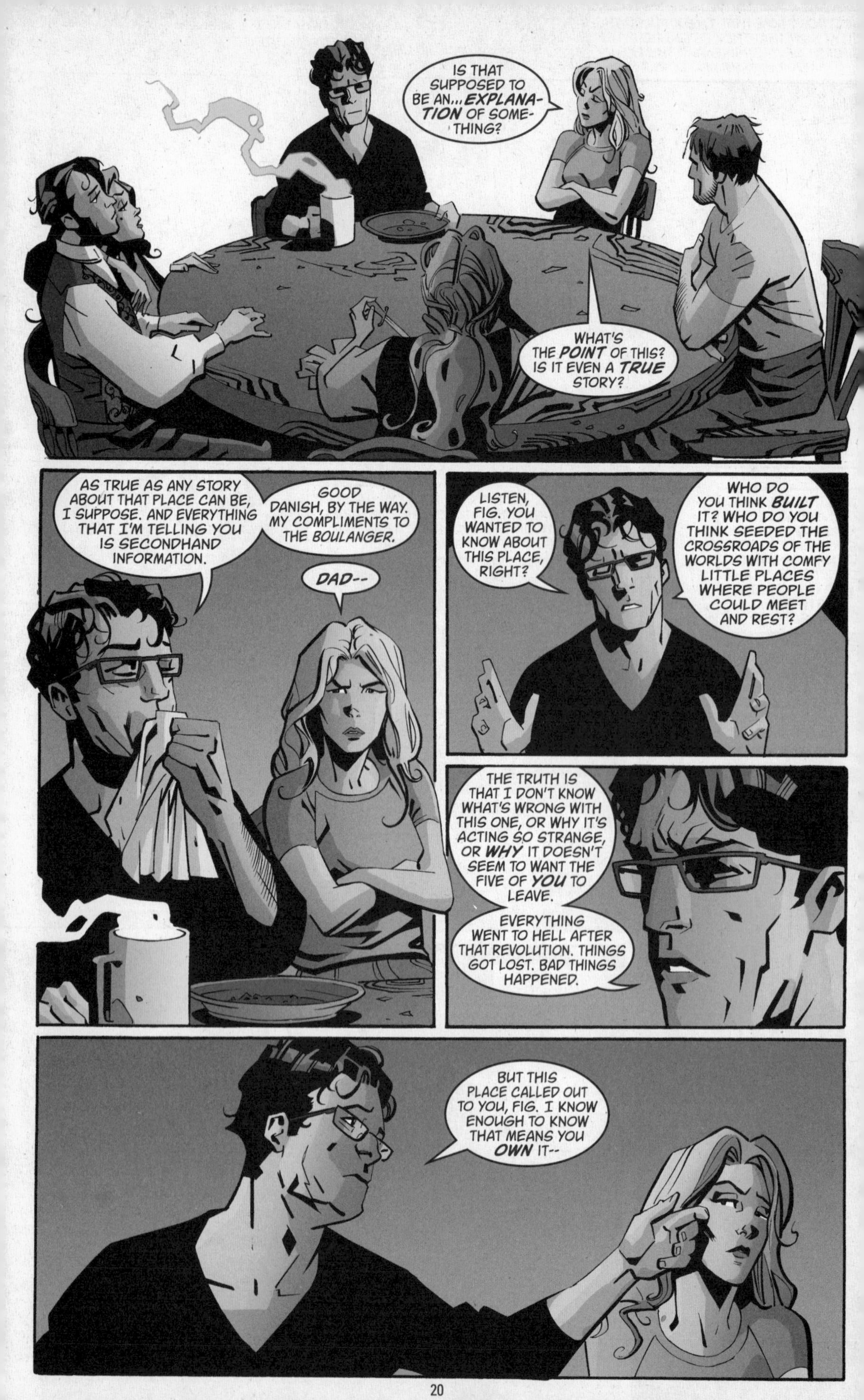
IS THAT SUPPOSED TO BE AN... EXPLANATION OF SOMETHING?
WHAT'S THE POINT OF THIS? IS IT EVEN A TRUE STORY?
AS TRUE AS ANY STORY ABOUT THAT PLACE CAN BE, I SUPPOSE. AND EVERYTHING THAT I'M TELLING YOU IS SECONDHAND INFORMATION.
GOOD DANISH, BY THE WAY. MY COMPLIMENTS TO THE BOULANGER.
DAD--
LISTEN, FIG. YOU WANTED TO KNOW ABOUT THIS PLACE, RIGHT?
WHO DO YOU THINK BUILT IT? WHO DO YOU THINK SEEDED THE CROSSROADS OF THE WORLDS WITH COMFY LITTLE PLACES WHERE PEOPLE COULD MEET AND REST?
THE TRUTH IS THAT I DON'T KNOW WHAT'S WRONG WITH THIS ONE, OR WHY IT'S ACTING SO STRANGE, OR WHY IT DOESN'T SEEM TO WANT THE FIVE OF YOU TO LEAVE.
EVERYTHING WENT TO HELL AFTER THAT REVOLUTION. THINGS GOT LOST. BAD THINGS HAPPENED.
BUT THIS PLACE CALLED OUT TO YOU, FIG. I KNOW ENOUGH TO KNOW THAT MEANS YOU OWN IT--

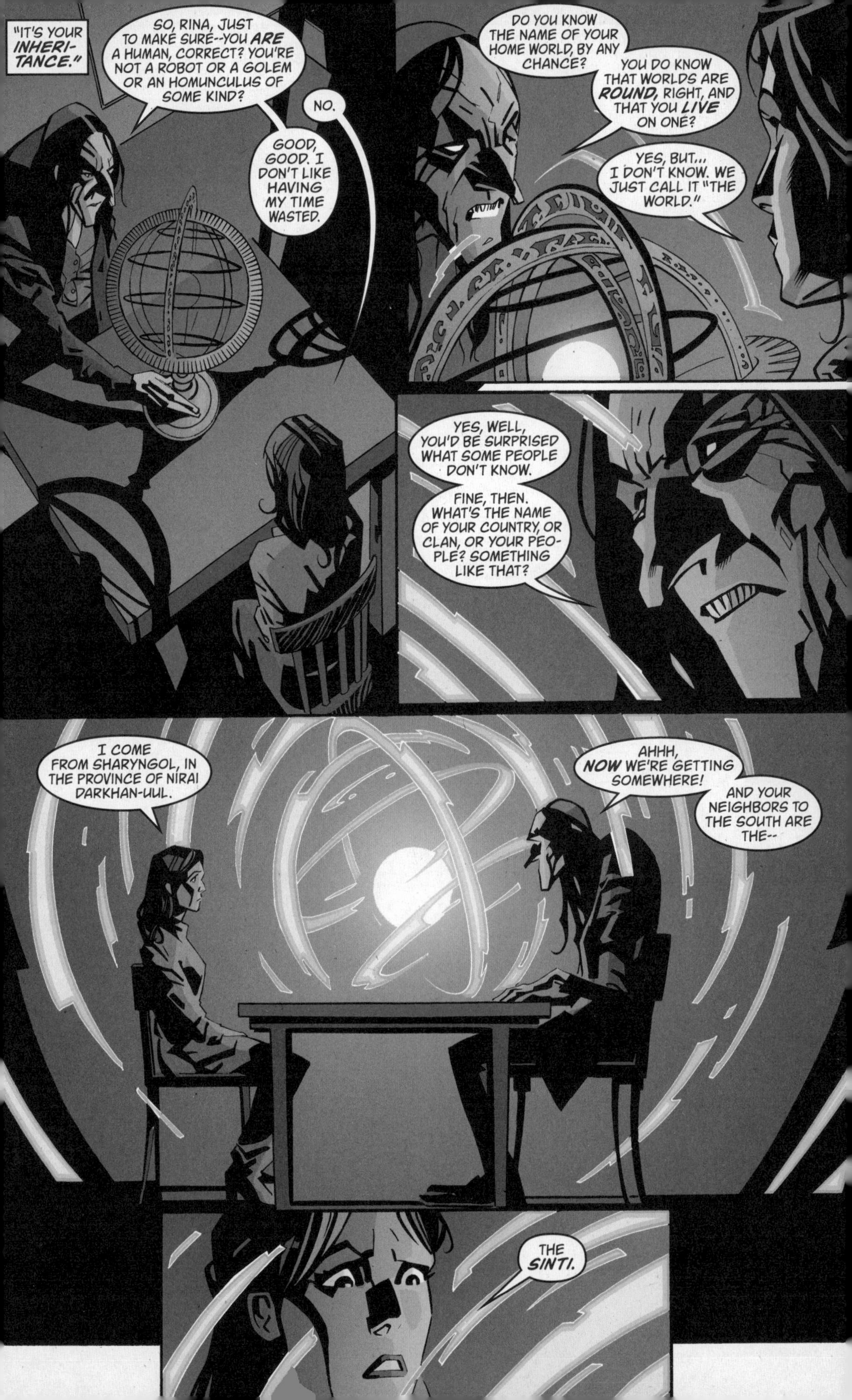
"IT'S YOUR INHERITANCE."
SO, RINA, JUST TO MAKE SURE--YOU ARE A HUMAN, CORRECT? YOU'RE NOT A ROBOT OR A GOLEM OR AN HOMUNCULUS OF SOME KIND?
NO.
GOOD, GOOD. I DON'T LIKE HAVING MY TIME WASTED.
DO YOU KNOW THE NAME OF YOUR HOME WORLD, BY ANY CHANCE?
YOU DO KNOW THAT WORLDS ARE ROUND, RIGHT, AND THAT YOU LIVE ON ONE?
YES, BUT... I DON'T KNOW. WE JUST CALL IT "THE WORLD."
YES, WELL, YOU'D BE SURPRISED WHAT SOME PEOPLE DON'T KNOW.
FINE, THEN. WHAT'S THE NAME OF YOUR COUNTRY, OR CLAN, OR YOUR PEOPLE? SOMETHING LIKE THAT?
I COME FROM SHARYNGOL, IN THE PROVINCE OF NIRAI DARKHAN-UUL.
AHHH, NOW WE'RE GETTING SOMEWHERE!
AND YOUR NEIGHBORS TO THE SOUTH ARE THE--
THE SINTI.

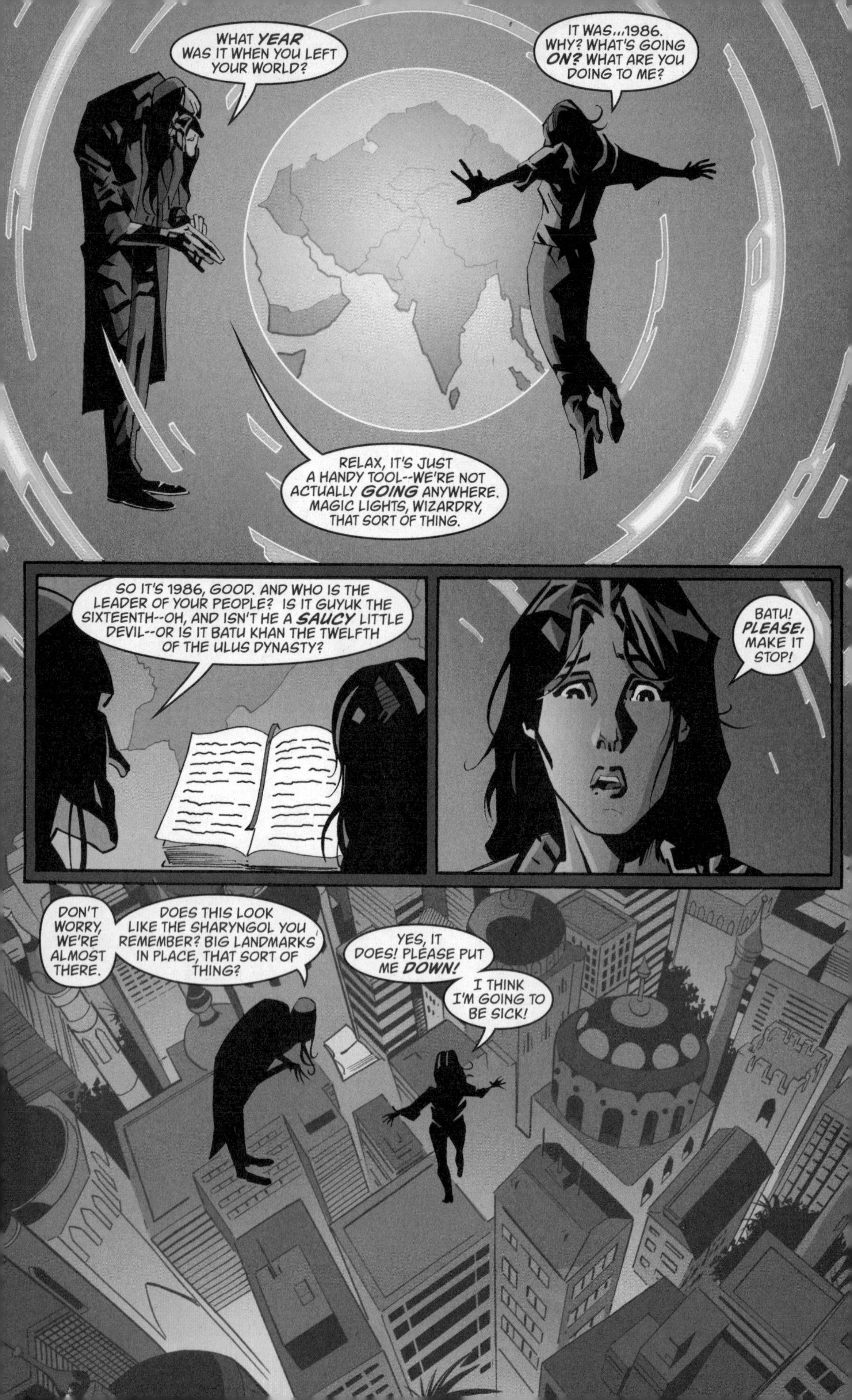

WHAT YEAR WAS IT WHEN YOU LEFT YOUR WORLD?
IT WAS...1986. WHY? WHAT'S GOING ON? WHAT ARE YOU DOING TO ME?
RELAX, IT'S JUST A HANDY TOOL--WE'RE NOT ACTUALLY GOING ANYWHERE. MAGIC LIGHTS, WIZARDRY, THAT SORT OF THING.
SO IT'S 1986, GOOD. AND WHO IS THE LEADER OF YOUR PEOPLE? IS IT GUYUK THE SIXTEENTH--OH, AND ISN'T HE A SAUCY LITTLE DEVIL--OR IS IT BATU KHAN THE TWELFTH OF THE ULUS DYNASTY?
BATU! PLEASE, MAKE IT STOP!
DON'T WORRY, WE'RE ALMOST THERE.
DOES THIS LOOK LIKE THE SHARYNGOL YOU REMEMBER? BIG LANDMARKS IN PLACE, THAT SORT OF THING?
YES, IT DOES! PLEASE PUT ME DOWN!
I THINK I'M GOING TO BE SICK!

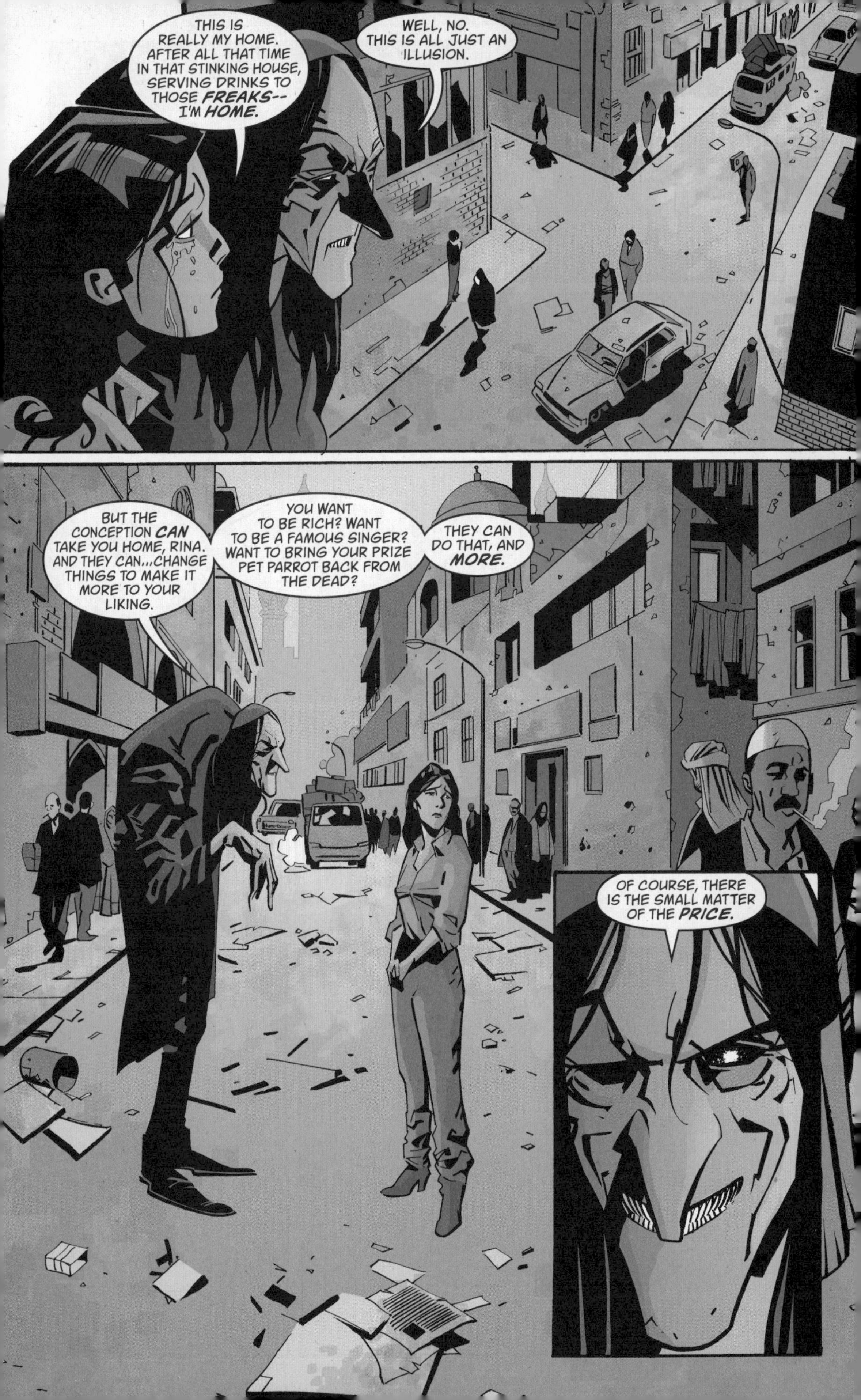
THIS IS REALLY MY HOME. AFTER ALL THAT TIME IN THAT STINKING HOUSE, SERVING DRINKS TO THOSE FREAKS-- I'M HOME.
WELL, NO. THIS IS ALL JUST AN ILLUSION.
BUT THE CONCEPTION CAN TAKE YOU HOME, RINA. AND THEY CAN...CHANGE THINGS TO MAKE IT MORE TO YOUR LIKING.
YOU WANT TO BE RICH? WANT TO BE A FAMOUS SINGER? WANT TO BRING YOUR PRIZE PET PARROT BACK FROM THE DEAD?
THEY CAN DO THAT, AND MORE.
OF COURSE, THERE IS THE SMALL MATTER OF THE PRICE.

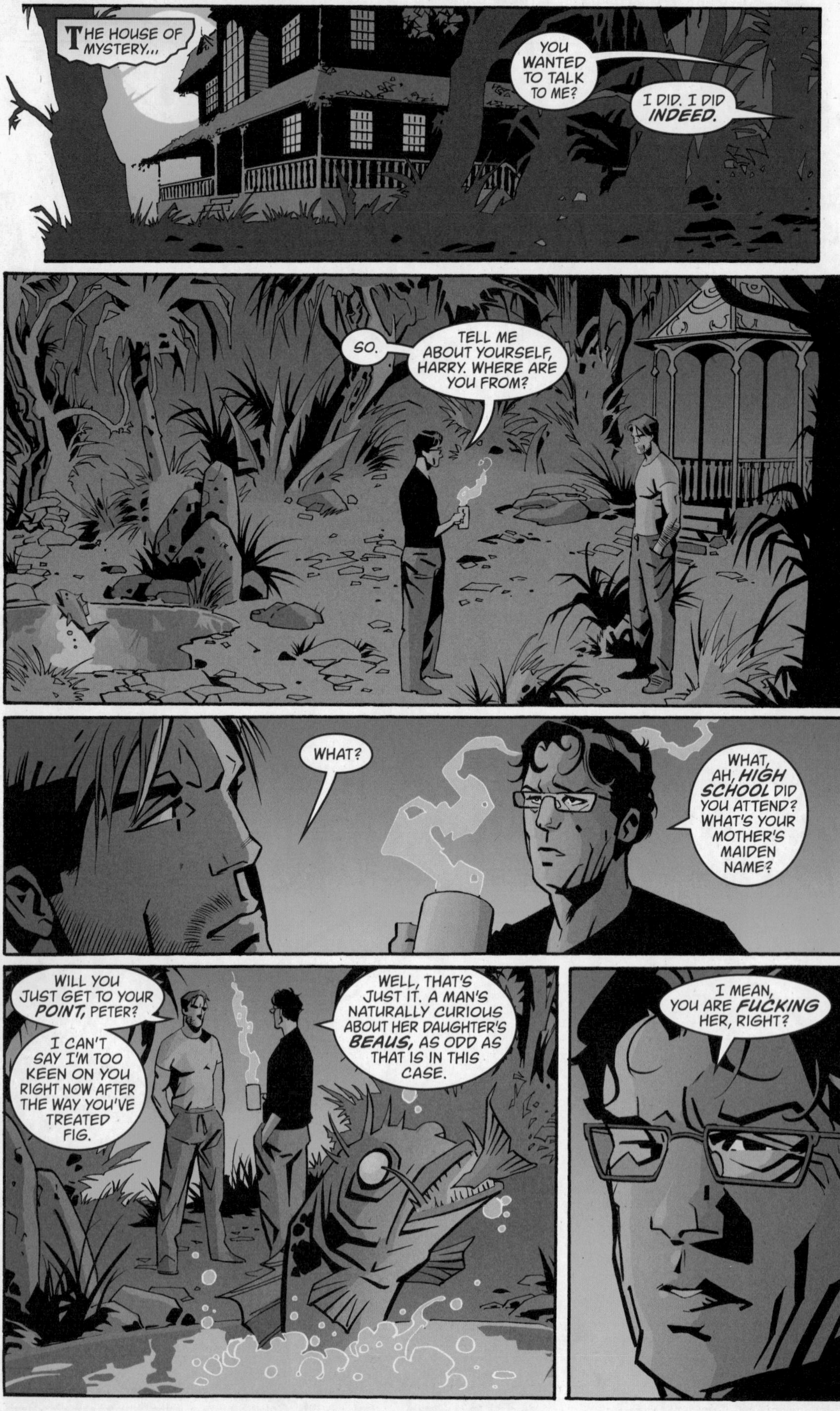
THE HOUSE OF MYSTERY...
YOU WANTED TO TALK TO ME?
I DID. I DID INDEED.
SO.
TELL ME ABOUT YOURSELF, HARRY. WHERE ARE YOU FROM?
WHAT?
WHAT, AH, HIGH SCHOOL DID YOU ATTEND? WHAT'S YOUR MOTHER'S MAIDEN NAME?
WILL YOU JUST GET TO YOUR POINT, PETER?
I CAN'T SAY I'M TOO KEEN ON YOU RIGHT NOW AFTER THE WAY YOU'VE TREATED FIG.
WELL, THAT'S JUST IT. A MAN'S NATURALLY CURIOUS ABOUT HER DAUGHTER'S BEAUS, AS ODD AS THAT IS IN THIS CASE.
I MEAN, YOU ARE FUCKING HER, RIGHT?

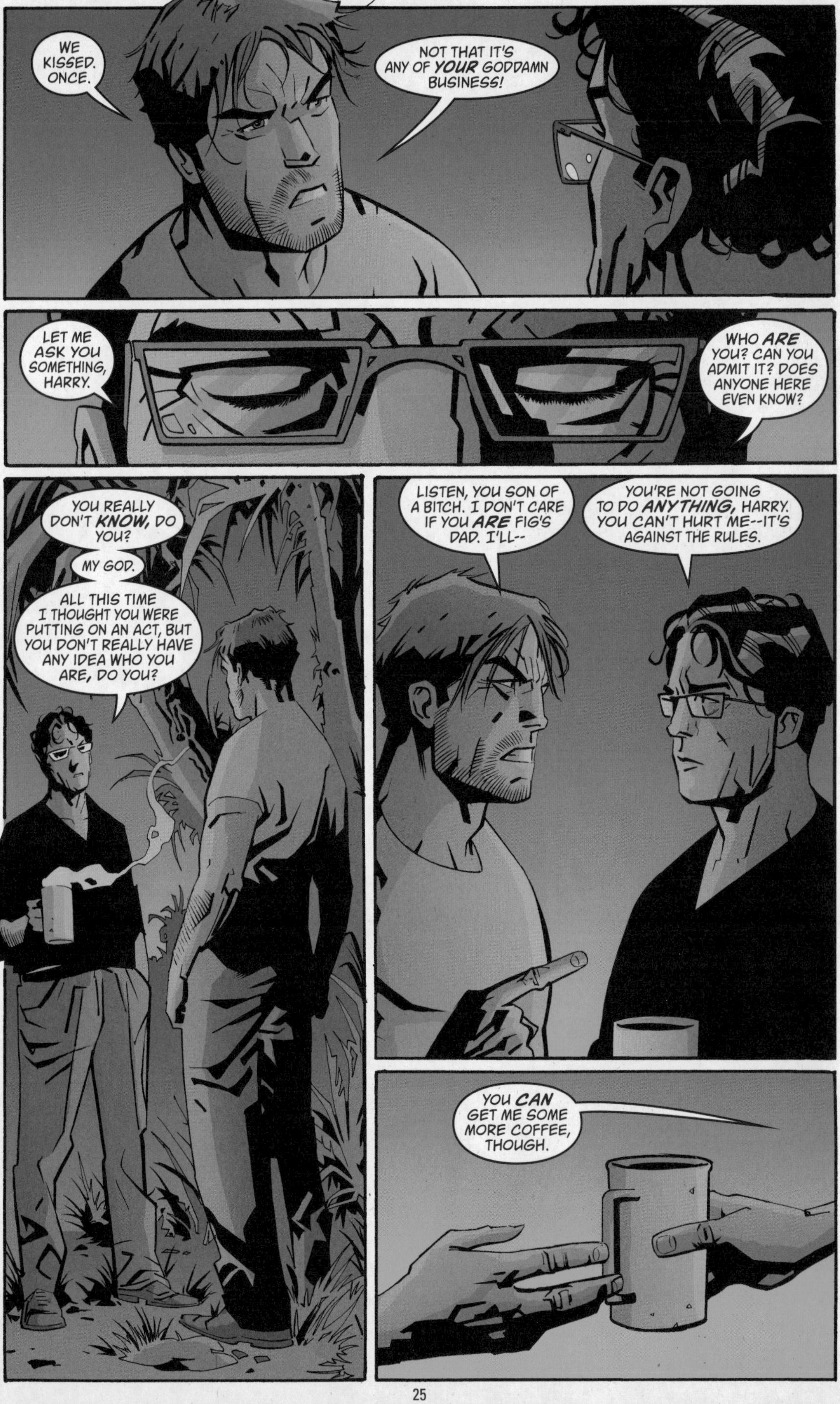
WE KISSED. ONCE.
NOT THAT IT'S ANY OF YOUR GODDAMN BUSINESS!
LET ME ASK YOU SOMETHING, HARRY.
WHO ARE YOU? CAN YOU ADMIT IT? DOES ANYONE HERE EVEN KNOW?
YOU REALLY DON'T KNOW, DO YOU?
MY GOD.
ALL THIS TIME I THOUGHT YOU WERE PUTTING ON AN ACT, BUT YOU DON'T REALLY HAVE ANY IDEA WHO YOU ARE, DO YOU?
LISTEN, YOU SON OF A BITCH. I DON'T CARE IF YOU ARE FIG'S DAD. I'LL--
YOU'RE NOT GOING TO DO ANYTHING, HARRY. YOU CAN'T HURT ME--IT'S AGAINST THE RULES.
YOU CAN GET ME SOME MORE COFFEE, THOUGH.

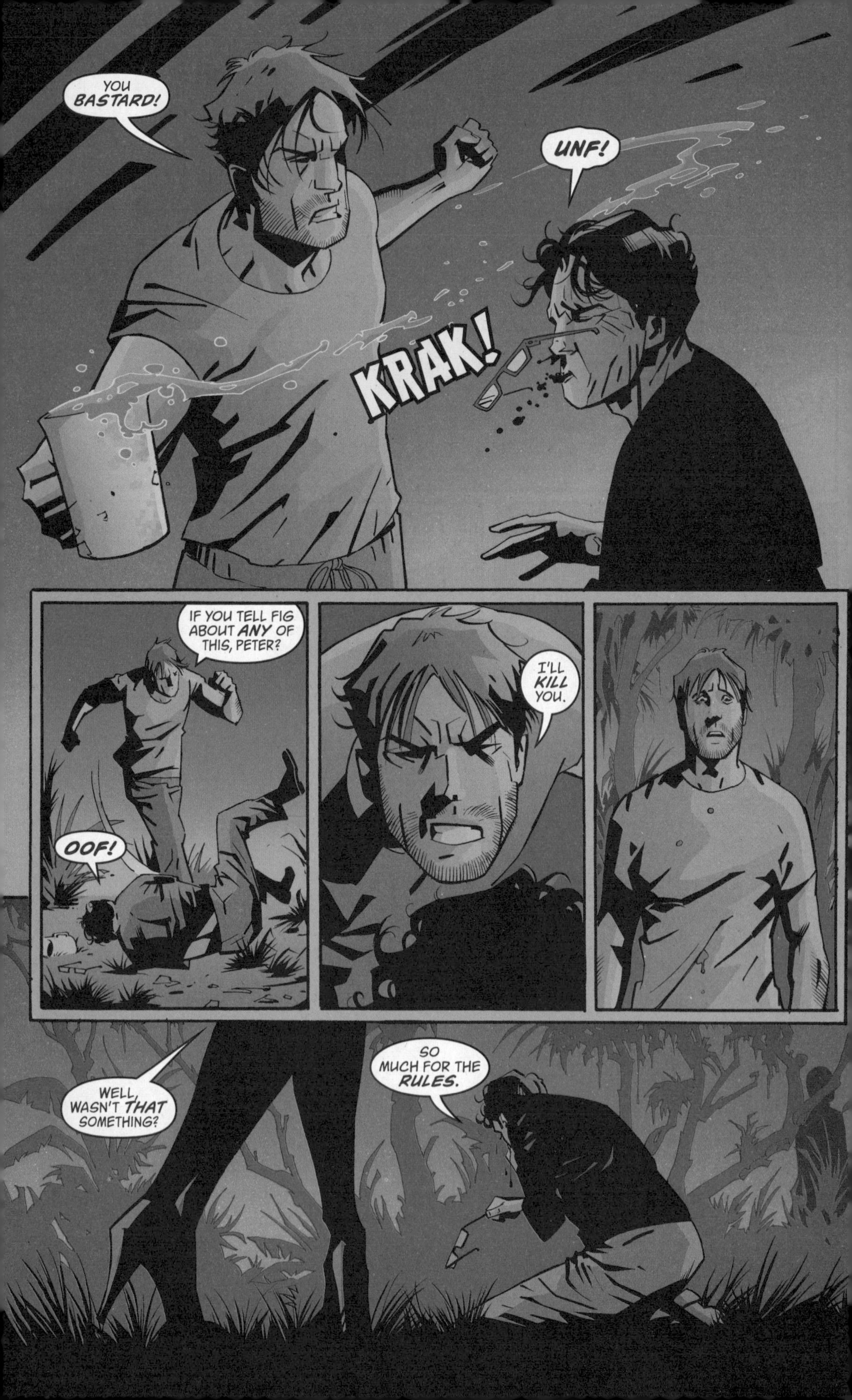
YOU BASTARD!
UNF!
KRAK!
IF YOU TELL FIG ABOUT ANY OF THIS, PETER?
OOF!
I'LL KILL YOU.
WELL, WASN'T THAT SOMETHING?
SO MUCH FOR THE RULES.

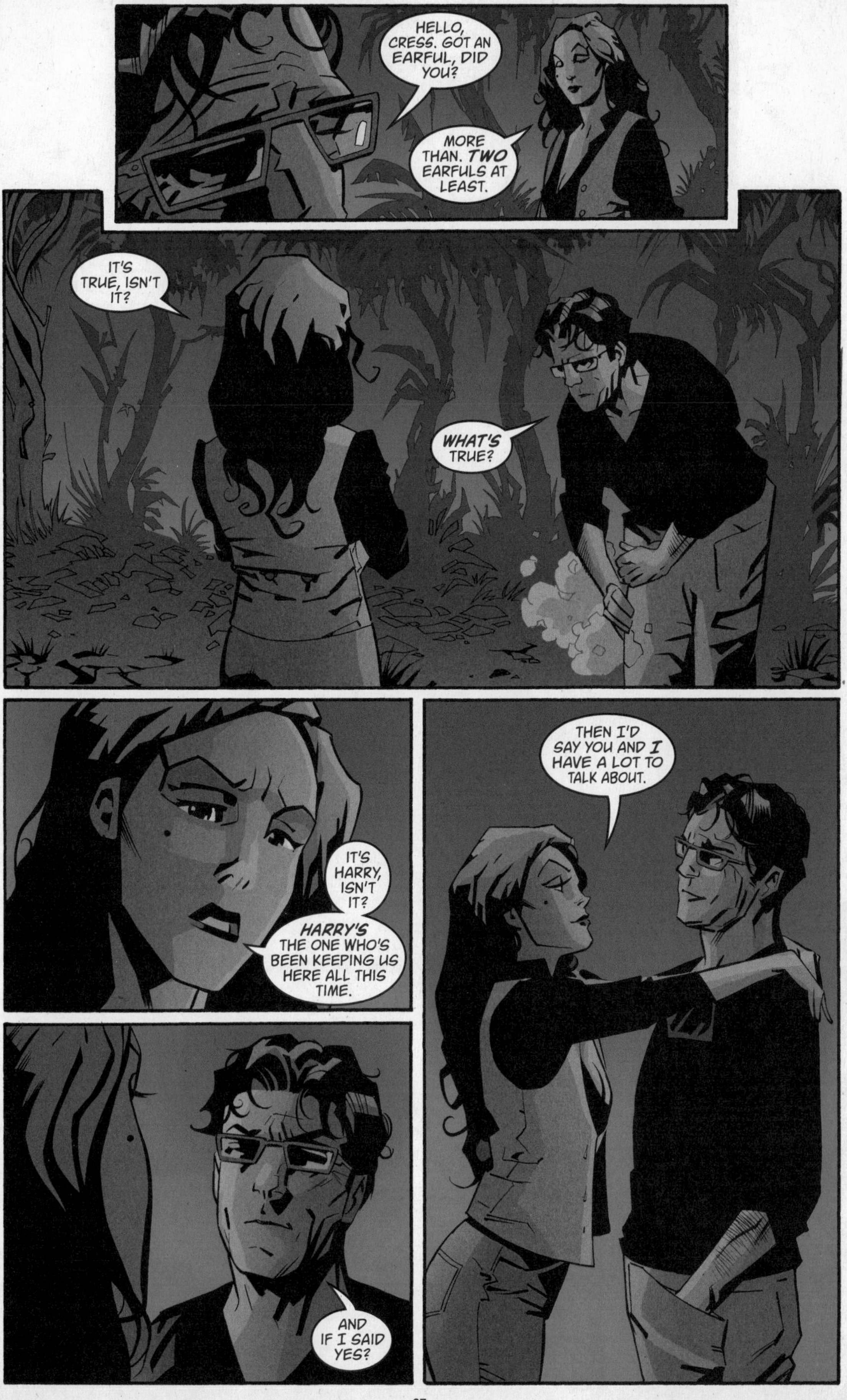
HELLO, CRESS. GOT AN EARFUL, DID YOU?
MORE THAN. TWO EARFULS AT LEAST.
IT'S TRUE, ISN'T IT?
WHAT'S TRUE?
IT'S HARRY, ISN'T IT?
HARRY'S THE ONE WHO'S BEEN KEEPING US HERE ALL THIS TIME.
AND IF I SAID YES?
THEN I'D SAY YOU AND I HAVE A LOT TO TALK ABOUT.

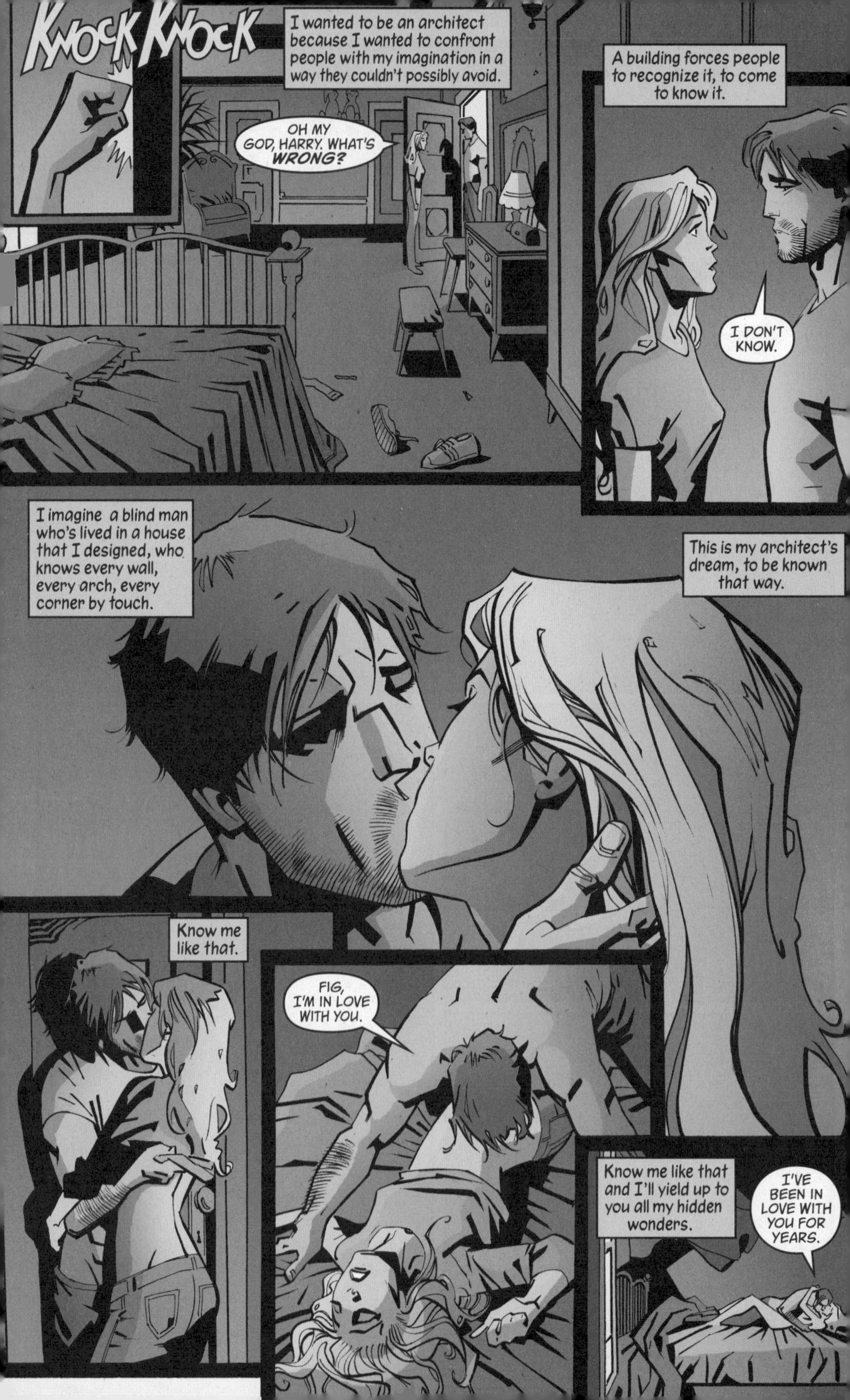
KNOCK KNOCK
I wanted to be an architect because I wanted to confront people with my imagination in a way they couldn't possibly avoid.
OH MY GOD, HARRY. WHAT'S WRONG?
A building forces people to recognize it, to come to know it.
I DON'T KNOW.
I imagine a blind man who's lived in a house that I designed, who knows every wall, every arch, every corner by touch.
This is my architect's dream, to be known that way.
Know me like that.
FIG, I'M IN LOVE WITH YOU.
Know me like that and I'll yield up to you all my hidden wonders.
I'VE BEEN IN LOVE WITH YOU FOR YEARS.

ISSUE #12 COVER ART BY ESAO ANDREWS.

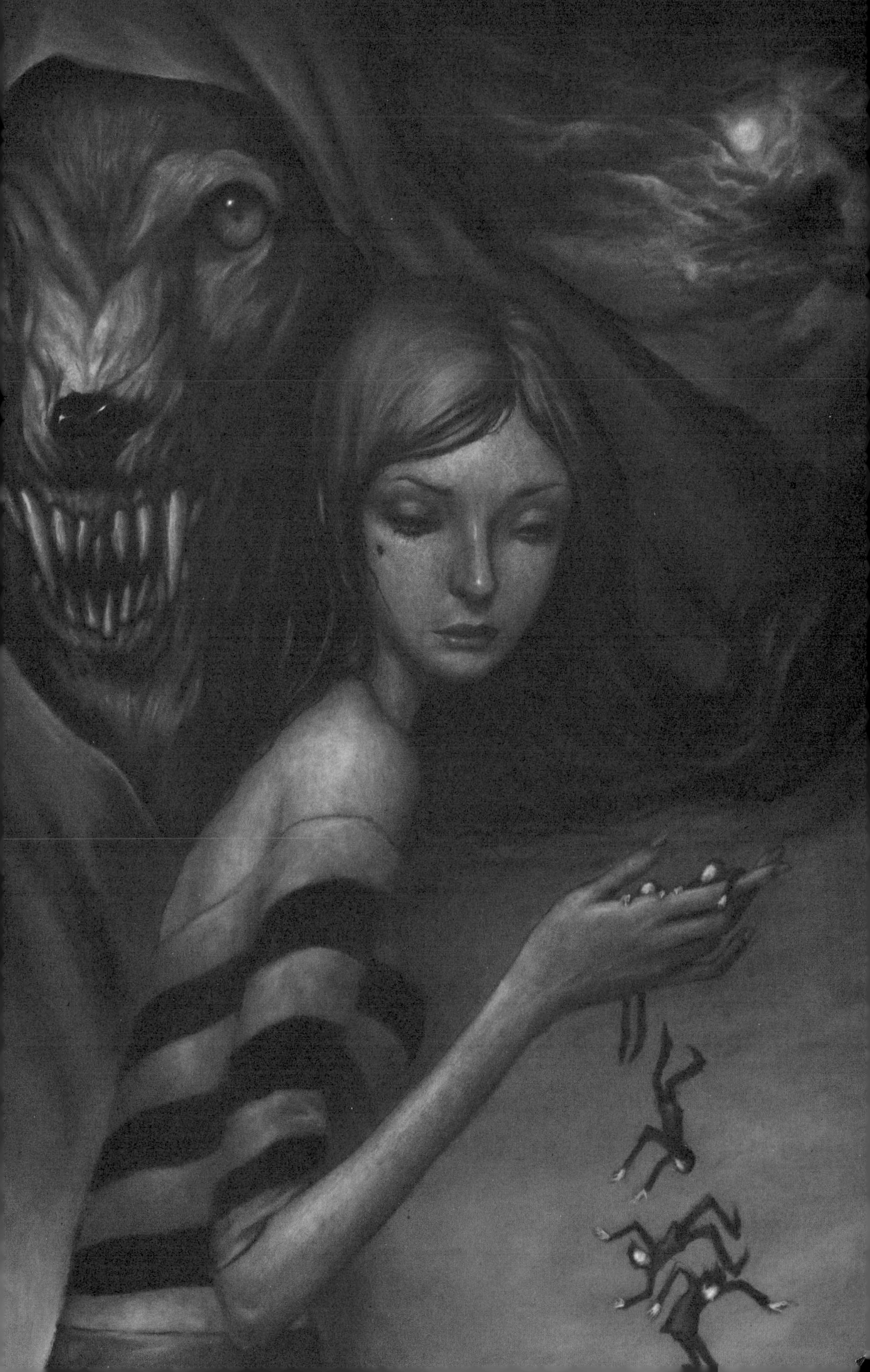

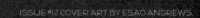

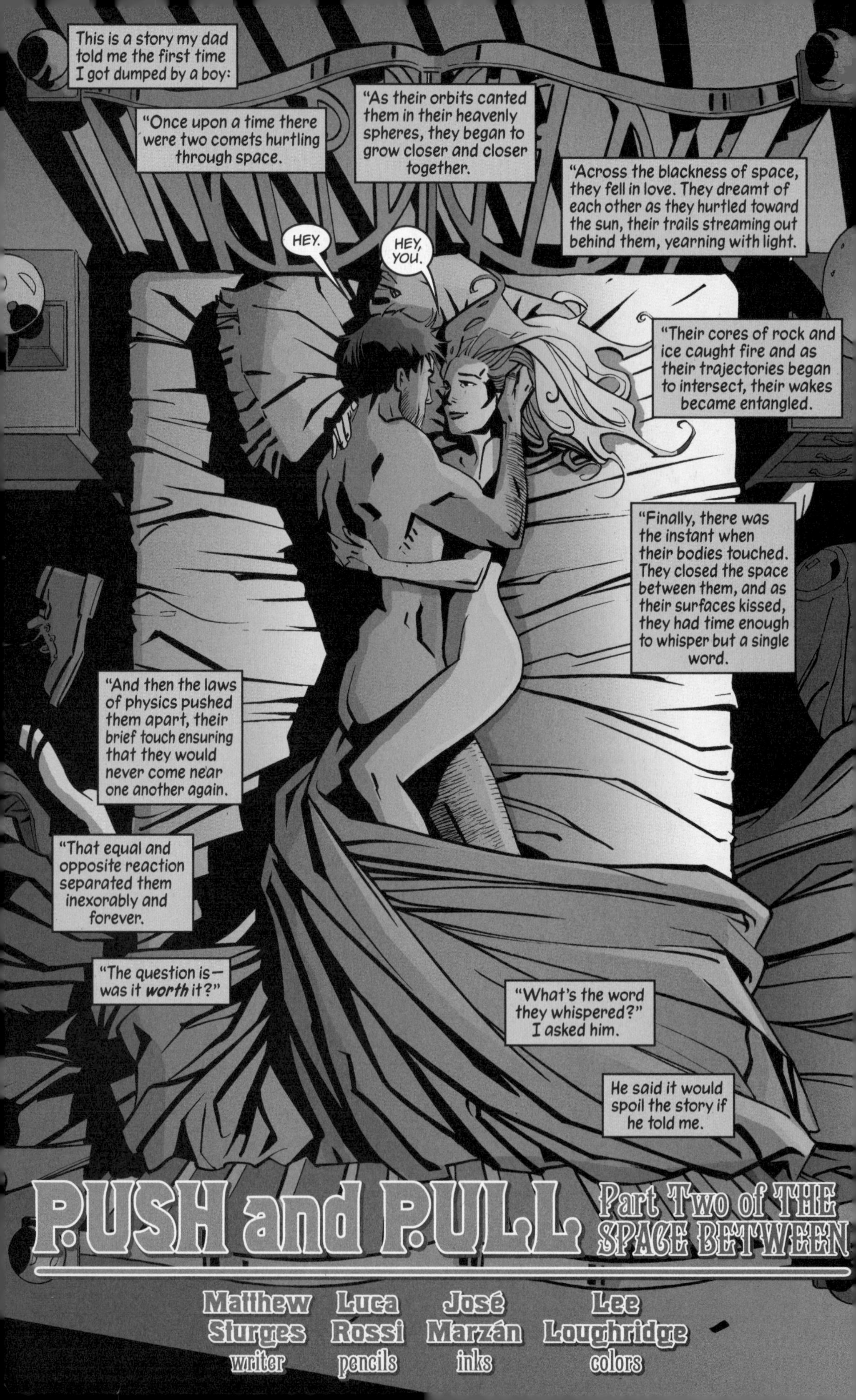

This is a story my dad told me the first time I got dumped by a boy:
"Once upon a time there were two comets hurtling through space.
"As their orbits canted them in their heavenly spheres, they began to grow closer and closer together.
"Across the blackness of space, they fell in love. They dreamt of each other as they hurtled toward the sun, their trails streaming out behind them, yearning with light.
HEY.
HEY, YOU.
"Their cores of rock and ice caught fire and as their trajectories began to intersect, their wakes became entangled.
"Finally, there was the instant when their bodies touched. They closed the space between them, and as their surfaces kissed, they had time enough to whisper but a single word.
"And then the laws of physics pushed them apart, their brief touch ensuring that they would never come near one another again.
"That equal and opposite reaction separated them inexorably and forever.
"The question is— was it *worth* it?"
"What's the word they whispered?" I asked him.
He said it would spoil the story if he told me.
PUSH and PULL
Part Two of THE SPACE BETWEEN
Matthew Sturges writer
Luca Rossi pencils
José Marzán inks
Lee Loughridge colors

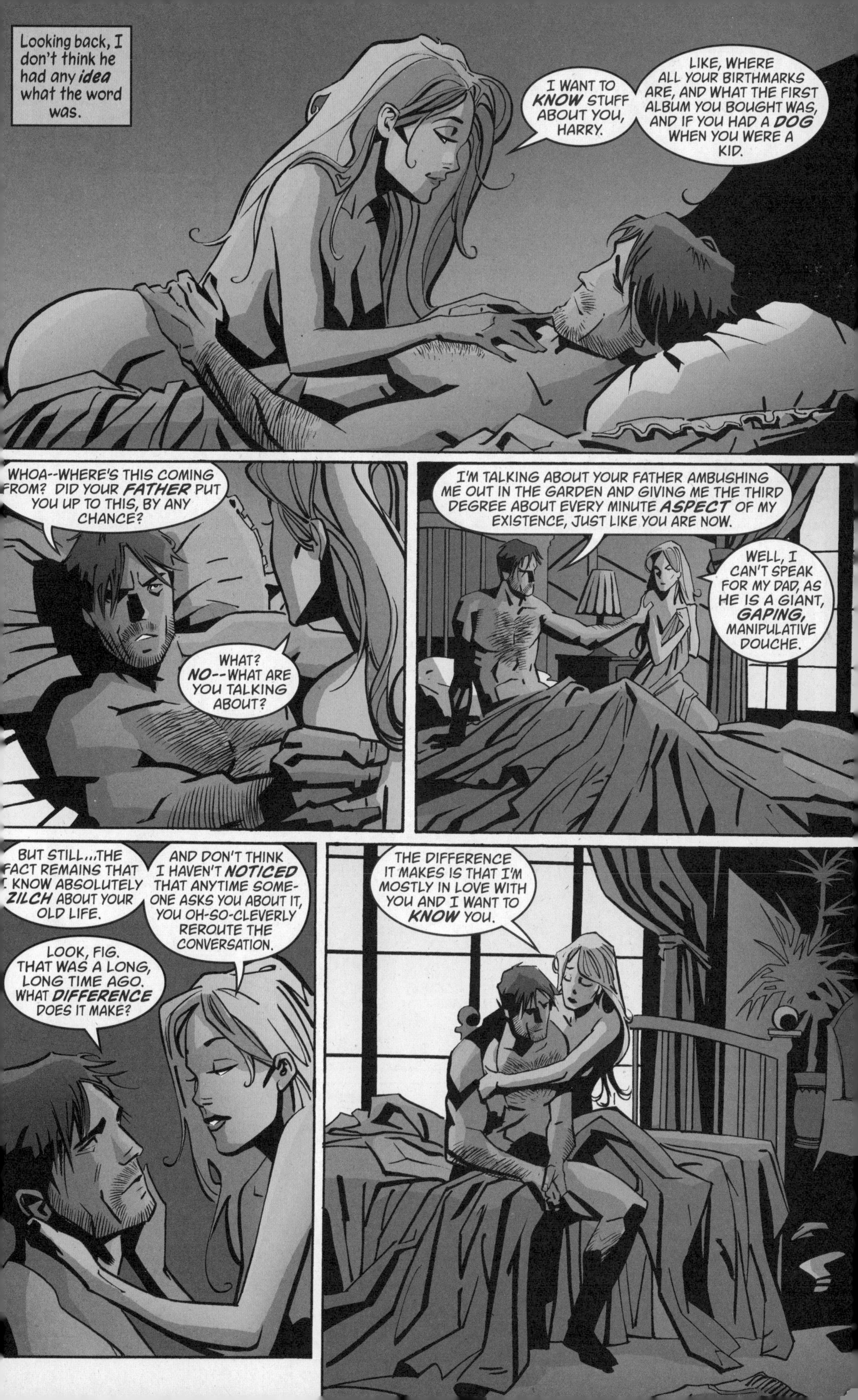
Looking back, I don't think he had any *idea* what the word was.
I WANT TO *KNOW* STUFF ABOUT YOU, HARRY.
LIKE, WHERE ALL YOUR BIRTHMARKS ARE, AND WHAT THE FIRST ALBUM YOU BOUGHT WAS, AND IF YOU HAD A *DOG* WHEN YOU WERE A KID.
WHOA--WHERE'S THIS COMING FROM? DID YOUR *FATHER* PUT YOU UP TO THIS, BY ANY CHANCE?
WHAT? *NO*--WHAT ARE YOU TALKING ABOUT?
I'M TALKING ABOUT YOUR FATHER AMBUSHING ME OUT IN THE GARDEN AND GIVING ME THE THIRD DEGREE ABOUT EVERY MINUTE *ASPECT* OF MY EXISTENCE, JUST LIKE YOU ARE NOW.
WELL, I CAN'T SPEAK FOR MY DAD, AS HE IS A GIANT, *GAPING,* MANIPULATIVE DOUCHE.
BUT STILL...THE FACT REMAINS THAT I KNOW ABSOLUTELY *ZILCH* ABOUT YOUR OLD LIFE.
AND DON'T THINK I HAVEN'T *NOTICED* THAT ANYTIME SOMEONE ASKS YOU ABOUT IT, YOU OH-SO-CLEVERLY REROUTE THE CONVERSATION.
LOOK, FIG. THAT WAS A LONG, LONG TIME AGO. WHAT *DIFFERENCE* DOES IT MAKE?
THE DIFFERENCE IT MAKES IS THAT I'M MOSTLY IN LOVE WITH YOU AND I WANT TO *KNOW* YOU.

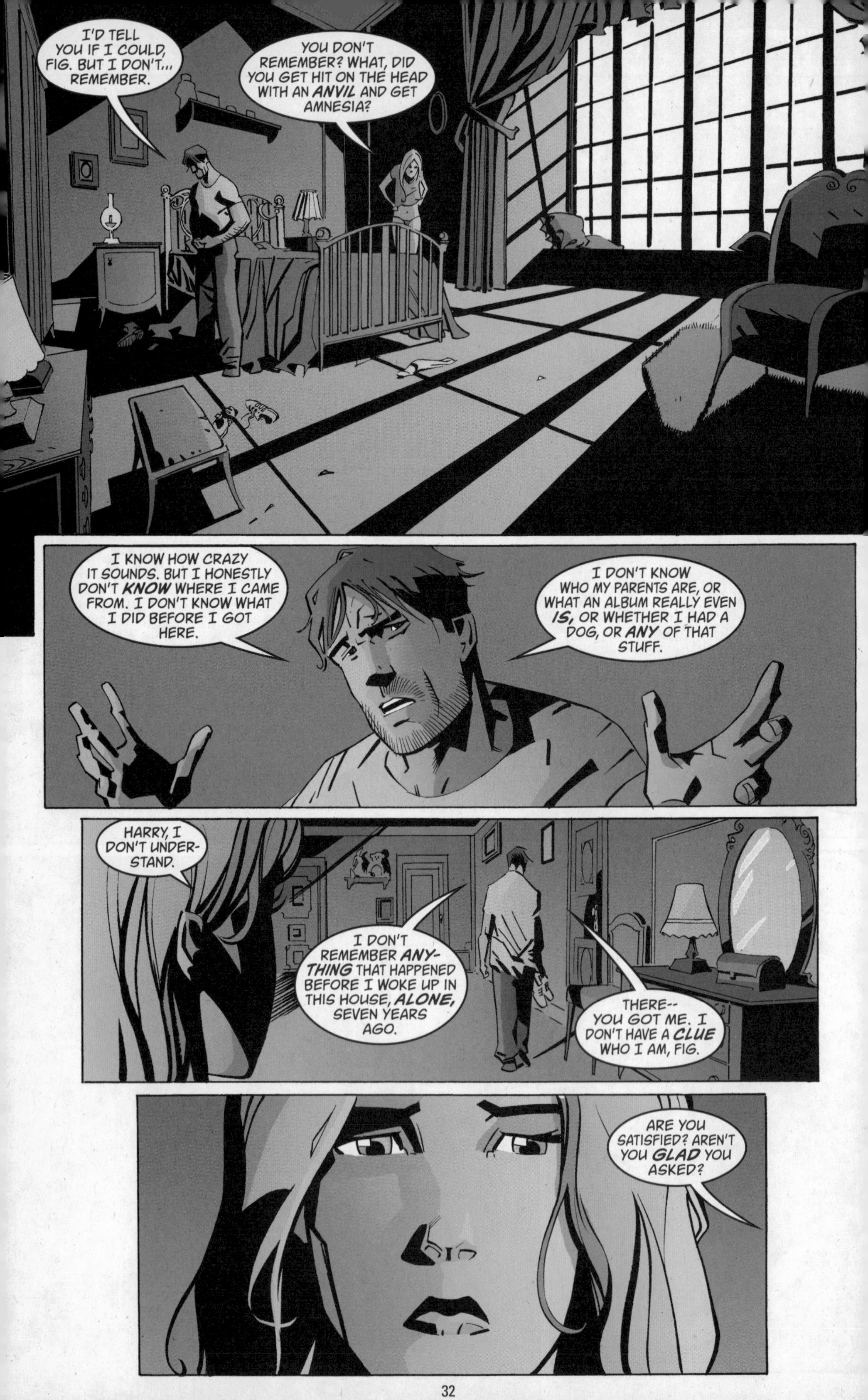
I'D TELL YOU IF I COULD, FIG. BUT I DON'T... REMEMBER.
YOU DON'T REMEMBER? WHAT, DID YOU GET HIT ON THE HEAD WITH AN ANVIL AND GET AMNESIA?
I KNOW HOW CRAZY IT SOUNDS. BUT I HONESTLY DON'T KNOW WHERE I CAME FROM. I DON'T KNOW WHAT I DID BEFORE I GOT HERE.
I DON'T KNOW WHO MY PARENTS ARE, OR WHAT AN ALBUM REALLY EVEN IS, OR WHETHER I HAD A DOG, OR ANY OF THAT STUFF.
HARRY, I DON'T UNDER-STAND.
I DON'T REMEMBER ANY-THING THAT HAPPENED BEFORE I WOKE UP IN THIS HOUSE, ALONE, SEVEN YEARS AGO.
THERE-- YOU GOT ME. I DON'T HAVE A CLUE WHO I AM, FIG.
ARE YOU SATISFIED? AREN'T YOU GLAD YOU ASKED?

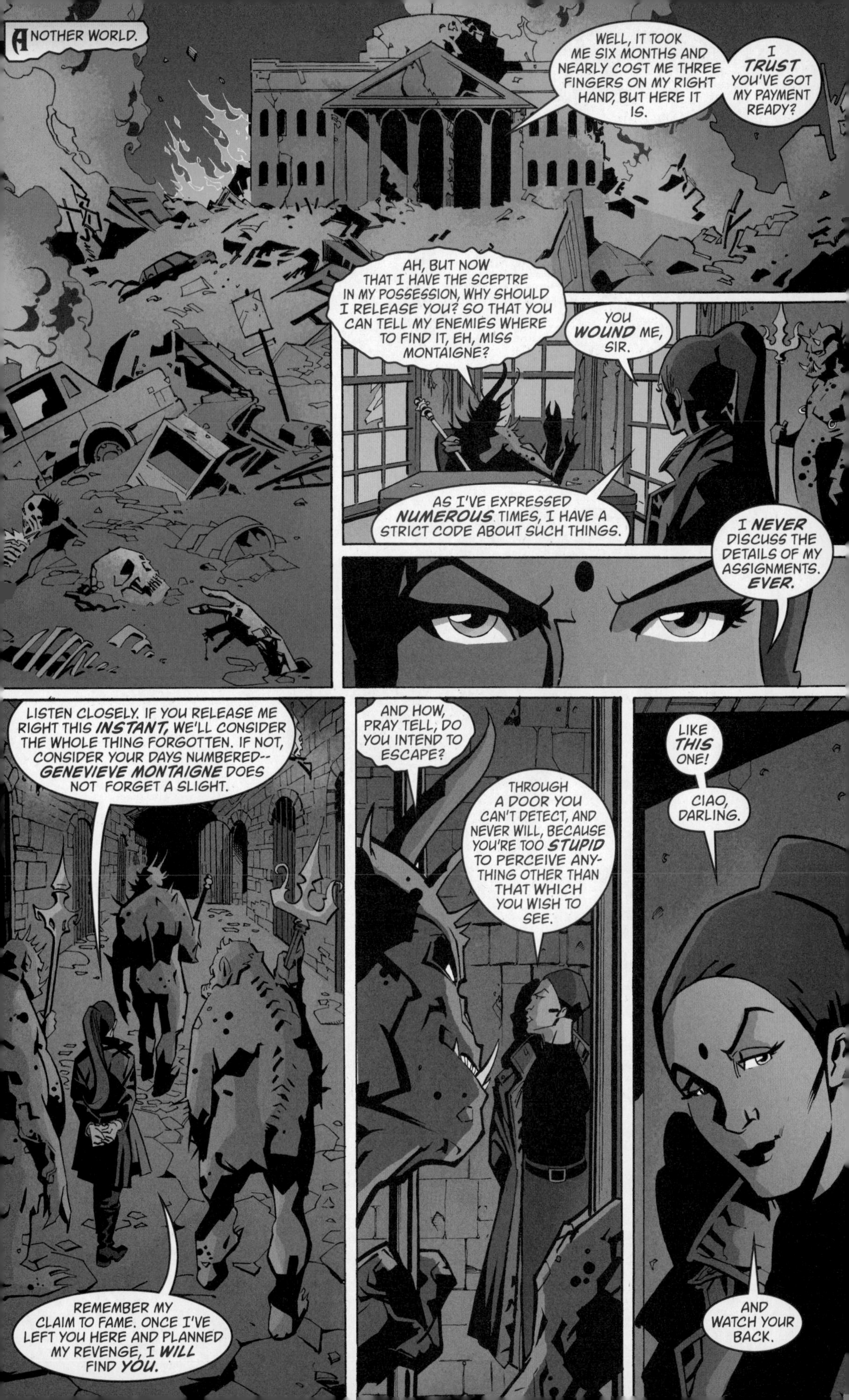
ANOTHER WORLD.
WELL, IT TOOK ME SIX MONTHS AND NEARLY COST ME THREE FINGERS ON MY RIGHT HAND, BUT HERE IT IS.
I TRUST YOU'VE GOT MY PAYMENT READY?
AH, BUT NOW THAT I HAVE THE SCEPTRE IN MY POSSESSION, WHY SHOULD I RELEASE YOU? SO THAT YOU CAN TELL MY ENEMIES WHERE TO FIND IT, EH, MISS MONTAIGNE?
YOU WOUND ME, SIR.
AS I'VE EXPRESSED NUMEROUS TIMES, I HAVE A STRICT CODE ABOUT SUCH THINGS.
I NEVER DISCUSS THE DETAILS OF MY ASSIGNMENTS. EVER.
LISTEN CLOSELY. IF YOU RELEASE ME RIGHT THIS INSTANT, WE'LL CONSIDER THE WHOLE THING FORGOTTEN. IF NOT, CONSIDER YOUR DAYS NUMBERED-- GENEVIEVE MONTAIGNE DOES NOT FORGET A SLIGHT.
REMEMBER MY CLAIM TO FAME. ONCE I'VE LEFT YOU HERE AND PLANNED MY REVENGE, I WILL FIND YOU.
AND HOW, PRAY TELL, DO YOU INTEND TO ESCAPE?
THROUGH A DOOR YOU CAN'T DETECT, AND NEVER WILL, BECAUSE YOU'RE TOO STUPID TO PERCEIVE ANYTHING OTHER THAN THAT WHICH YOU WISH TO SEE.
LIKE THIS ONE!
CIAO, DARLING.
AND WATCH YOUR BACK.

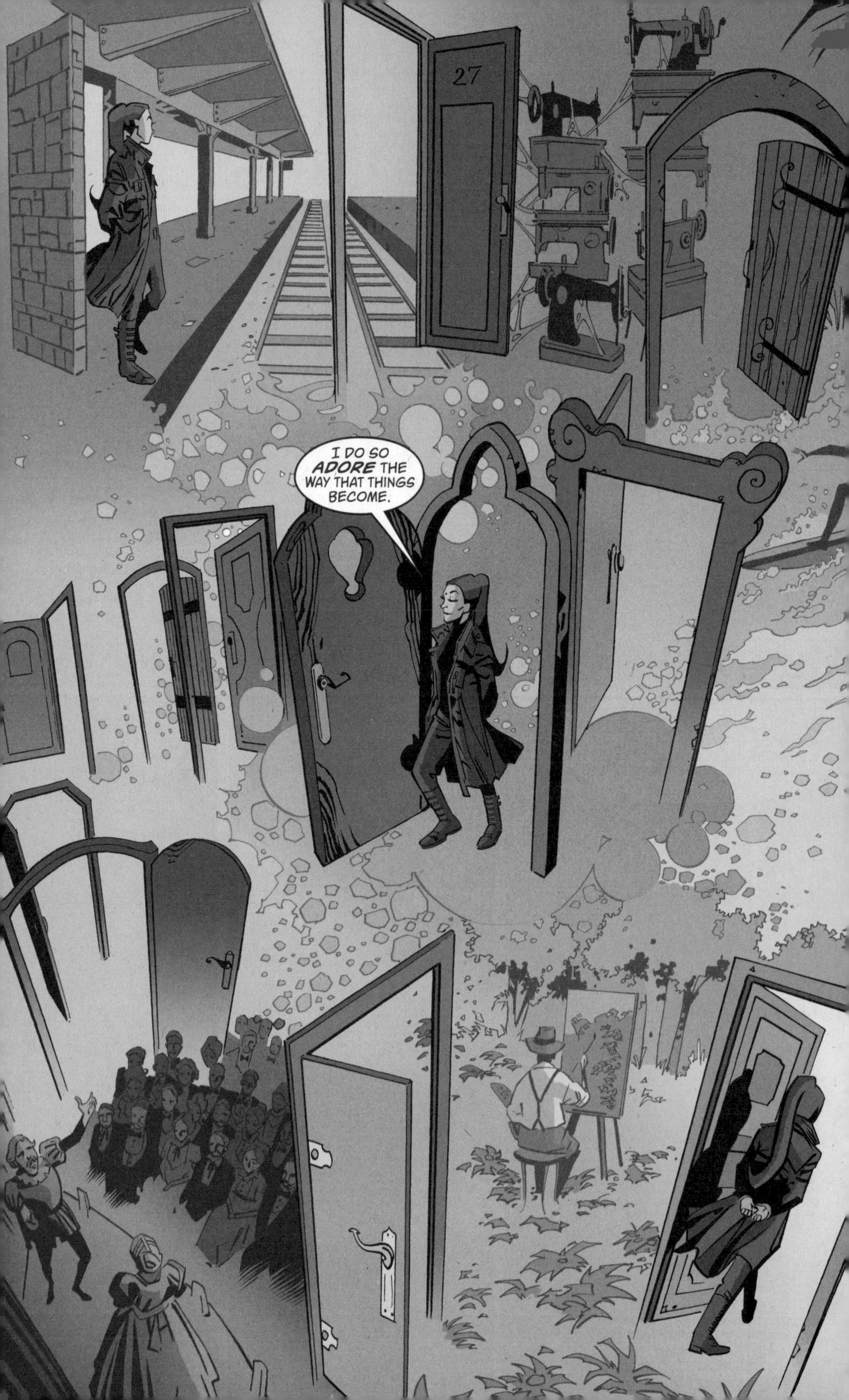
27
I DO SO ADORE THE WAY THAT THINGS BECOME.

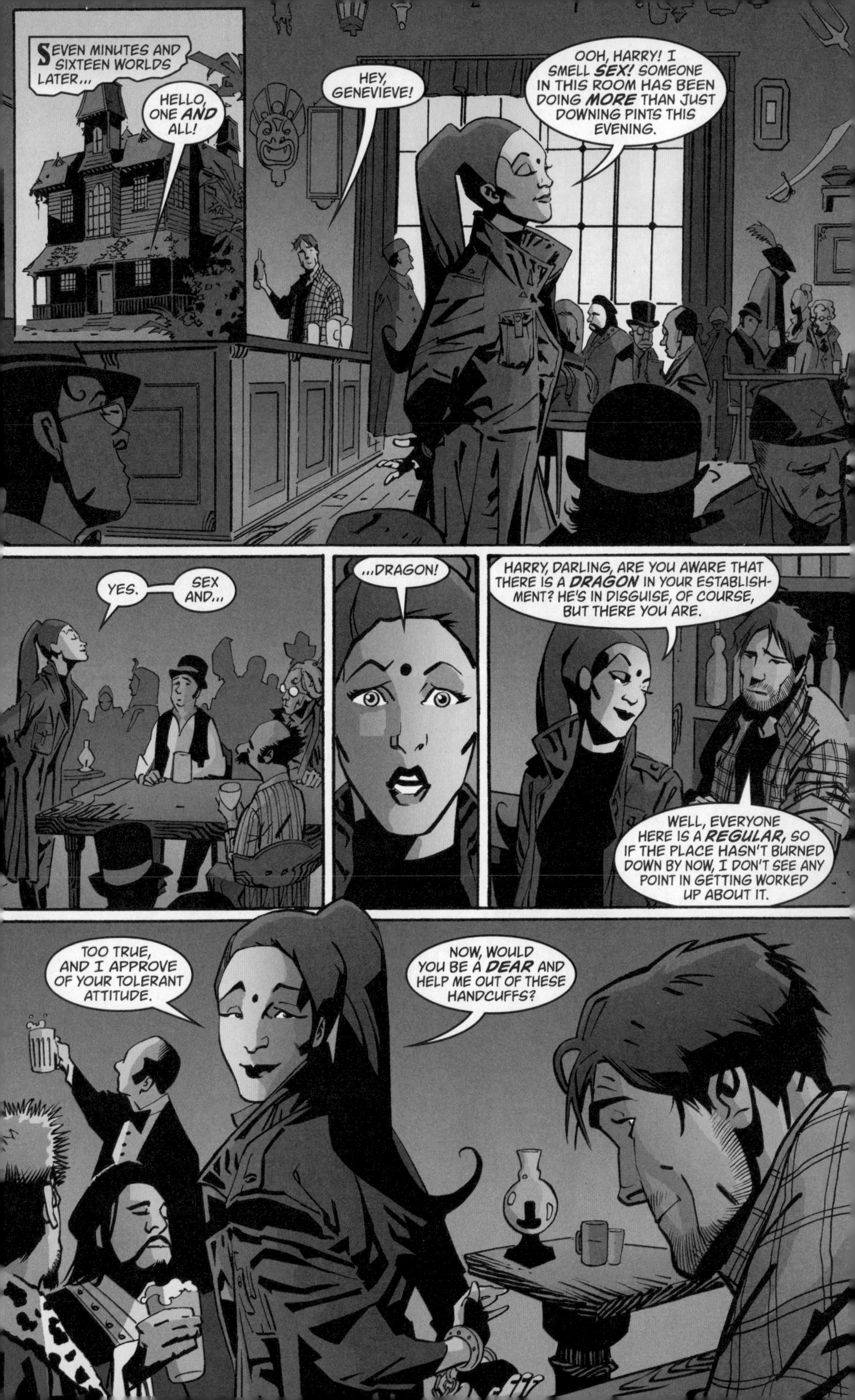
SEVEN MINUTES AND SIXTEEN WORLDS LATER...
HELLO, ONE AND ALL!
HEY, GENEVIEVE!
OOH, HARRY! I SMELL SEX! SOMEONE IN THIS ROOM HAS BEEN DOING MORE THAN JUST DOWNING PINTS THIS EVENING.
YES.
SEX AND...
...DRAGON!
HARRY, DARLING, ARE YOU AWARE THAT THERE IS A DRAGON IN YOUR ESTABLISHMENT? HE'S IN DISGUISE, OF COURSE, BUT THERE YOU ARE.
WELL, EVERYONE HERE IS A REGULAR, SO IF THE PLACE HASN'T BURNED DOWN BY NOW, I DON'T SEE ANY POINT IN GETTING WORKED UP ABOUT IT.
TOO TRUE, AND I APPROVE OF YOUR TOLERANT ATTITUDE.
NOW, WOULD YOU BE A DEAR AND HELP ME OUT OF THESE HANDCUFFS?

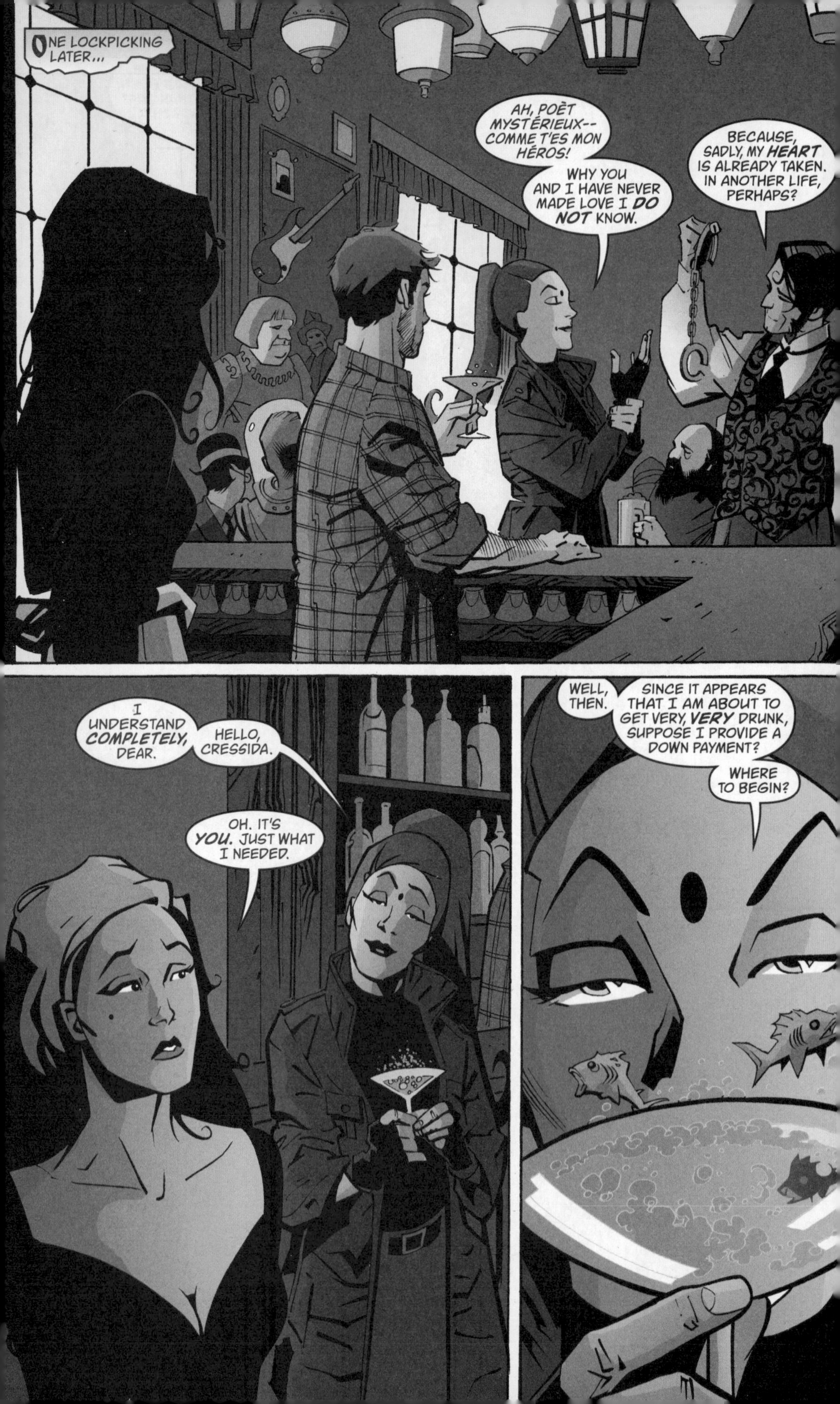
ONE LOCKPICKING LATER...
AH, POÈT MYSTÉRIEUX-- COMME T'ES MON HÉROS!
WHY YOU AND I HAVE NEVER MADE LOVE I DO NOT KNOW.
BECAUSE, SADLY, MY HEART IS ALREADY TAKEN. IN ANOTHER LIFE, PERHAPS?
I UNDERSTAND COMPLETELY, DEAR.
HELLO, CRESSIDA.
OH. IT'S YOU. JUST WHAT I NEEDED.
WELL, THEN.
SINCE IT APPEARS THAT I AM ABOUT TO GET VERY, VERY DRUNK, SUPPOSE I PROVIDE A DOWN PAYMENT?
WHERE TO BEGIN?

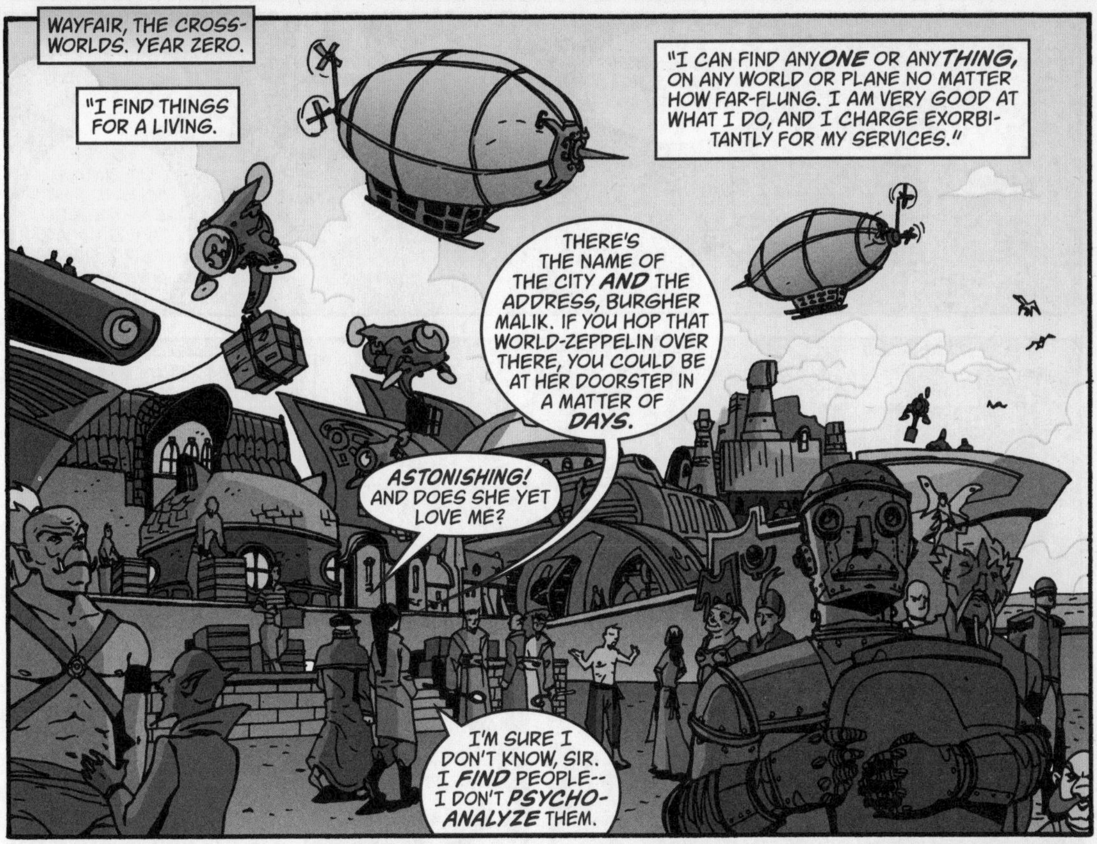
WAYFAIR, THE CROSS-WORLDS. YEAR ZERO.
"I FIND THINGS FOR A LIVING.
"I CAN FIND ANY*ONE* OR ANY*THING*, ON ANY WORLD OR PLANE NO MATTER HOW FAR-FLUNG. I AM VERY GOOD AT WHAT I DO, AND I CHARGE EXORBITANTLY FOR MY SERVICES."
THERE'S THE NAME OF THE CITY *AND* THE ADDRESS, BURGHER MALIK. IF YOU HOP THAT WORLD-ZEPPELIN OVER THERE, YOU COULD BE AT HER DOORSTEP IN A MATTER OF *DAYS*.
ASTONISHING! AND DOES SHE YET LOVE ME?
I'M SURE I DON'T KNOW, SIR. I *FIND* PEOPLE-- I DON'T *PSYCHOANALYZE* THEM.

A CRESS IN EVERY PORT

MATTHEW STURGES writer · GRAZIA LOBACCARO pencils · STEFANO LANDINI inks · LEE LOUGHRIDGE colors

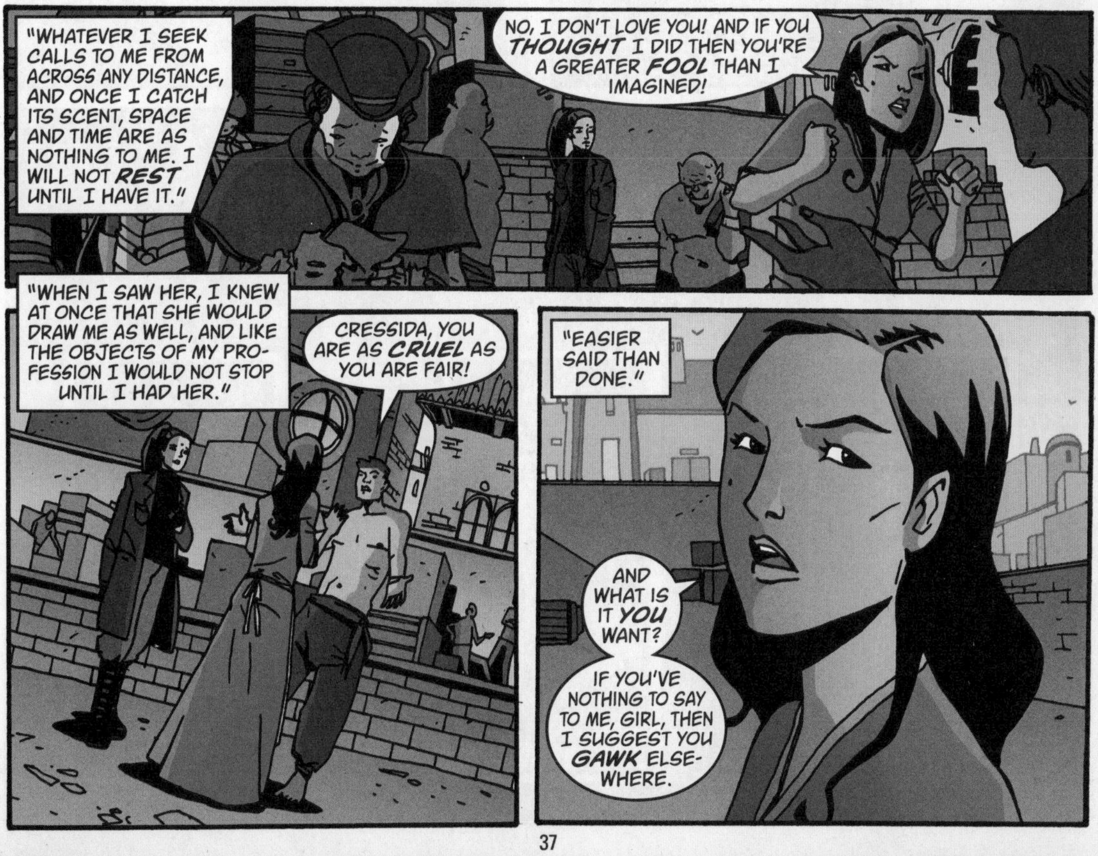
"WHATEVER I SEEK CALLS TO ME FROM ACROSS ANY DISTANCE, AND ONCE I CATCH ITS SCENT, SPACE AND TIME ARE AS NOTHING TO ME. I WILL NOT *REST* UNTIL I HAVE IT."
NO, I DON'T LOVE YOU! AND IF YOU *THOUGHT* I DID THEN YOU'RE A GREATER *FOOL* THAN I IMAGINED!
"WHEN I SAW HER, I KNEW AT ONCE THAT SHE WOULD DRAW ME AS WELL, AND LIKE THE OBJECTS OF MY PROFESSION I WOULD NOT STOP UNTIL I HAD HER."
CRESSIDA, YOU ARE AS *CRUEL* AS YOU ARE FAIR!
"EASIER SAID THAN DONE."
AND WHAT IS IT *YOU* WANT?
IF YOU'VE NOTHING TO SAY TO ME, GIRL, THEN I SUGGEST YOU *GAWK* ELSEWHERE.

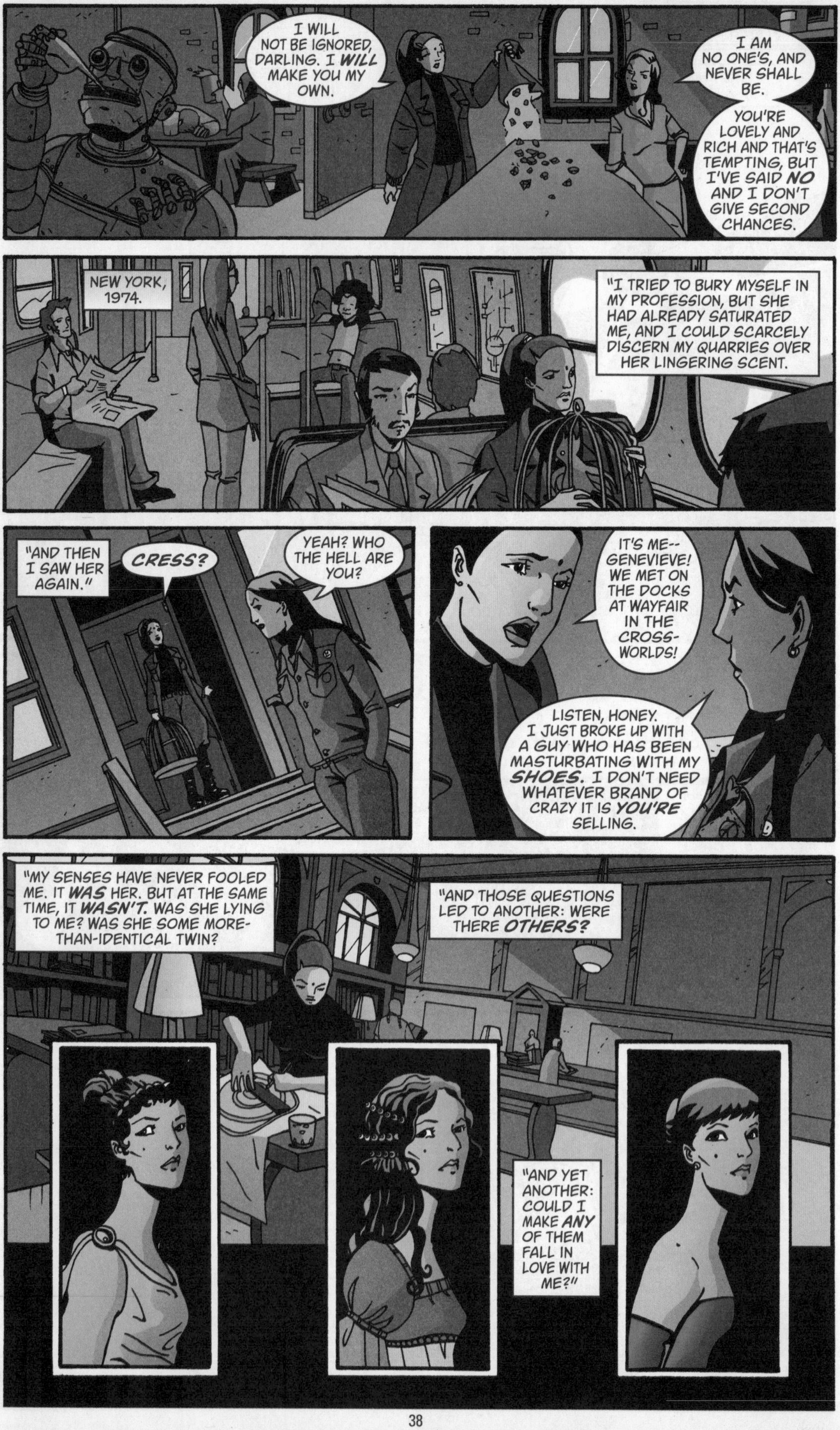
I WILL NOT BE IGNORED, DARLING. I WILL MAKE YOU MY OWN.
I AM NO ONE'S, AND NEVER SHALL BE.
YOU'RE LOVELY AND RICH AND THAT'S TEMPTING, BUT I'VE SAID NO AND I DON'T GIVE SECOND CHANCES.
NEW YORK, 1974.
"I TRIED TO BURY MYSELF IN MY PROFESSION, BUT SHE HAD ALREADY SATURATED ME, AND I COULD SCARCELY DISCERN MY QUARRIES OVER HER LINGERING SCENT.
"AND THEN I SAW HER AGAIN."
CRESS?
YEAH? WHO THE HELL ARE YOU?
IT'S ME-- GENEVIEVE! WE MET ON THE DOCKS AT WAYFAIR IN THE CROSS-WORLDS!
LISTEN, HONEY. I JUST BROKE UP WITH A GUY WHO HAS BEEN MASTURBATING WITH MY SHOES. I DON'T NEED WHATEVER BRAND OF CRAZY IT IS YOU'RE SELLING.
"MY SENSES HAVE NEVER FOOLED ME. IT WAS HER. BUT AT THE SAME TIME, IT WASN'T. WAS SHE LYING TO ME? WAS SHE SOME MORE-THAN-IDENTICAL TWIN?
"AND THOSE QUESTIONS LED TO ANOTHER: WERE THERE OTHERS?
"AND YET ANOTHER: COULD I MAKE ANY OF THEM FALL IN LOVE WITH ME?"

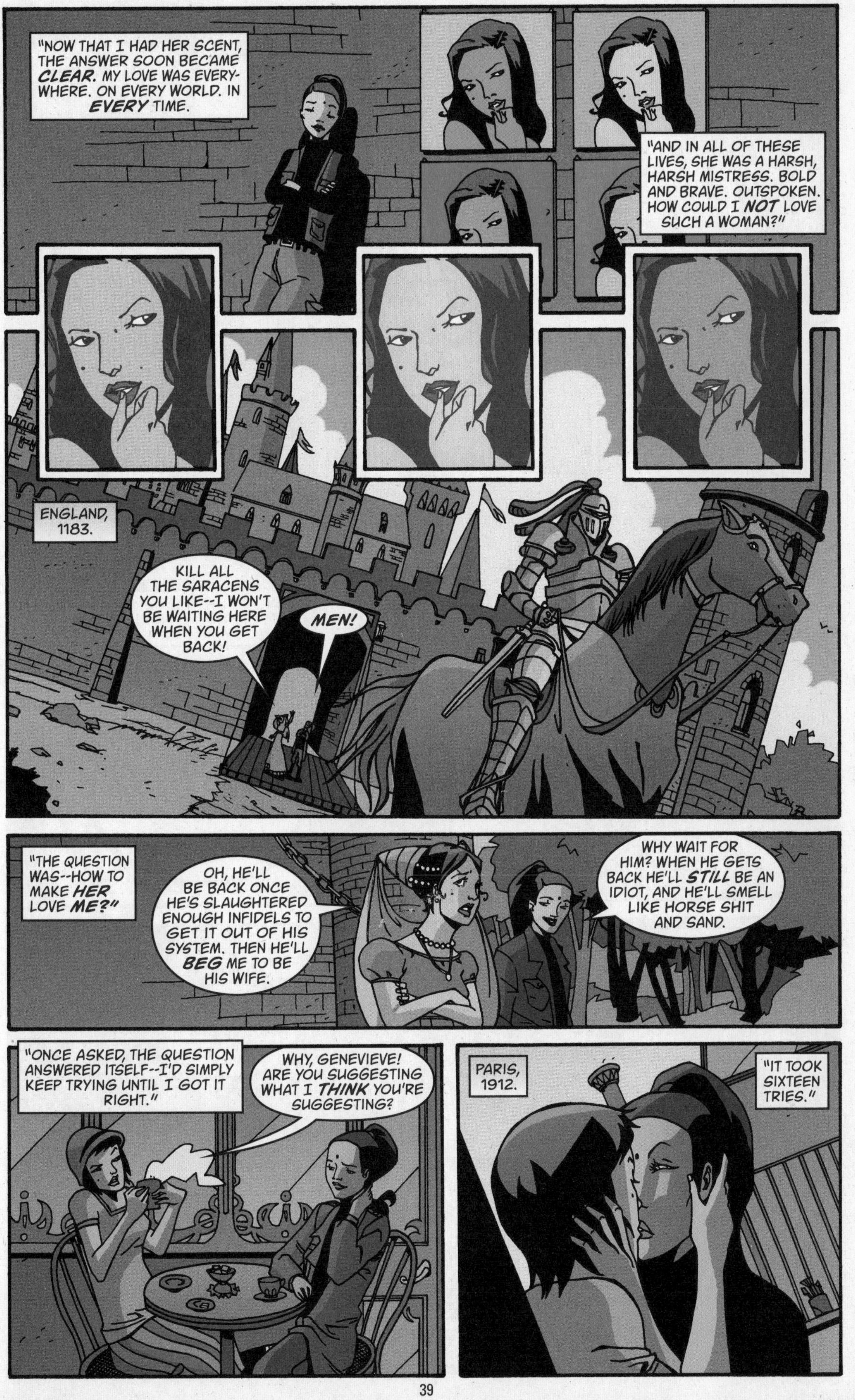
"NOW THAT I HAD HER SCENT, THE ANSWER SOON BECAME **CLEAR.** MY LOVE WAS EVERYWHERE. ON EVERY WORLD. IN **EVERY** TIME.
"AND IN ALL OF THESE LIVES, SHE WAS A HARSH, HARSH MISTRESS. BOLD AND BRAVE. OUTSPOKEN. HOW COULD I **NOT** LOVE SUCH A WOMAN?"
ENGLAND, 1183.
KILL ALL THE SARACENS YOU LIKE--I WON'T BE WAITING HERE WHEN YOU GET BACK!
MEN!
"THE QUESTION WAS--HOW TO MAKE **HER** LOVE **ME?"**
OH, HE'LL BE BACK ONCE HE'S SLAUGHTERED ENOUGH INFIDELS TO GET IT OUT OF HIS SYSTEM. THEN HE'LL **BEG** ME TO BE HIS WIFE.
WHY WAIT FOR HIM? WHEN HE GETS BACK HE'LL **STILL** BE AN IDIOT, AND HE'LL SMELL LIKE HORSE SHIT AND SAND.
"ONCE ASKED, THE QUESTION ANSWERED ITSELF--I'D SIMPLY KEEP TRYING UNTIL I GOT IT RIGHT."
WHY, GENEVIEVE! ARE YOU SUGGESTING WHAT I **THINK** YOU'RE SUGGESTING?
PARIS, 1912.
"IT TOOK SIXTEEN TRIES."

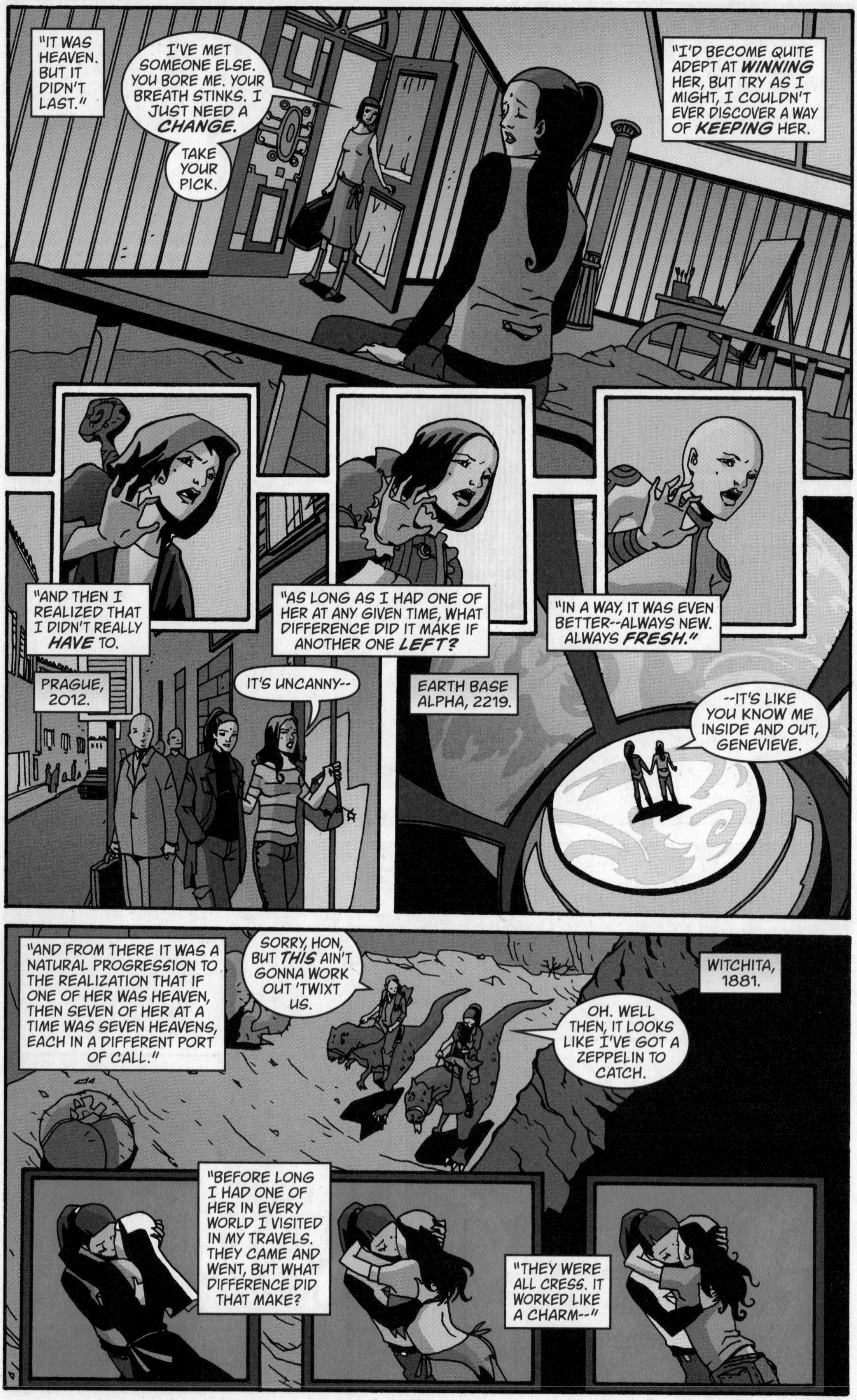
"IT WAS HEAVEN. BUT IT DIDN'T LAST."
I'VE MET SOMEONE ELSE. YOU BORE ME. YOUR BREATH STINKS. I JUST NEED A CHANGE.
TAKE YOUR PICK.
"I'D BECOME QUITE ADEPT AT WINNING HER, BUT TRY AS I MIGHT, I COULDN'T EVER DISCOVER A WAY OF KEEPING HER.
"AND THEN I REALIZED THAT I DIDN'T REALLY HAVE TO.
"AS LONG AS I HAD ONE OF HER AT ANY GIVEN TIME, WHAT DIFFERENCE DID IT MAKE IF ANOTHER ONE LEFT?
"IN A WAY, IT WAS EVEN BETTER--ALWAYS NEW. ALWAYS FRESH."
PRAGUE, 2012.
IT'S UNCANNY--
EARTH BASE ALPHA, 2219.
--IT'S LIKE YOU KNOW ME INSIDE AND OUT, GENEVIEVE.
"AND FROM THERE IT WAS A NATURAL PROGRESSION TO THE REALIZATION THAT IF ONE OF HER WAS HEAVEN, THEN SEVEN OF HER AT A TIME WAS SEVEN HEAVENS, EACH IN A DIFFERENT PORT OF CALL."
SORRY, HON, BUT THIS AIN'T GONNA WORK OUT 'TWIXT US.
WITCHITA, 1881.
OH. WELL THEN, IT LOOKS LIKE I'VE GOT A ZEPPELIN TO CATCH.
"BEFORE LONG I HAD ONE OF HER IN EVERY WORLD I VISITED IN MY TRAVELS. THEY CAME AND WENT, BUT WHAT DIFFERENCE DID THAT MAKE?
"THEY WERE ALL CRESS. IT WORKED LIKE A CHARM--"

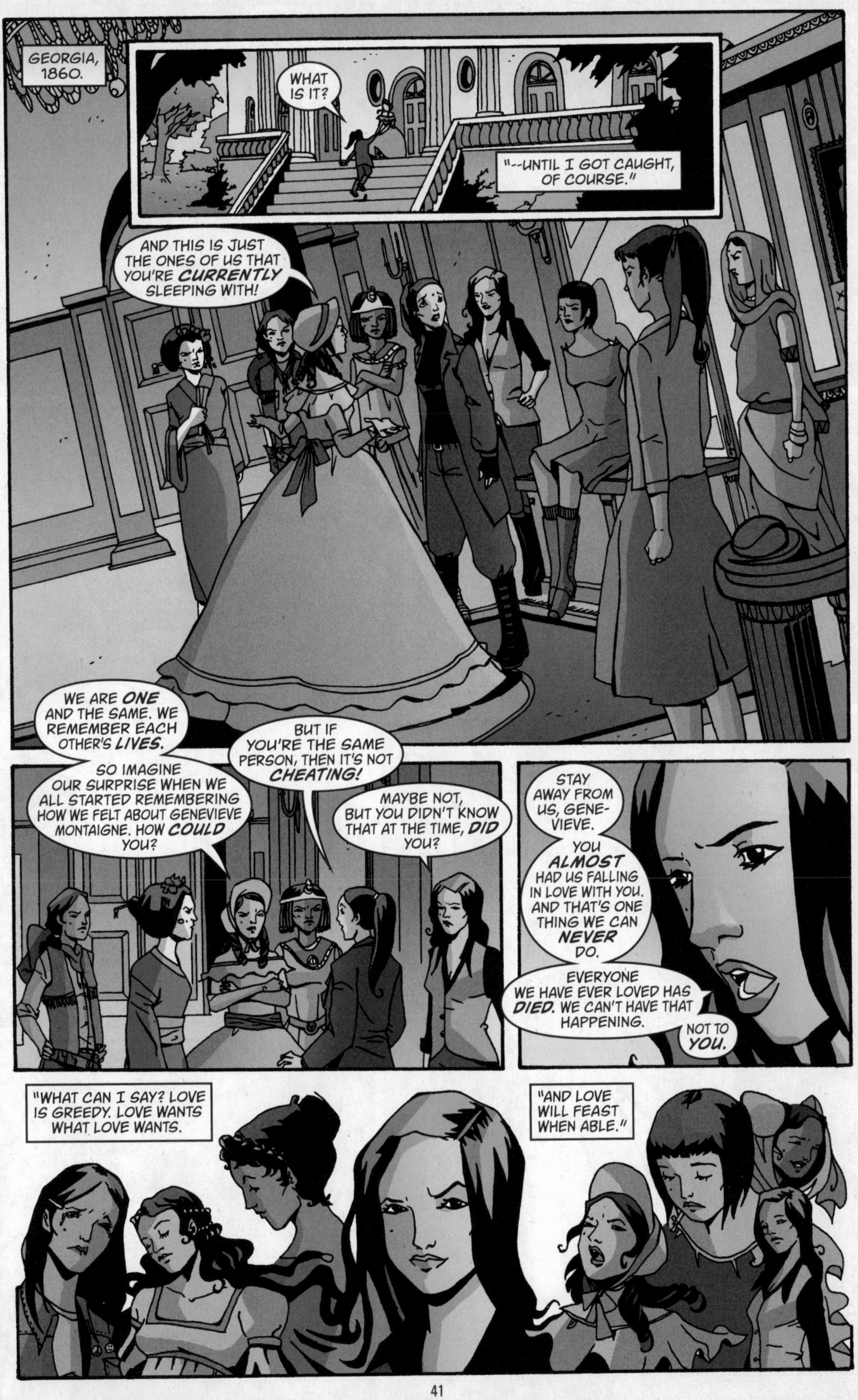
GEORGIA, 1860.
WHAT IS IT?
"--UNTIL I GOT CAUGHT, OF COURSE."
AND THIS IS JUST THE ONES OF US THAT YOU'RE CURRENTLY SLEEPING WITH!
WE ARE ONE AND THE SAME. WE REMEMBER EACH OTHER'S LIVES.
SO IMAGINE OUR SURPRISE WHEN WE ALL STARTED REMEMBERING HOW WE FELT ABOUT GENEVIEVE MONTAIGNE. HOW COULD YOU?
BUT IF YOU'RE THE SAME PERSON, THEN IT'S NOT CHEATING!
MAYBE NOT, BUT YOU DIDN'T KNOW THAT AT THE TIME, DID YOU?
STAY AWAY FROM US, GENE-VIEVE.
YOU ALMOST HAD US FALLING IN LOVE WITH YOU. AND THAT'S ONE THING WE CAN NEVER DO.
EVERYONE WE HAVE EVER LOVED HAS DIED. WE CAN'T HAVE THAT HAPPENING.
NOT TO YOU.
"WHAT CAN I SAY? LOVE IS GREEDY. LOVE WANTS WHAT LOVE WANTS.
"AND LOVE WILL FEAST WHEN ABLE."

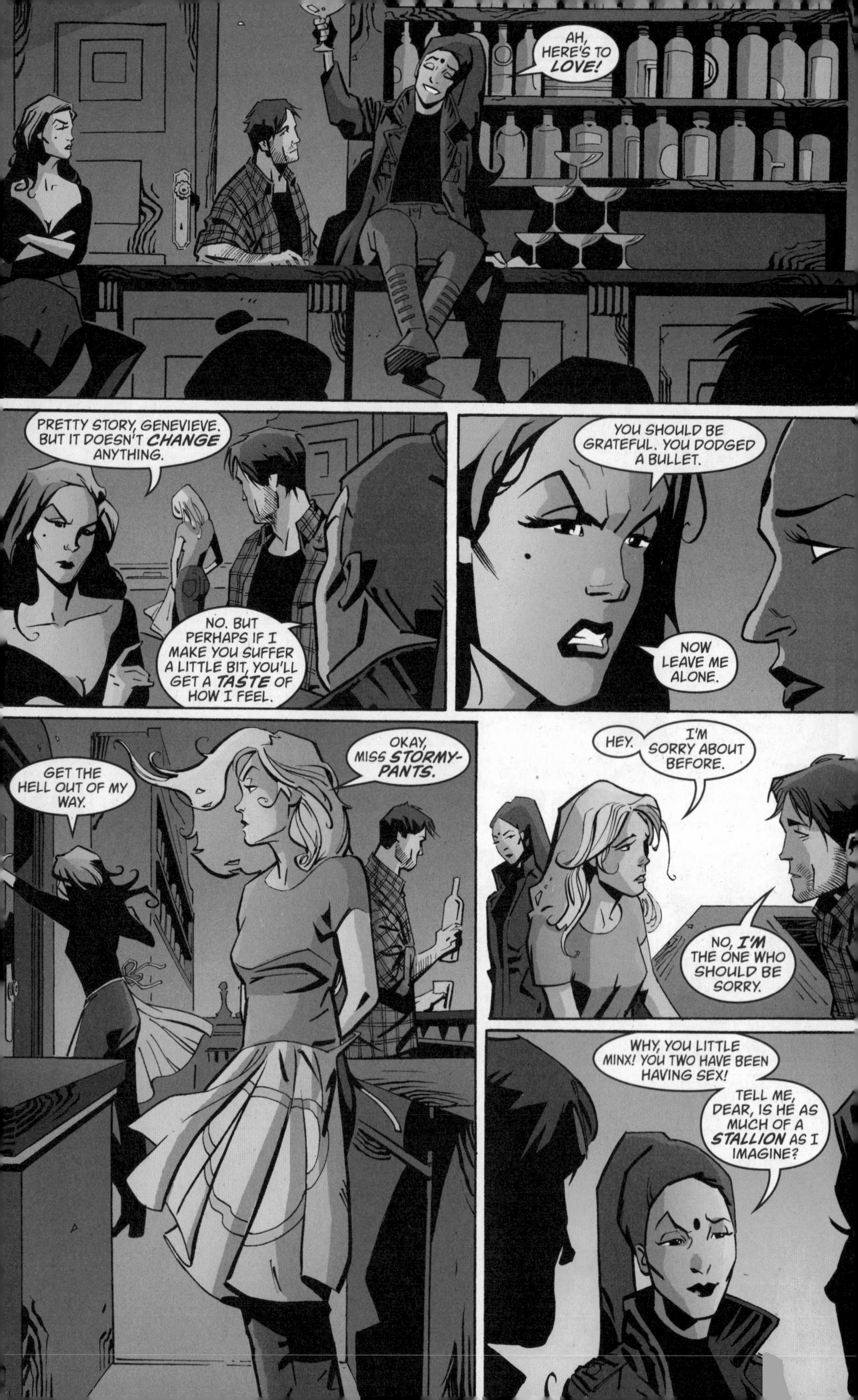
AH, HERE'S TO LOVE!
PRETTY STORY, GENEVIEVE. BUT IT DOESN'T CHANGE ANYTHING.
NO. BUT PERHAPS IF I MAKE YOU SUFFER A LITTLE BIT, YOU'LL GET A TASTE OF HOW I FEEL.
YOU SHOULD BE GRATEFUL. YOU DODGED A BULLET.
NOW LEAVE ME ALONE.
GET THE HELL OUT OF MY WAY.
OKAY, MISS STORMY-PANTS.
HEY.
I'M SORRY ABOUT BEFORE.
NO, I'M THE ONE WHO SHOULD BE SORRY.
WHY, YOU LITTLE MINX! YOU TWO HAVE BEEN HAVING SEX!
TELL ME, DEAR, IS HE AS MUCH OF A STALLION AS I IMAGINE?

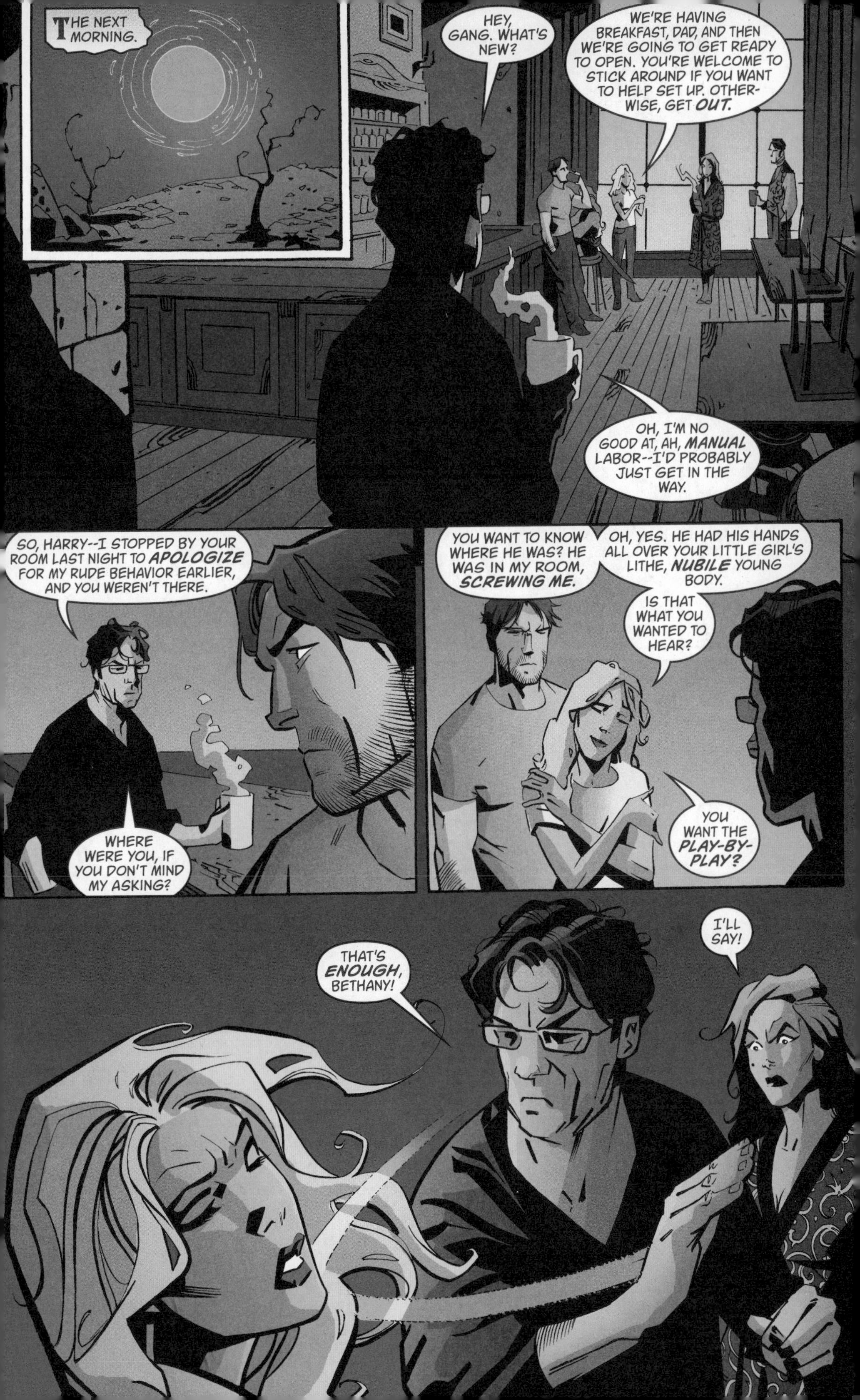
THE NEXT MORNING.
HEY, GANG. WHAT'S NEW?
WE'RE HAVING BREAKFAST, DAD, AND THEN WE'RE GOING TO GET READY TO OPEN. YOU'RE WELCOME TO STICK AROUND IF YOU WANT TO HELP SET UP. OTHER-WISE, GET OUT.
OH, I'M NO GOOD AT, AH, MANUAL LABOR--I'D PROBABLY JUST GET IN THE WAY.
SO, HARRY--I STOPPED BY YOUR ROOM LAST NIGHT TO APOLOGIZE FOR MY RUDE BEHAVIOR EARLIER, AND YOU WEREN'T THERE.
WHERE WERE YOU, IF YOU DON'T MIND MY ASKING?
YOU WANT TO KNOW WHERE HE WAS? HE WAS IN MY ROOM, SCREWING ME.
OH, YES. HE HAD HIS HANDS ALL OVER YOUR LITTLE GIRL'S LITHE, NUBILE YOUNG BODY.
IS THAT WHAT YOU WANTED TO HEAR?
YOU WANT THE PLAY-BY-PLAY?
THAT'S ENOUGH, BETHANY!
I'LL SAY!

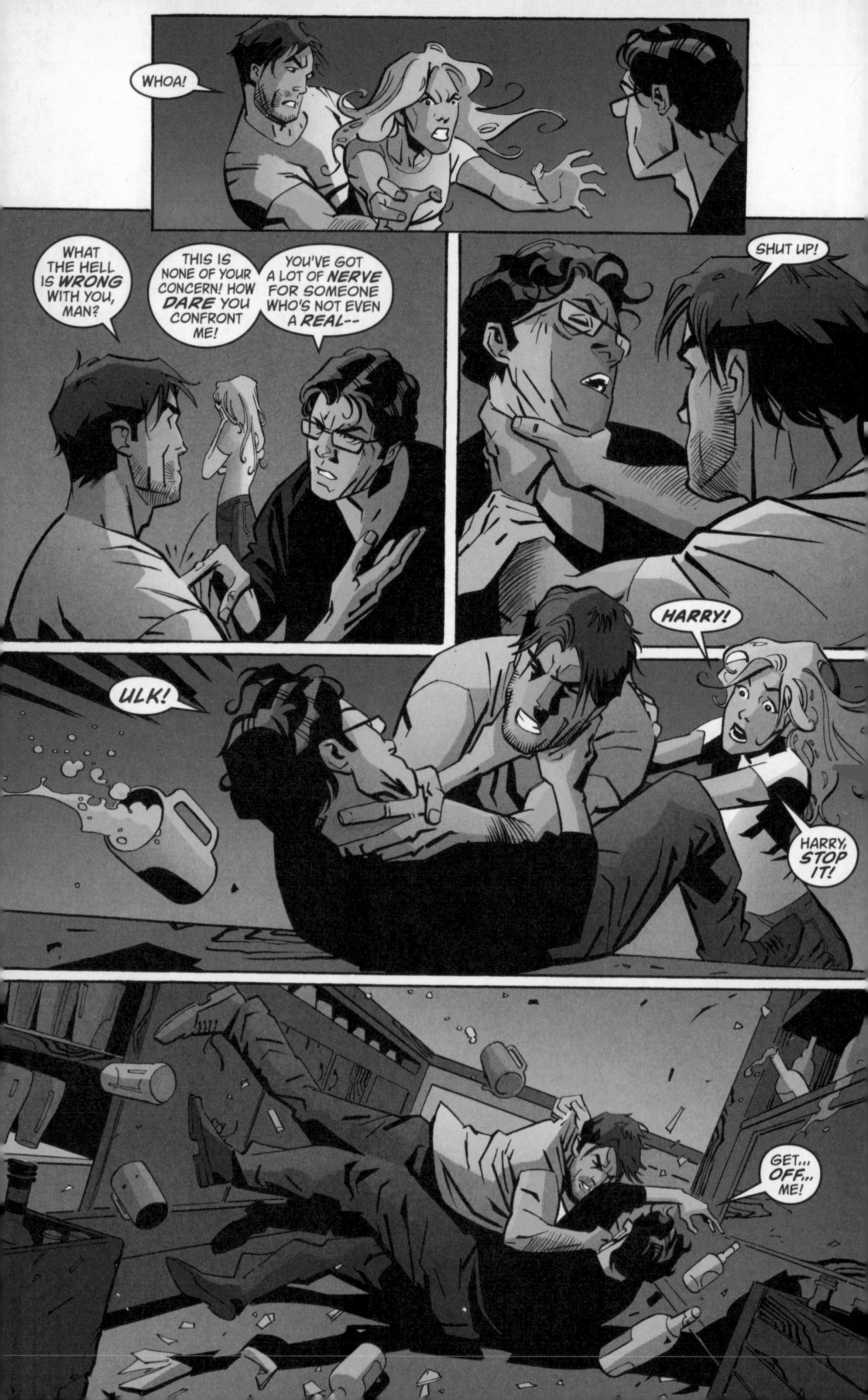
WHOA!
WHAT THE HELL IS WRONG WITH YOU, MAN?
THIS IS NONE OF YOUR CONCERN! HOW DARE YOU CONFRONT ME!
YOU'VE GOT A LOT OF NERVE FOR SOMEONE WHO'S NOT EVEN A REAL--
SHUT UP!
ULK!
HARRY!
HARRY, STOP IT!
GET... OFF... ME!

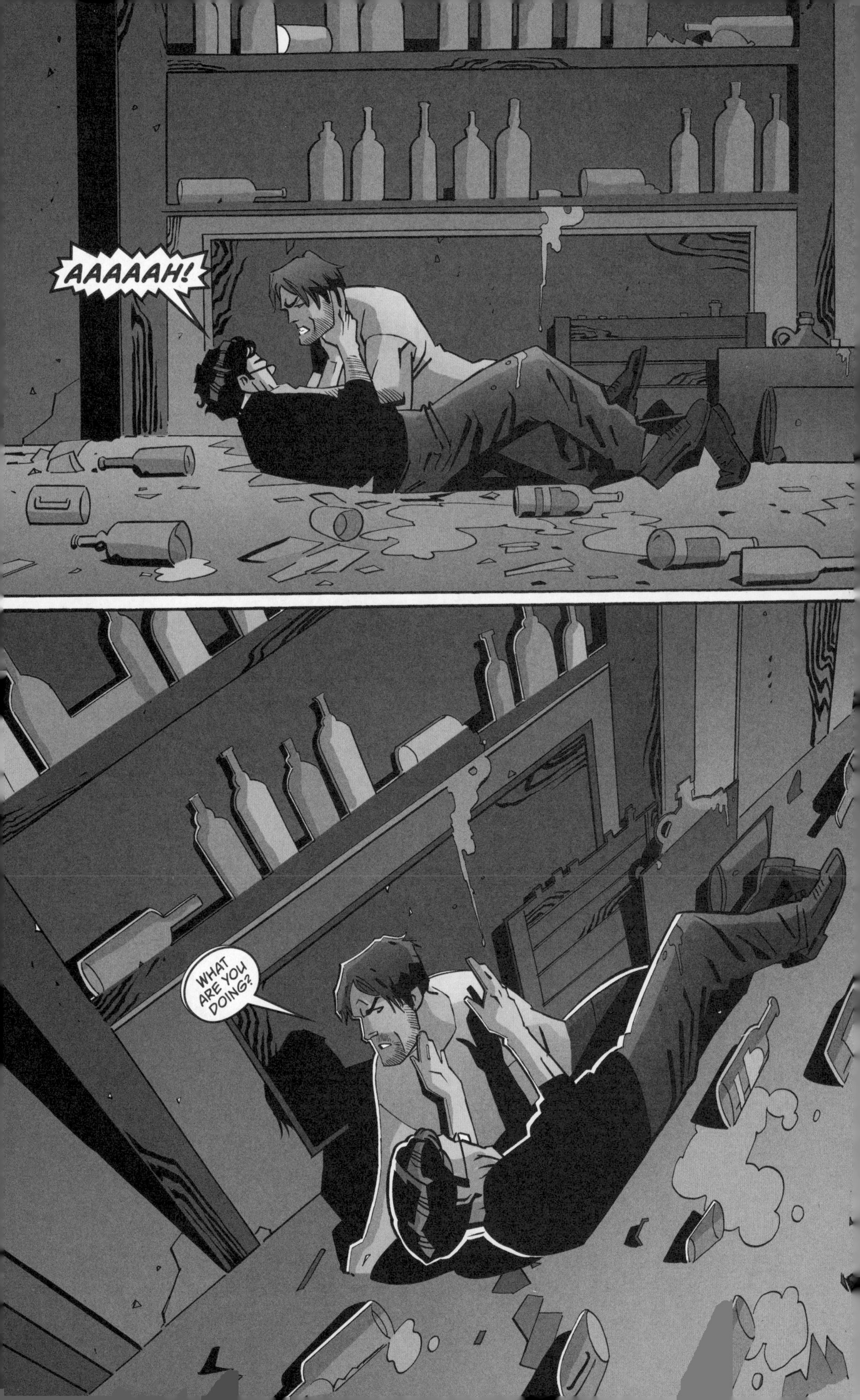
AAAAAH!
WHAT ARE YOU DOING?

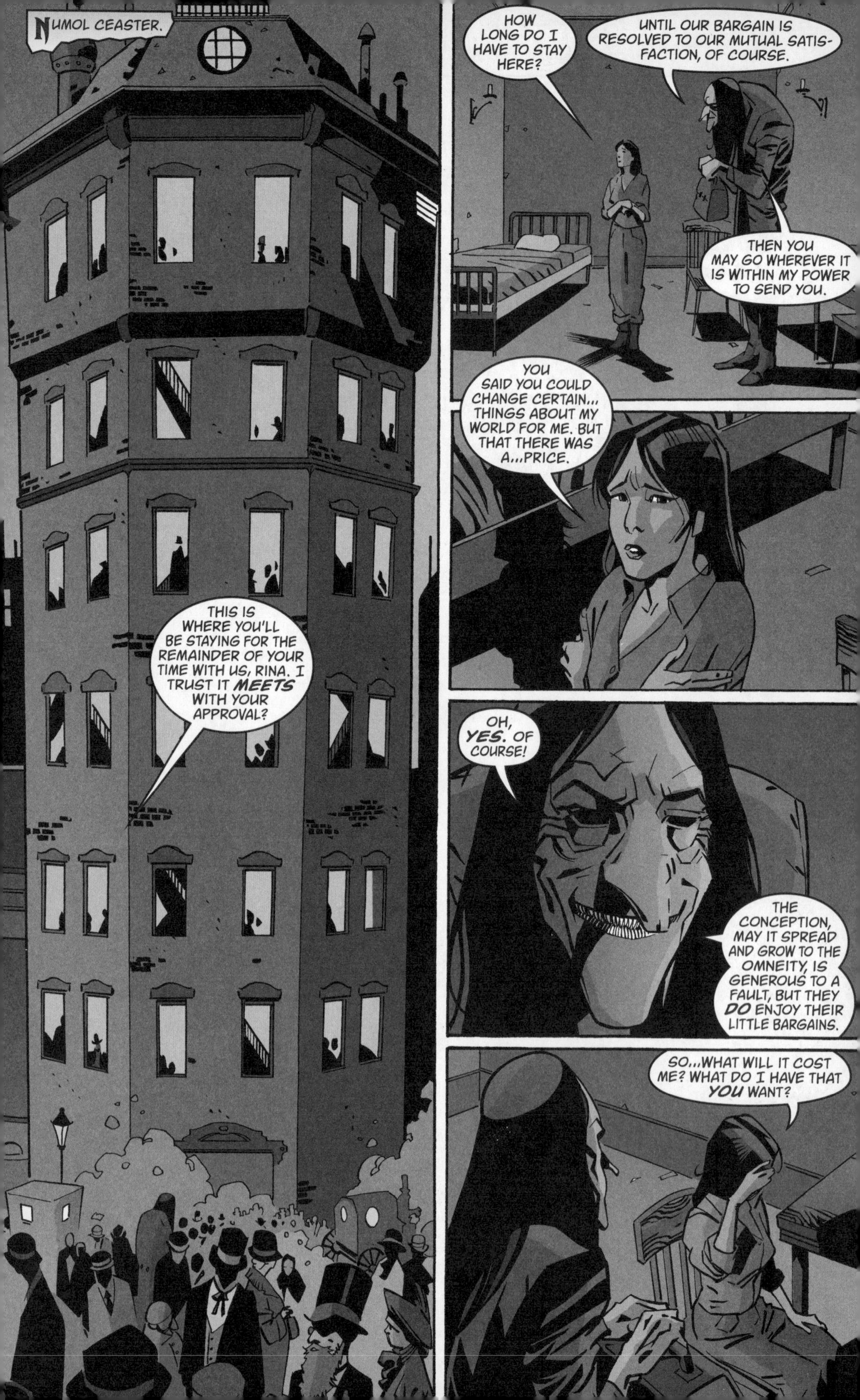
NUMOL CEASTER.
THIS IS WHERE YOU'LL BE STAYING FOR THE REMAINDER OF YOUR TIME WITH US, RINA. I TRUST IT MEETS WITH YOUR APPROVAL?
HOW LONG DO I HAVE TO STAY HERE?
UNTIL OUR BARGAIN IS RESOLVED TO OUR MUTUAL SATISFACTION, OF COURSE.
THEN YOU MAY GO WHEREVER IT IS WITHIN MY POWER TO SEND YOU.
YOU SAID YOU COULD CHANGE CERTAIN... THINGS ABOUT MY WORLD FOR ME. BUT THAT THERE WAS A...PRICE.
OH, YES. OF COURSE!
THE CONCEPTION, MAY IT SPREAD AND GROW TO THE OMNEITY, IS GENEROUS TO A FAULT, BUT THEY DO ENJOY THEIR LITTLE BARGAINS.
SO...WHAT WILL IT COST ME? WHAT DO I HAVE THAT YOU WANT?

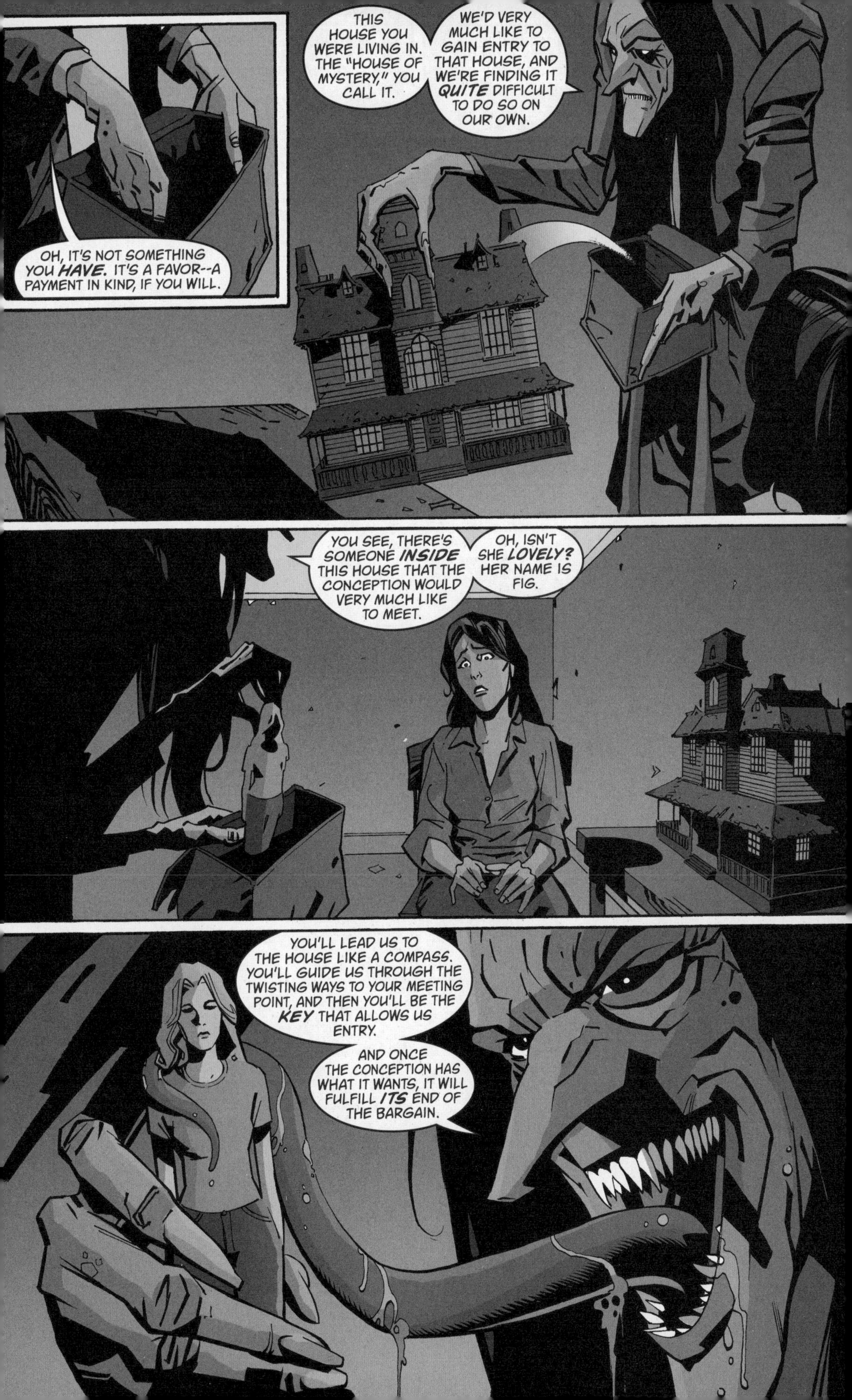
OH, IT'S NOT SOMETHING YOU HAVE. IT'S A FAVOR--A PAYMENT IN KIND, IF YOU WILL.
THIS HOUSE YOU WERE LIVING IN. THE "HOUSE OF MYSTERY," YOU CALL IT.
WE'D VERY MUCH LIKE TO GAIN ENTRY TO THAT HOUSE, AND WE'RE FINDING IT QUITE DIFFICULT TO DO SO ON OUR OWN.
YOU SEE, THERE'S SOMEONE INSIDE THIS HOUSE THAT THE CONCEPTION WOULD VERY MUCH LIKE TO MEET.
OH, ISN'T SHE LOVELY? HER NAME IS FIG.
YOU'LL LEAD US TO THE HOUSE LIKE A COMPASS. YOU'LL GUIDE US THROUGH THE TWISTING WAYS TO YOUR MEETING POINT, AND THEN YOU'LL BE THE KEY THAT ALLOWS US ENTRY.
AND ONCE THE CONCEPTION HAS WHAT IT WANTS, IT WILL FULFILL ITS END OF THE BARGAIN.

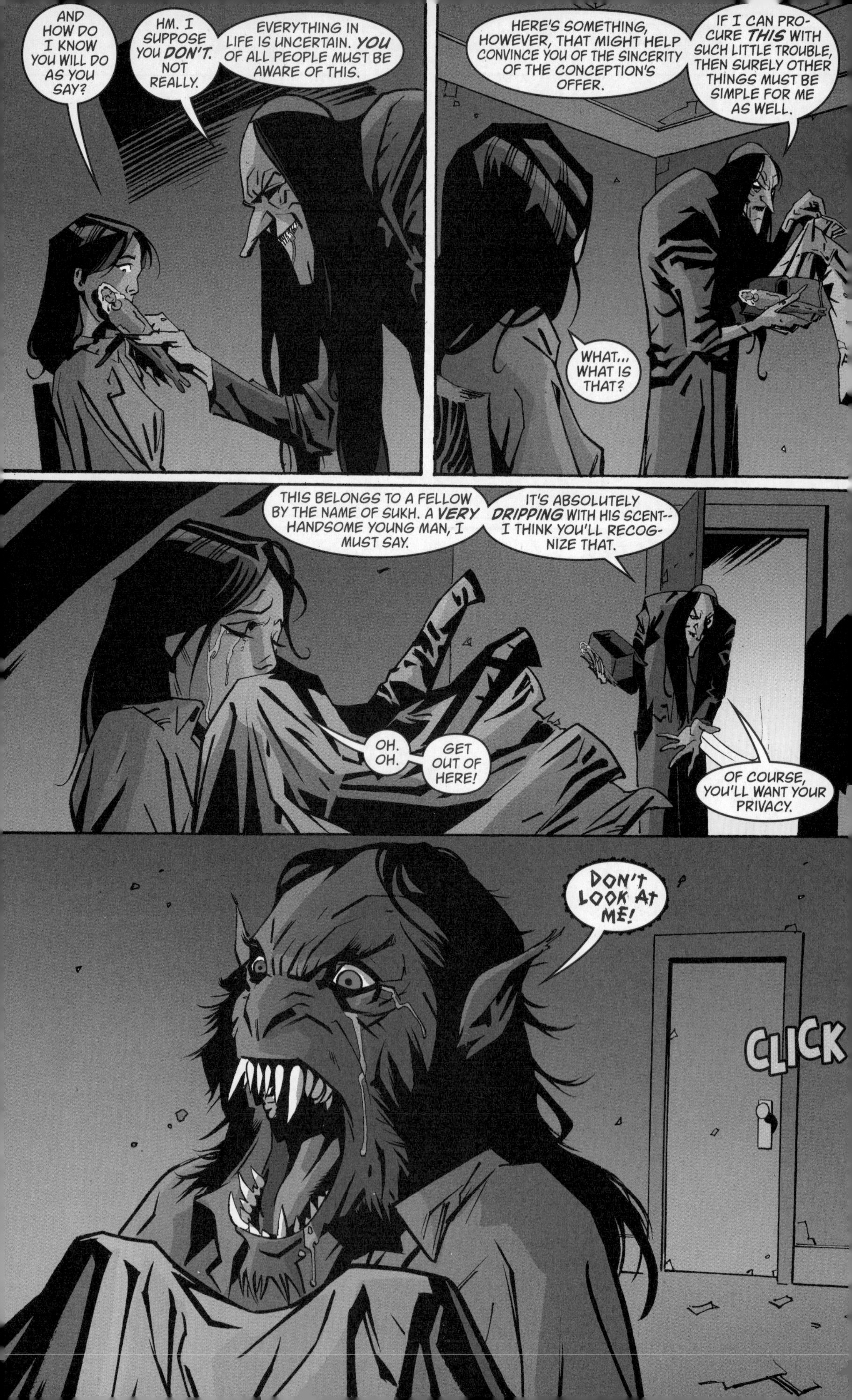
AND HOW DO I KNOW YOU WILL DO AS YOU SAY?
HM. I SUPPOSE YOU DON'T. NOT REALLY.
EVERYTHING IN LIFE IS UNCERTAIN. YOU OF ALL PEOPLE MUST BE AWARE OF THIS.
HERE'S SOMETHING, HOWEVER, THAT MIGHT HELP CONVINCE YOU OF THE SINCERITY OF THE CONCEPTION'S OFFER.
IF I CAN PROCURE THIS WITH SUCH LITTLE TROUBLE, THEN SURELY OTHER THINGS MUST BE SIMPLE FOR ME AS WELL.
WHAT... WHAT IS THAT?
THIS BELONGS TO A FELLOW BY THE NAME OF SUKH. A VERY HANDSOME YOUNG MAN, I MUST SAY.
IT'S ABSOLUTELY DRIPPING WITH HIS SCENT-- I THINK YOU'LL RECOGNIZE THAT.
OH. OH.
GET OUT OF HERE!
OF COURSE, YOU'LL WANT YOUR PRIVACY.
DON'T LOOK AT ME!
CLICK

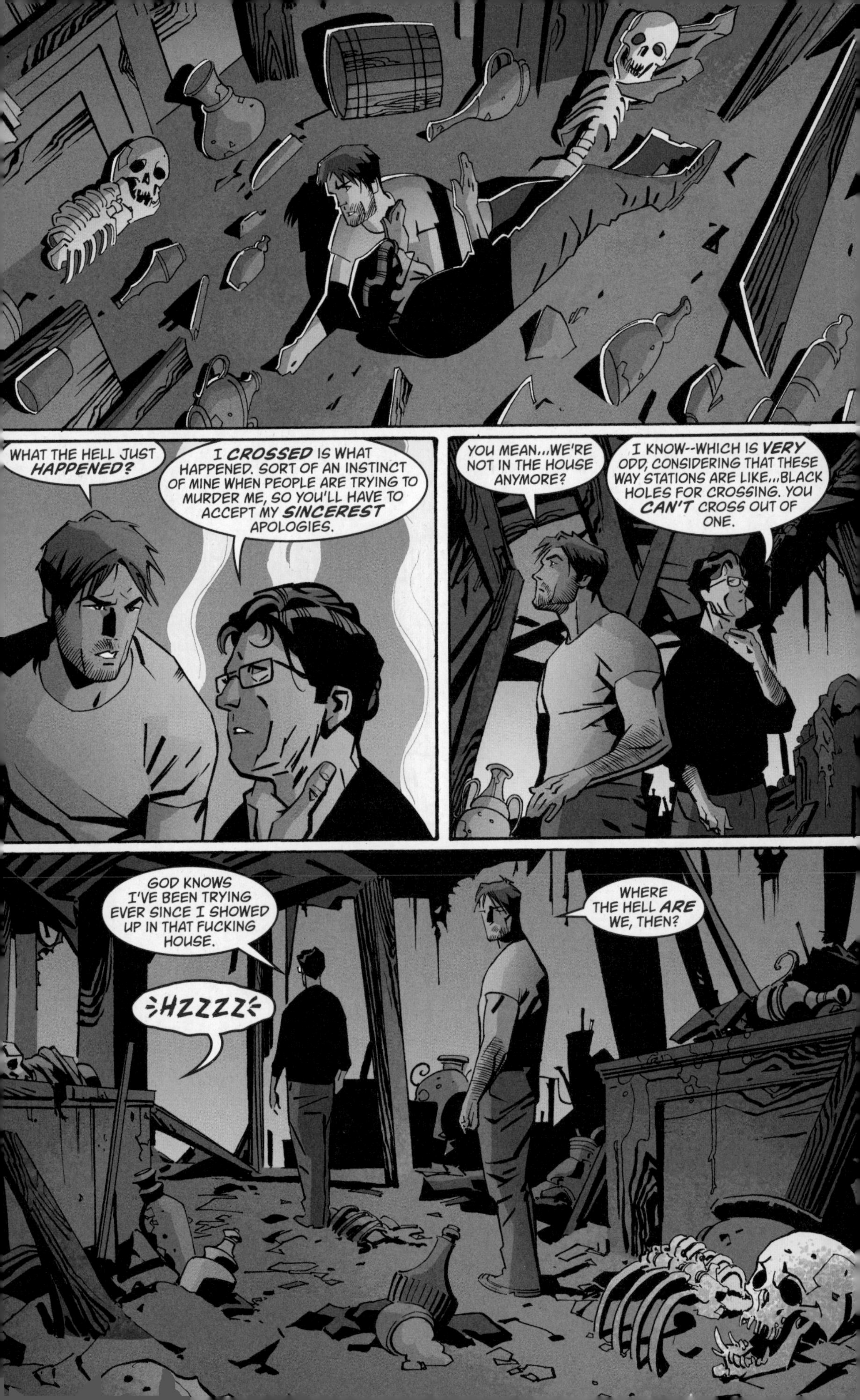

WHAT THE HELL JUST HAPPENED?
I CROSSED IS WHAT HAPPENED. SORT OF AN INSTINCT OF MINE WHEN PEOPLE ARE TRYING TO MURDER ME, SO YOU'LL HAVE TO ACCEPT MY SINCEREST APOLOGIES.
YOU MEAN...WE'RE NOT IN THE HOUSE ANYMORE?
I KNOW--WHICH IS VERY ODD, CONSIDERING THAT THESE WAY STATIONS ARE LIKE...BLACK HOLES FOR CROSSING. YOU CAN'T CROSS OUT OF ONE.
GOD KNOWS I'VE BEEN TRYING EVER SINCE I SHOWED UP IN THAT FUCKING HOUSE.
HZZZZ
WHERE THE HELL ARE WE, THEN?

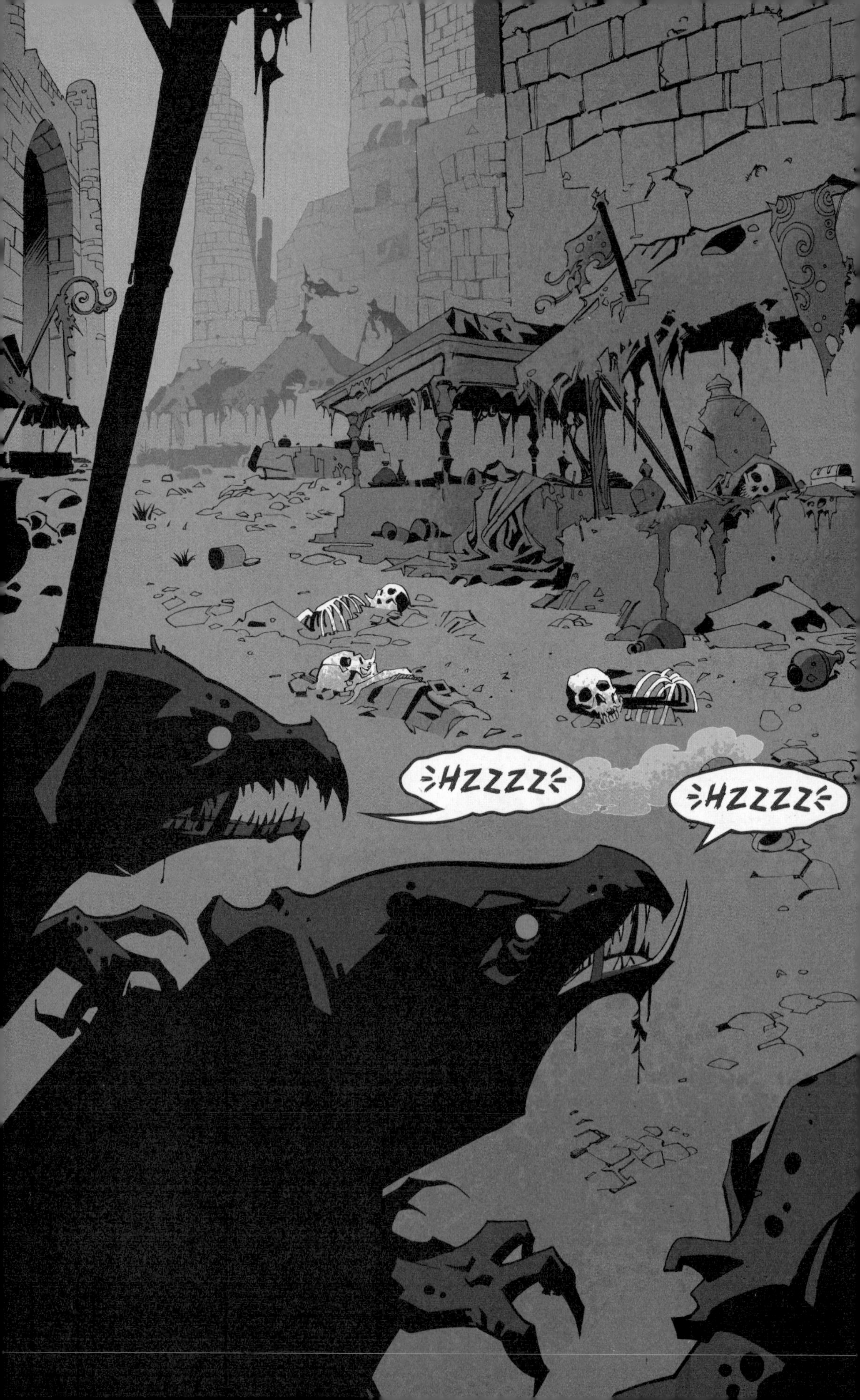
HZZZZ
HZZZZ

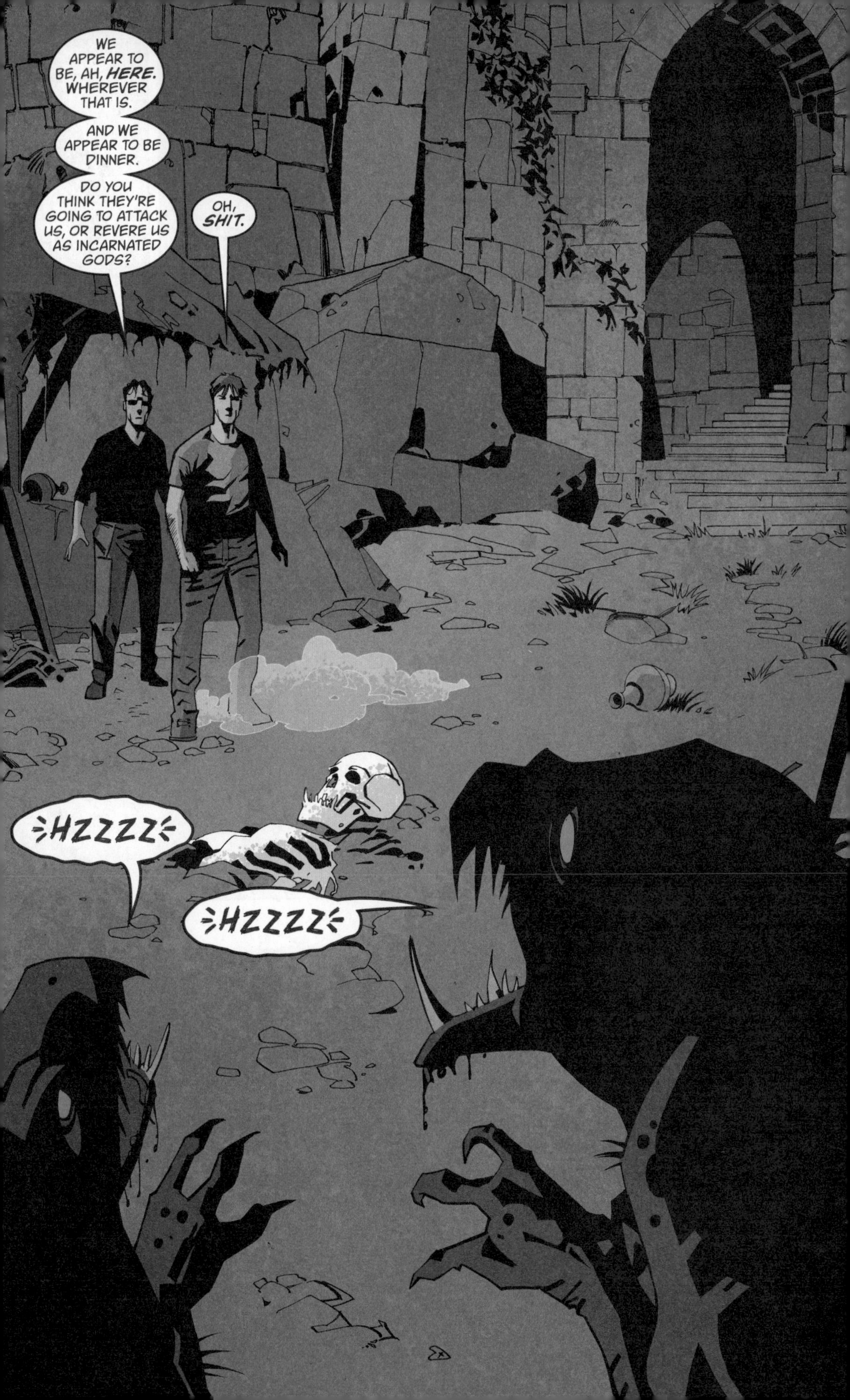
WE APPEAR TO BE, AH, *HERE*. WHEREVER THAT IS.
AND WE APPEAR TO BE DINNER.
DO YOU THINK THEY'RE GOING TO ATTACK US, OR REVERE US AS INCARNATED GODS?
OH, *SHIT*.
HZZZZ
HZZZZ

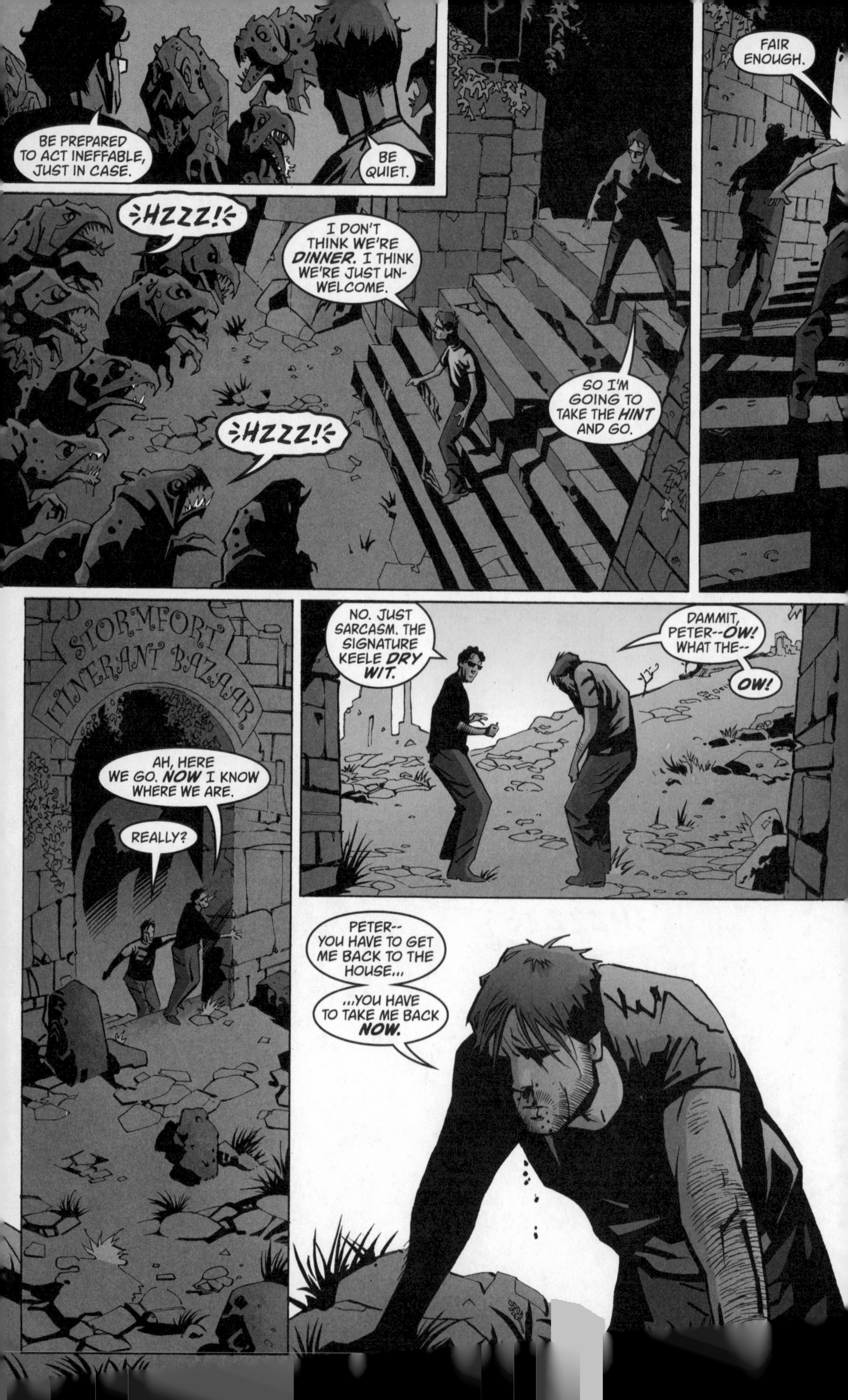
BE PREPARED TO ACT INEFFABLE, JUST IN CASE.
BE QUIET.
FAIR ENOUGH.
HZZZ!
I DON'T THINK WE'RE DINNER. I THINK WE'RE JUST UN-WELCOME.
SO I'M GOING TO TAKE THE HINT AND GO.
HZZZ!
STORMFORT ITINERANT BAZAAR
AH, HERE WE GO. NOW I KNOW WHERE WE ARE.
REALLY?
NO. JUST SARCASM. THE SIGNATURE KEELE DRY WIT.
DAMMIT, PETER--OW! WHAT THE--
OW!
PETER-- YOU HAVE TO GET ME BACK TO THE HOUSE...
...YOU HAVE TO TAKE ME BACK NOW.

ISSUE #13 COVER ART BY ESAO ANDREWS.

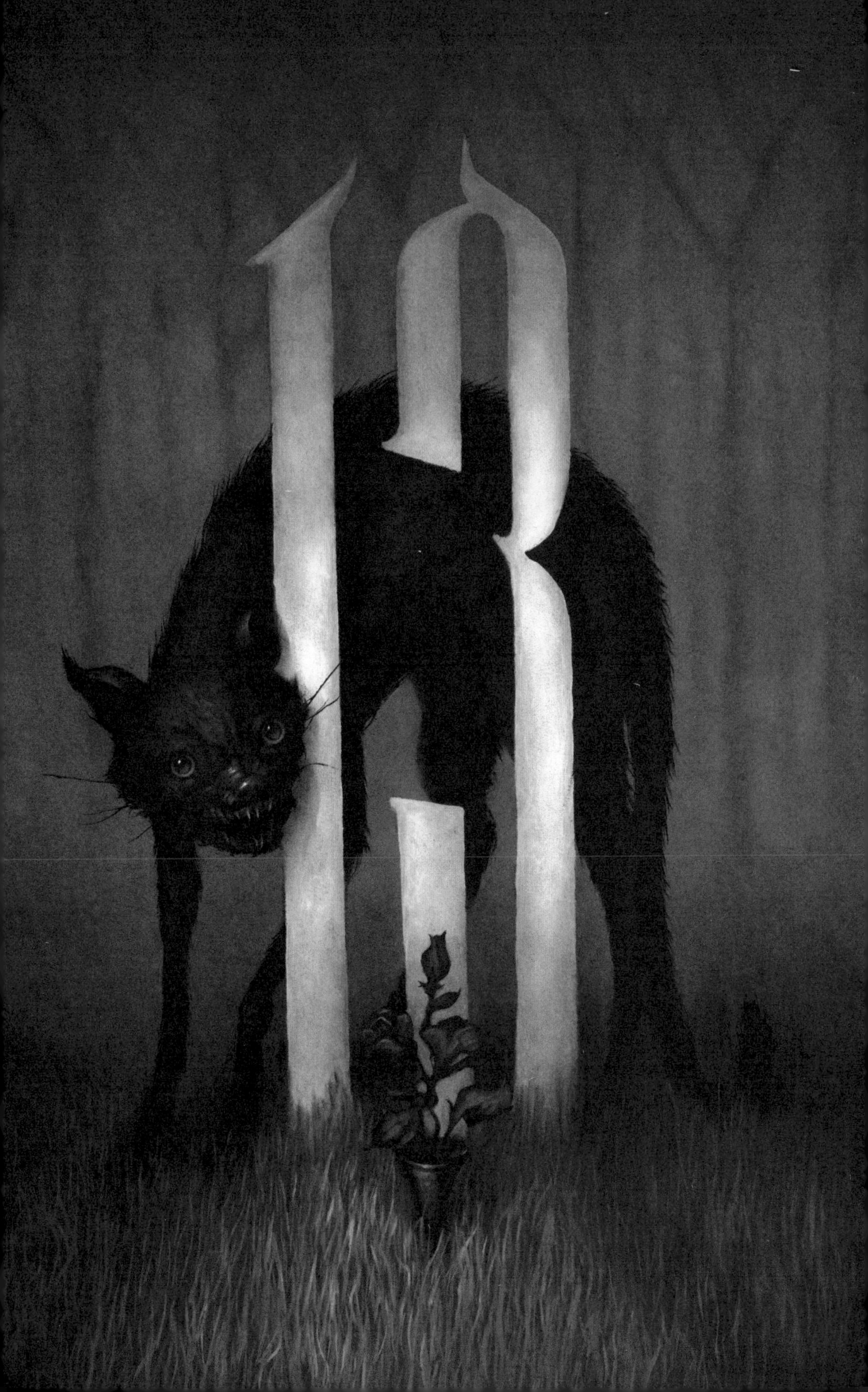
13

ISSUE #13 VARIANT COVER ART BY NEAL ADAMS.
COLOR BY MOOSE BAUMANN.

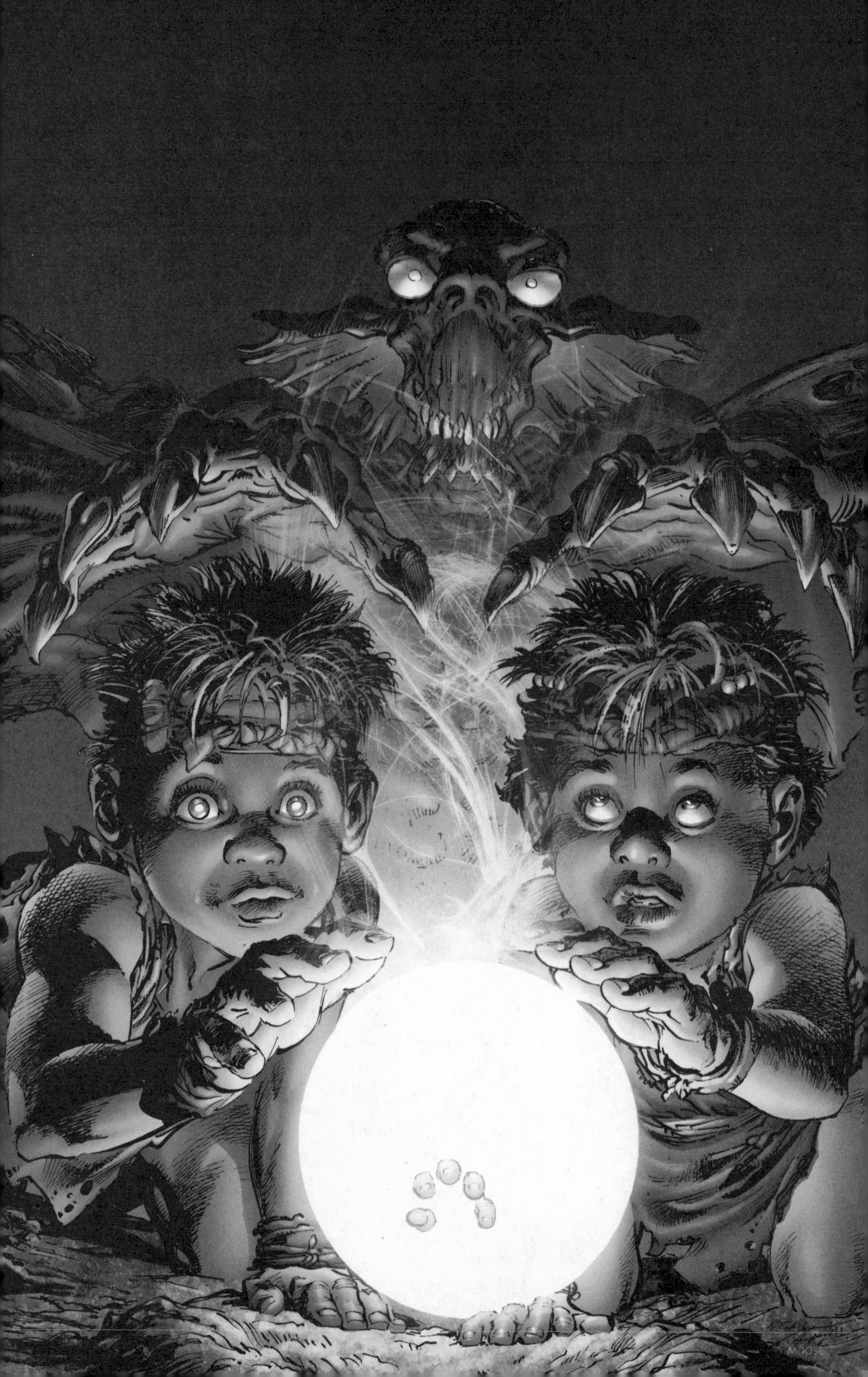

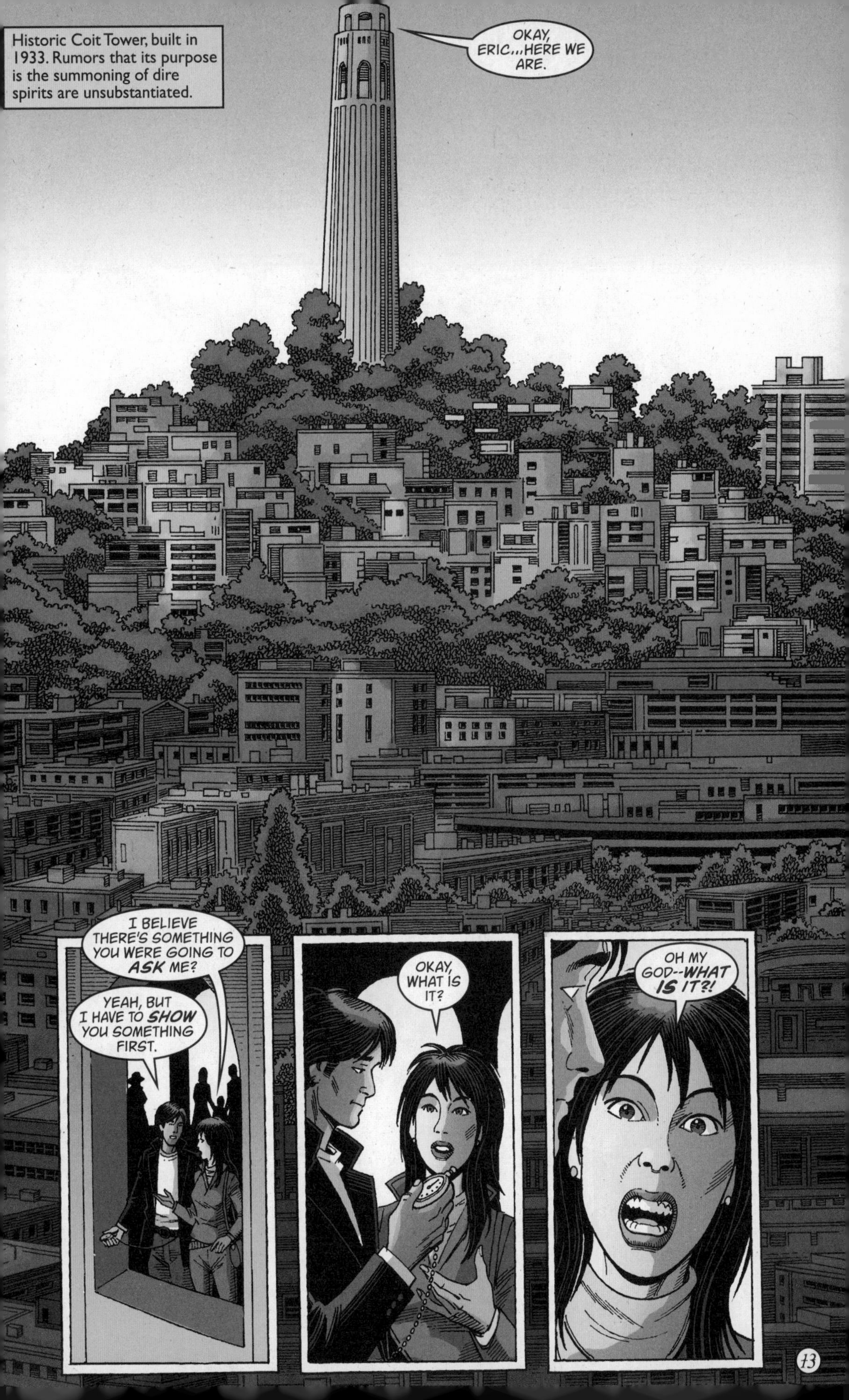
Historic Coit Tower, built in 1933. Rumors that its purpose is the summoning of dire spirits are unsubstantiated.
OKAY, ERIC...HERE WE ARE.
I BELIEVE THERE'S SOMETHING YOU WERE GOING TO ASK ME?
YEAH, BUT I HAVE TO SHOW YOU SOMETHING FIRST.
OKAY, WHAT IS IT?
OH MY GOD--WHAT IS IT?!

THE THIRTEENTH HOUR

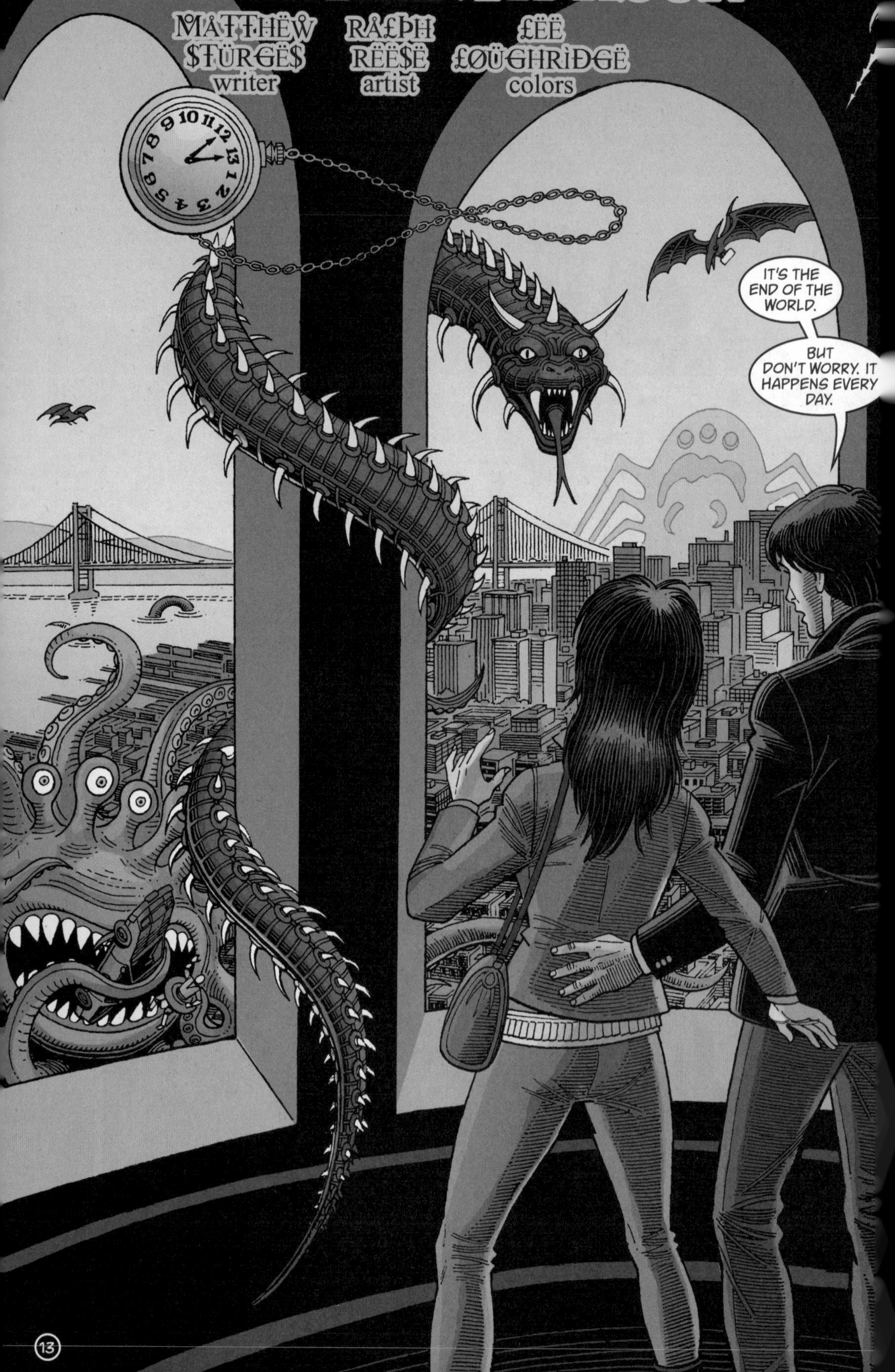
MATTHEW STURGES writer
RALPH REESE artist
LEE LOUGHRIDGE colors
IT'S THE END OF THE WORLD.
BUT DON'T WORRY. IT HAPPENS EVERY DAY.

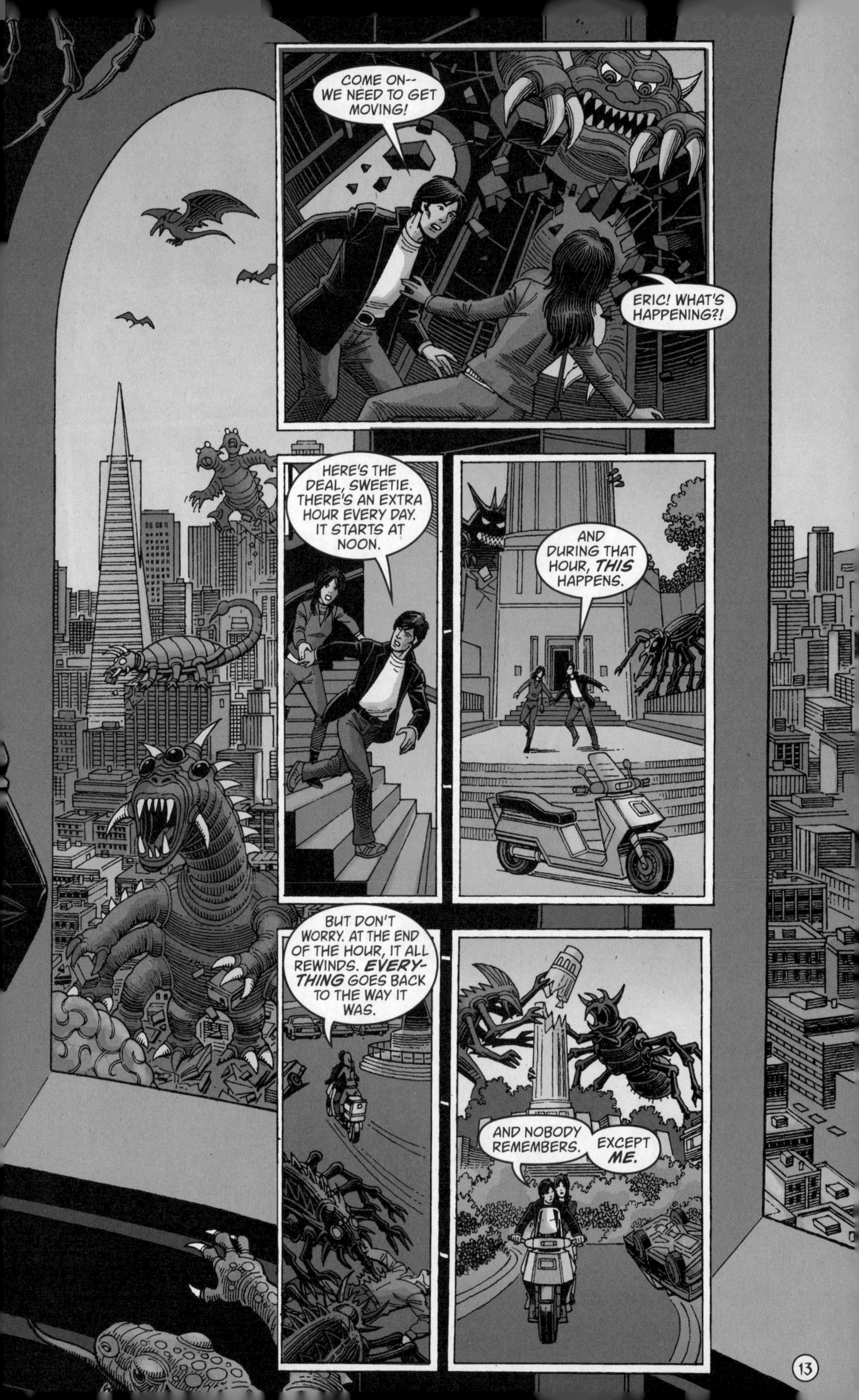
COME ON-- WE NEED TO GET MOVING!
ERIC! WHAT'S HAPPENING?!
HERE'S THE DEAL, SWEETIE. THERE'S AN EXTRA HOUR EVERY DAY. IT STARTS AT NOON.
AND DURING THAT HOUR, THIS HAPPENS.
BUT DON'T WORRY. AT THE END OF THE HOUR, IT ALL REWINDS. EVERY-THING GOES BACK TO THE WAY IT WAS.
AND NOBODY REMEMBERS.
EXCEPT ME.

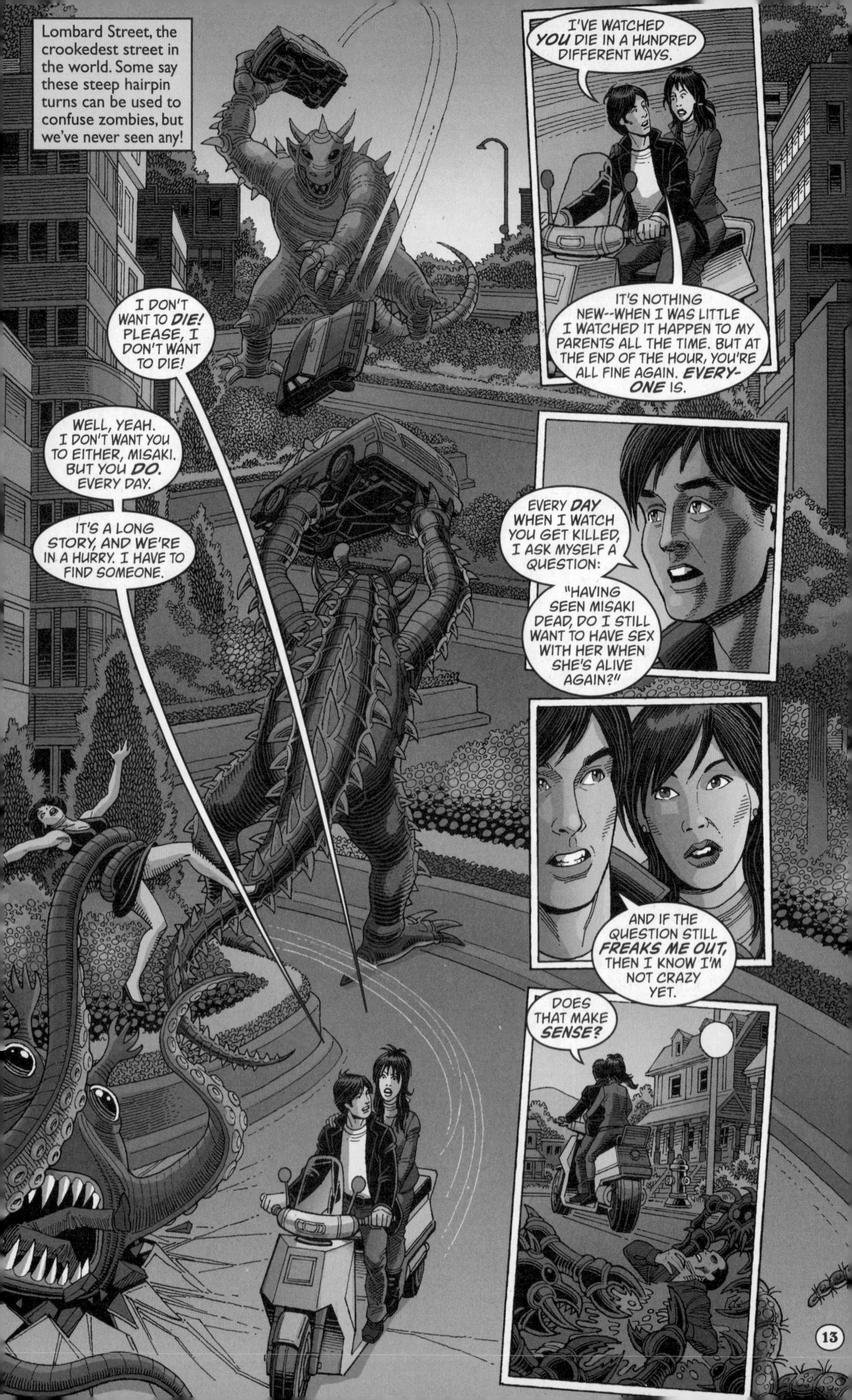

Lombard Street, the crookedest street in the world. Some say these steep hairpin turns can be used to confuse zombies, but we've never seen any!
I DON'T WANT TO DIE! PLEASE, I DON'T WANT TO DIE!
WELL, YEAH. I DON'T WANT YOU TO EITHER, MISAKI. BUT YOU DO. EVERY DAY.
IT'S A LONG STORY, AND WE'RE IN A HURRY. I HAVE TO FIND SOMEONE.
I'VE WATCHED YOU DIE IN A HUNDRED DIFFERENT WAYS.
IT'S NOTHING NEW--WHEN I WAS LITTLE I WATCHED IT HAPPEN TO MY PARENTS ALL THE TIME. BUT AT THE END OF THE HOUR, YOU'RE ALL FINE AGAIN. EVERY-ONE IS.
EVERY DAY WHEN I WATCH YOU GET KILLED, I ASK MYSELF A QUESTION:
"HAVING SEEN MISAKI DEAD, DO I STILL WANT TO HAVE SEX WITH HER WHEN SHE'S ALIVE AGAIN?"
AND IF THE QUESTION STILL FREAKS ME OUT, THEN I KNOW I'M NOT CRAZY YET.
DOES THAT MAKE SENSE?

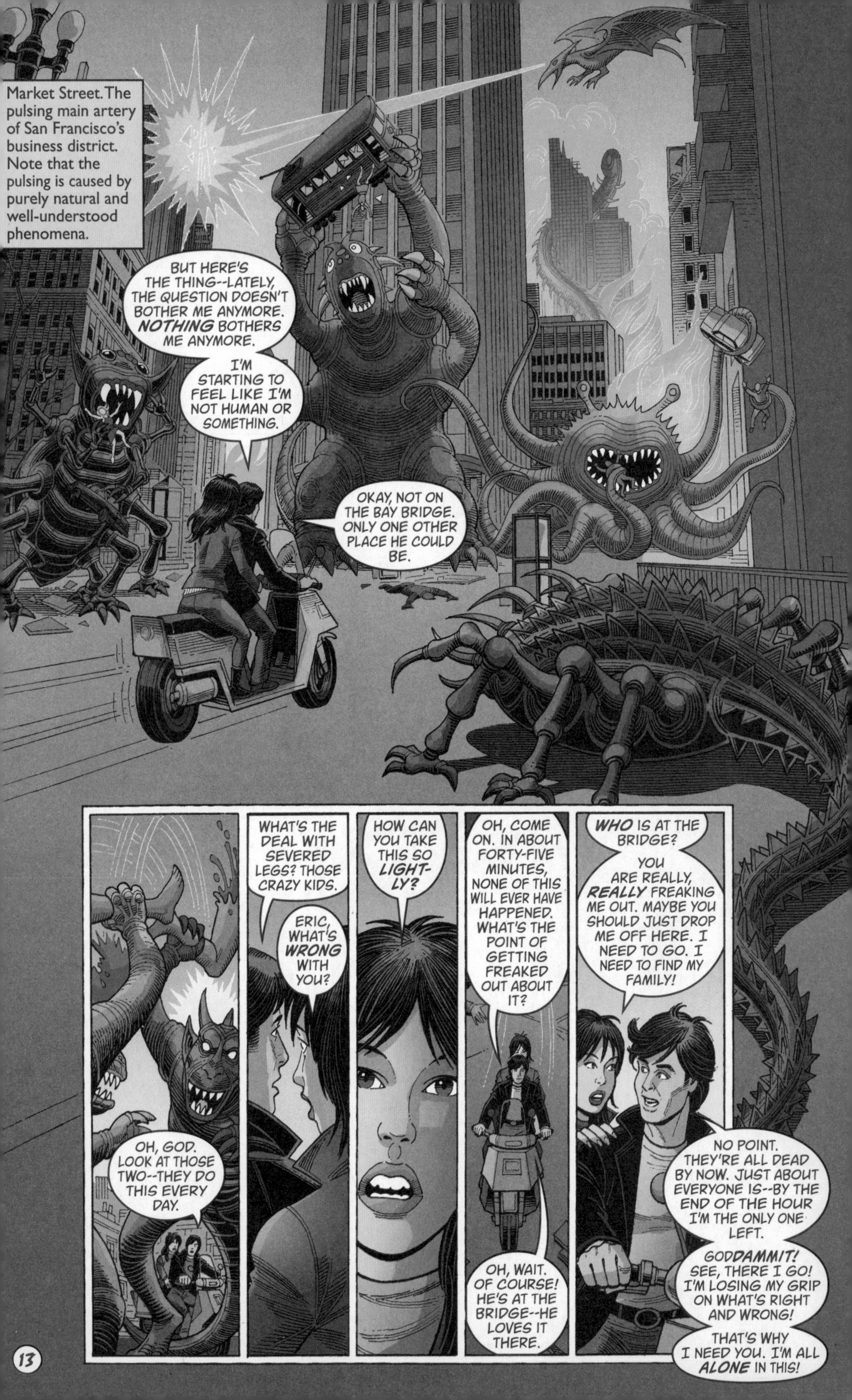
Market Street. The pulsing main artery of San Francisco's business district. Note that the pulsing is caused by purely natural and well-understood phenomena.
BUT HERE'S THE THING--LATELY, THE QUESTION DOESN'T BOTHER ME ANYMORE. NOTHING BOTHERS ME ANYMORE.
I'M STARTING TO FEEL LIKE I'M NOT HUMAN OR SOMETHING.
OKAY, NOT ON THE BAY BRIDGE. ONLY ONE OTHER PLACE HE COULD BE.
OH, GOD. LOOK AT THOSE TWO--THEY DO THIS EVERY DAY.
WHAT'S THE DEAL WITH SEVERED LEGS? THOSE CRAZY KIDS.
ERIC, WHAT'S WRONG WITH YOU?
HOW CAN YOU TAKE THIS SO LIGHT-LY?
OH, COME ON. IN ABOUT FORTY-FIVE MINUTES, NONE OF THIS WILL EVER HAVE HAPPENED. WHAT'S THE POINT OF GETTING FREAKED OUT ABOUT IT?
OH, WAIT. OF COURSE! HE'S AT THE BRIDGE--HE LOVES IT THERE.
WHO IS AT THE BRIDGE?
YOU ARE REALLY, REALLY FREAKING ME OUT. MAYBE YOU SHOULD JUST DROP ME OFF HERE. I NEED TO GO. I NEED TO FIND MY FAMILY!
NO POINT. THEY'RE ALL DEAD BY NOW. JUST ABOUT EVERYONE IS--BY THE END OF THE HOUR I'M THE ONLY ONE LEFT.
GODDAMMIT! SEE, THERE I GO! I'M LOSING MY GRIP ON WHAT'S RIGHT AND WRONG!
THAT'S WHY I NEED YOU. I'M ALL ALONE IN THIS!

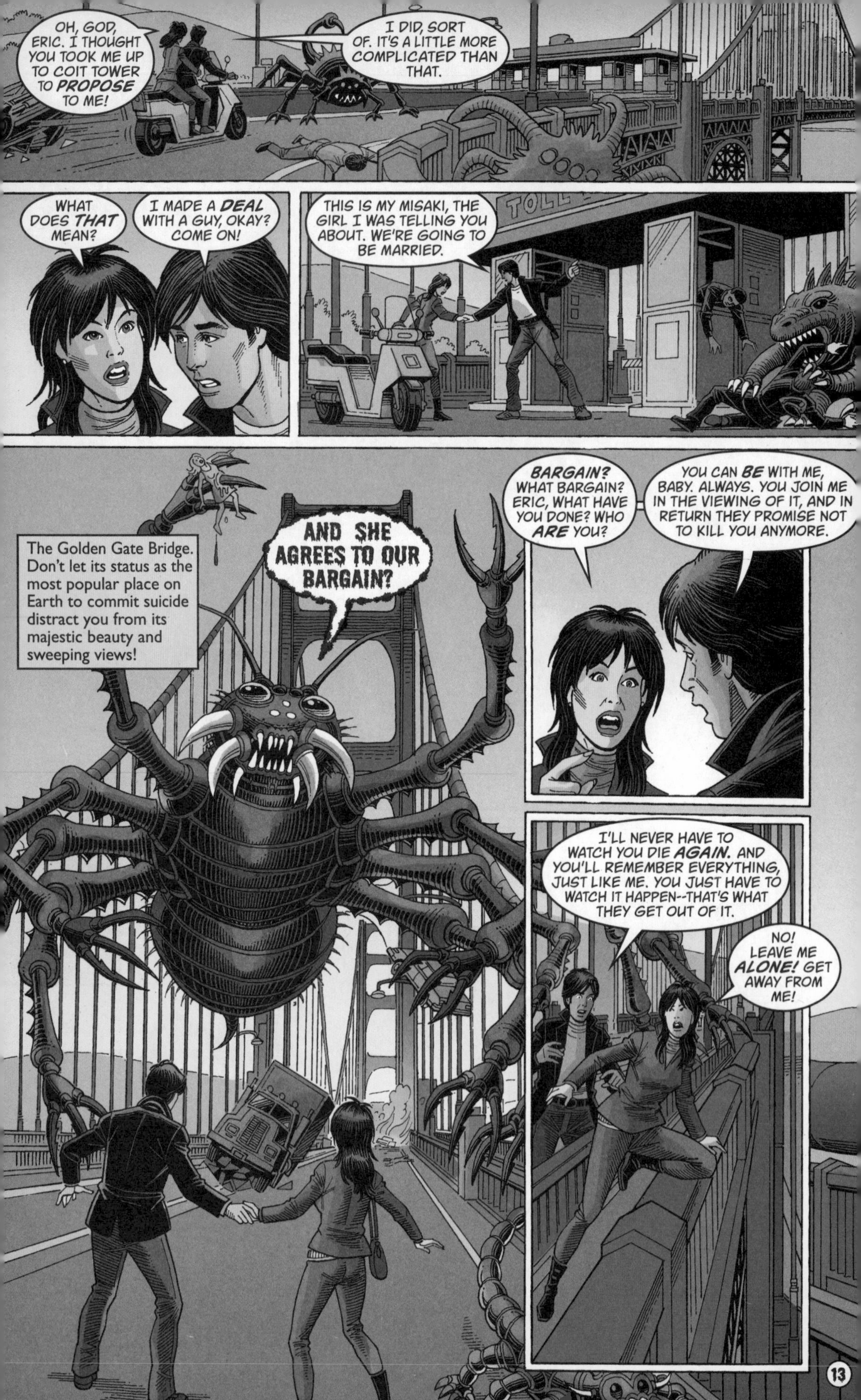
OH, GOD, ERIC. I THOUGHT YOU TOOK ME UP TO COIT TOWER TO PROPOSE TO ME!
I DID, SORT OF. IT'S A LITTLE MORE COMPLICATED THAN THAT.
WHAT DOES THAT MEAN?
I MADE A DEAL WITH A GUY, OKAY? COME ON!
TOLL
THIS IS MY MISAKI, THE GIRL I WAS TELLING YOU ABOUT. WE'RE GOING TO BE MARRIED.
The Golden Gate Bridge. Don't let its status as the most popular place on Earth to commit suicide distract you from its majestic beauty and sweeping views!
AND SHE AGREES TO OUR BARGAIN?
BARGAIN? WHAT BARGAIN? ERIC, WHAT HAVE YOU DONE? WHO ARE YOU?
YOU CAN BE WITH ME, BABY. ALWAYS. YOU JOIN ME IN THE VIEWING OF IT, AND IN RETURN THEY PROMISE NOT TO KILL YOU ANYMORE.
I'LL NEVER HAVE TO WATCH YOU DIE AGAIN. AND YOU'LL REMEMBER EVERYTHING, JUST LIKE ME. YOU JUST HAVE TO WATCH IT HAPPEN--THAT'S WHAT THEY GET OUT OF IT.
NO! LEAVE ME ALONE! GET AWAY FROM ME!

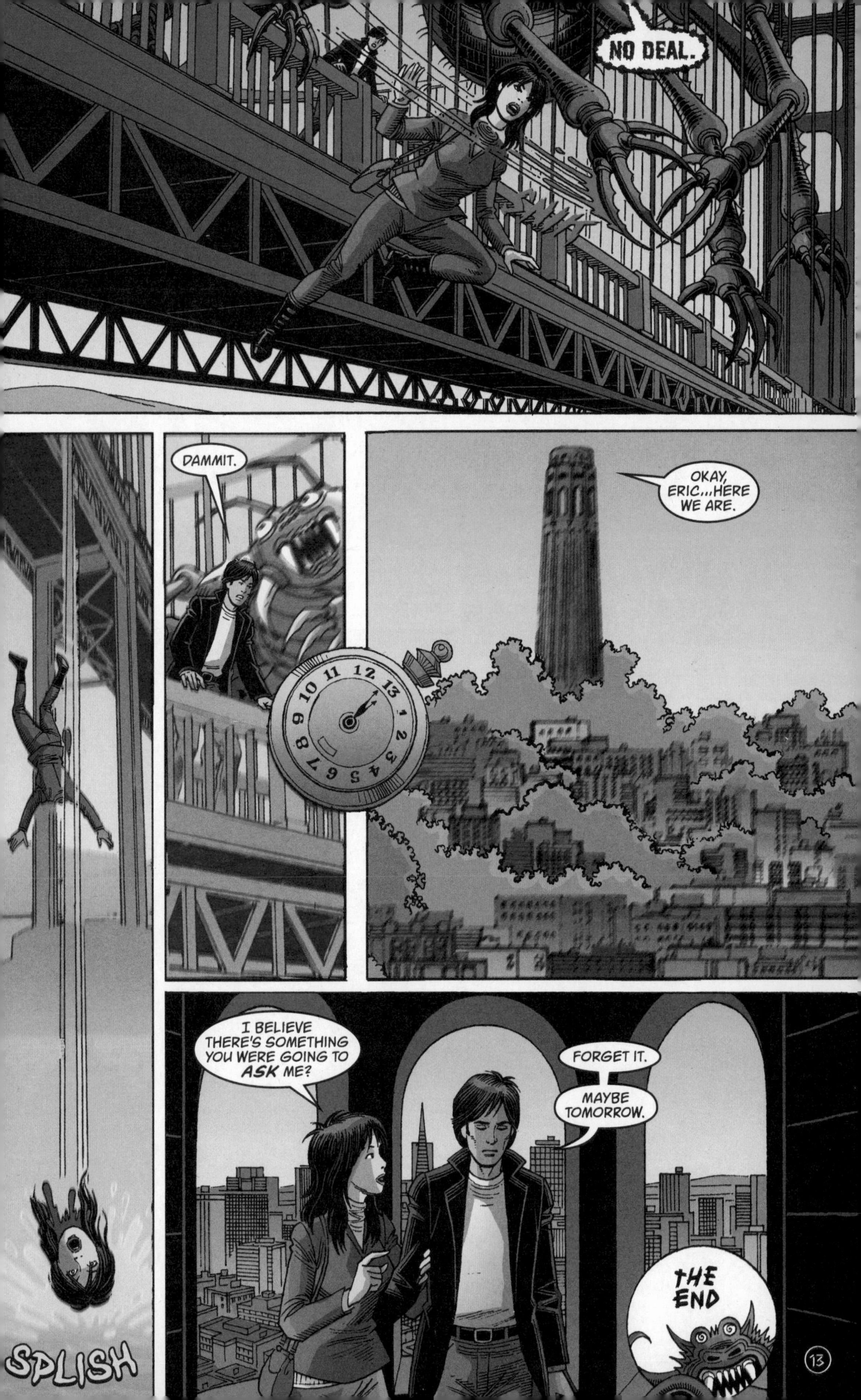
NO DEAL.
DAMMIT.
OKAY, ERIC...HERE WE ARE.
I BELIEVE THERE'S SOMETHING YOU WERE GOING TO ASK ME?
FORGET IT.
MAYBE TOMORROW.
SPLISH
THE END

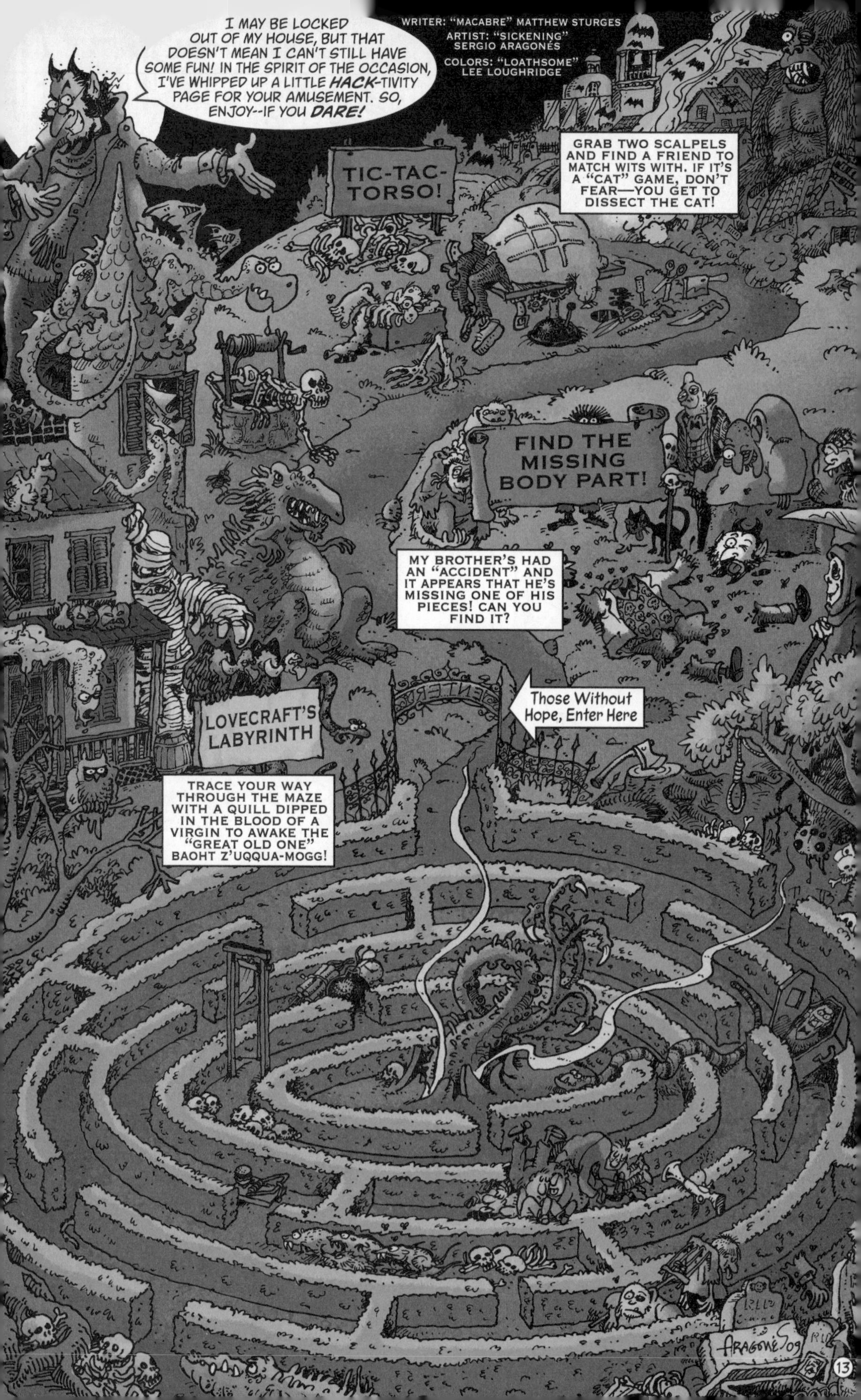

I MAY BE LOCKED OUT OF MY HOUSE, BUT THAT DOESN'T MEAN I CAN'T STILL HAVE SOME FUN! IN THE SPIRIT OF THE OCCASION, I'VE WHIPPED UP A LITTLE HACK-TIVITY PAGE FOR YOUR AMUSEMENT. SO, ENJOY--IF YOU DARE!
WRITER: "MACABRE" MATTHEW STURGES
ARTIST: "SICKENING" SERGIO ARAGONÉS
COLORS: "LOATHSOME" LEE LOUGHRIDGE
TIC-TAC-TORSO!
GRAB TWO SCALPELS AND FIND A FRIEND TO MATCH WITS WITH. IF IT'S A "CAT" GAME, DON'T FEAR—YOU GET TO DISSECT THE CAT!
FIND THE MISSING BODY PART!
MY BROTHER'S HAD AN "ACCIDENT" AND IT APPEARS THAT HE'S MISSING ONE OF HIS PIECES! CAN YOU FIND IT?
ENTER
Those Without Hope, Enter Here
LOVECRAFT'S LABYRINTH
TRACE YOUR WAY THROUGH THE MAZE WITH A QUILL DIPPED IN THE BLOOD OF A VIRGIN TO AWAKE THE "GREAT OLD ONE" BAOHT Z'UQQUA-MOGG!
ARAGONÉS 09

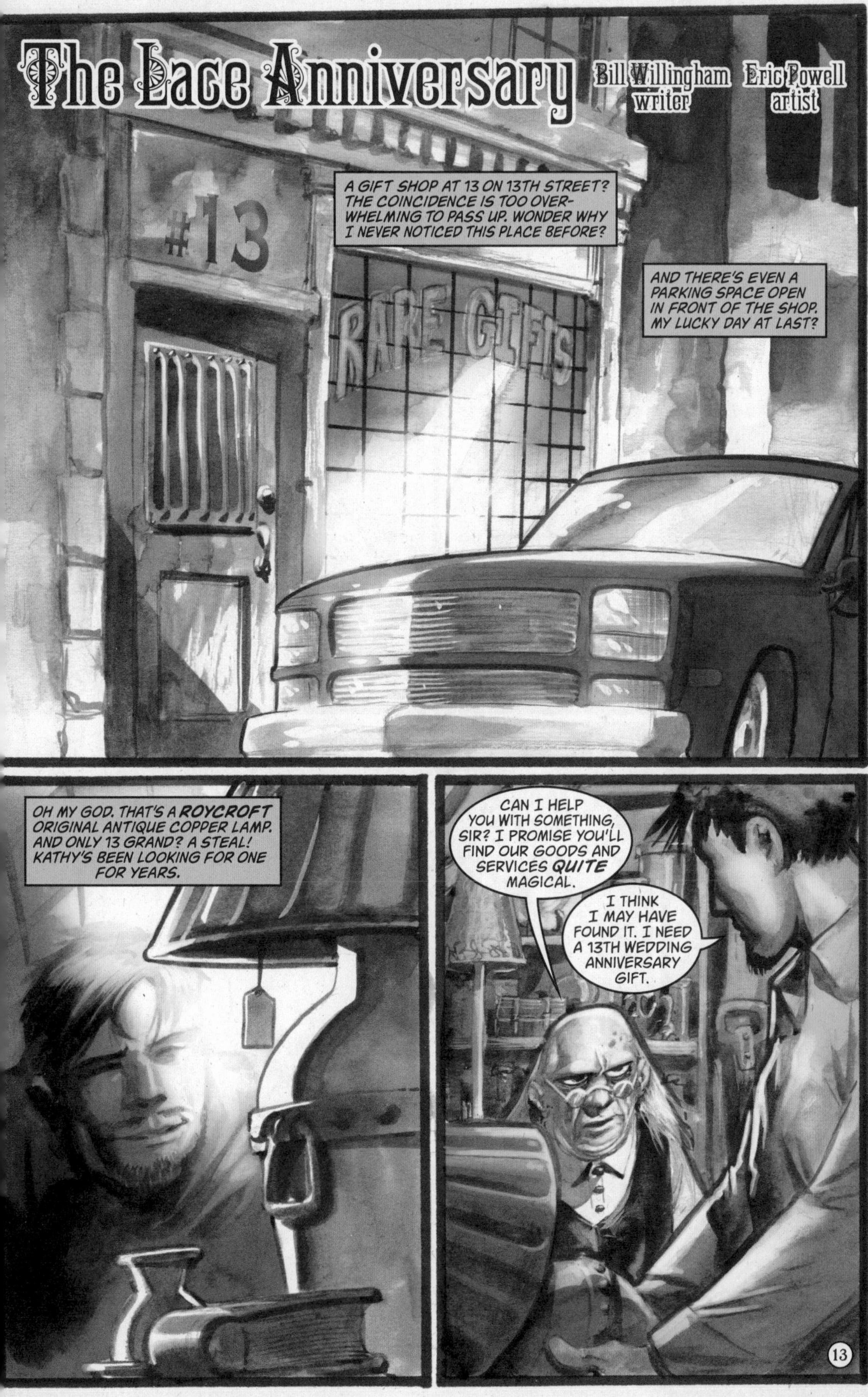
The Lace Anniversary
Bill Willingham writer
Eric Powell artist
A GIFT SHOP AT 13 ON 13TH STREET? THE COINCIDENCE IS TOO OVERWHELMING TO PASS UP. WONDER WHY I NEVER NOTICED THIS PLACE BEFORE?
#13
RARE GIFTS
AND THERE'S EVEN A PARKING SPACE OPEN IN FRONT OF THE SHOP. MY LUCKY DAY AT LAST?
OH MY GOD. THAT'S A ROYCROFT ORIGINAL ANTIQUE COPPER LAMP. AND ONLY 13 GRAND? A STEAL! KATHY'S BEEN LOOKING FOR ONE FOR YEARS.
CAN I HELP YOU WITH SOMETHING, SIR? I PROMISE YOU'LL FIND OUR GOODS AND SERVICES QUITE MAGICAL.
I THINK I MAY HAVE FOUND IT. I NEED A 13TH WEDDING ANNIVERSARY GIFT.
13

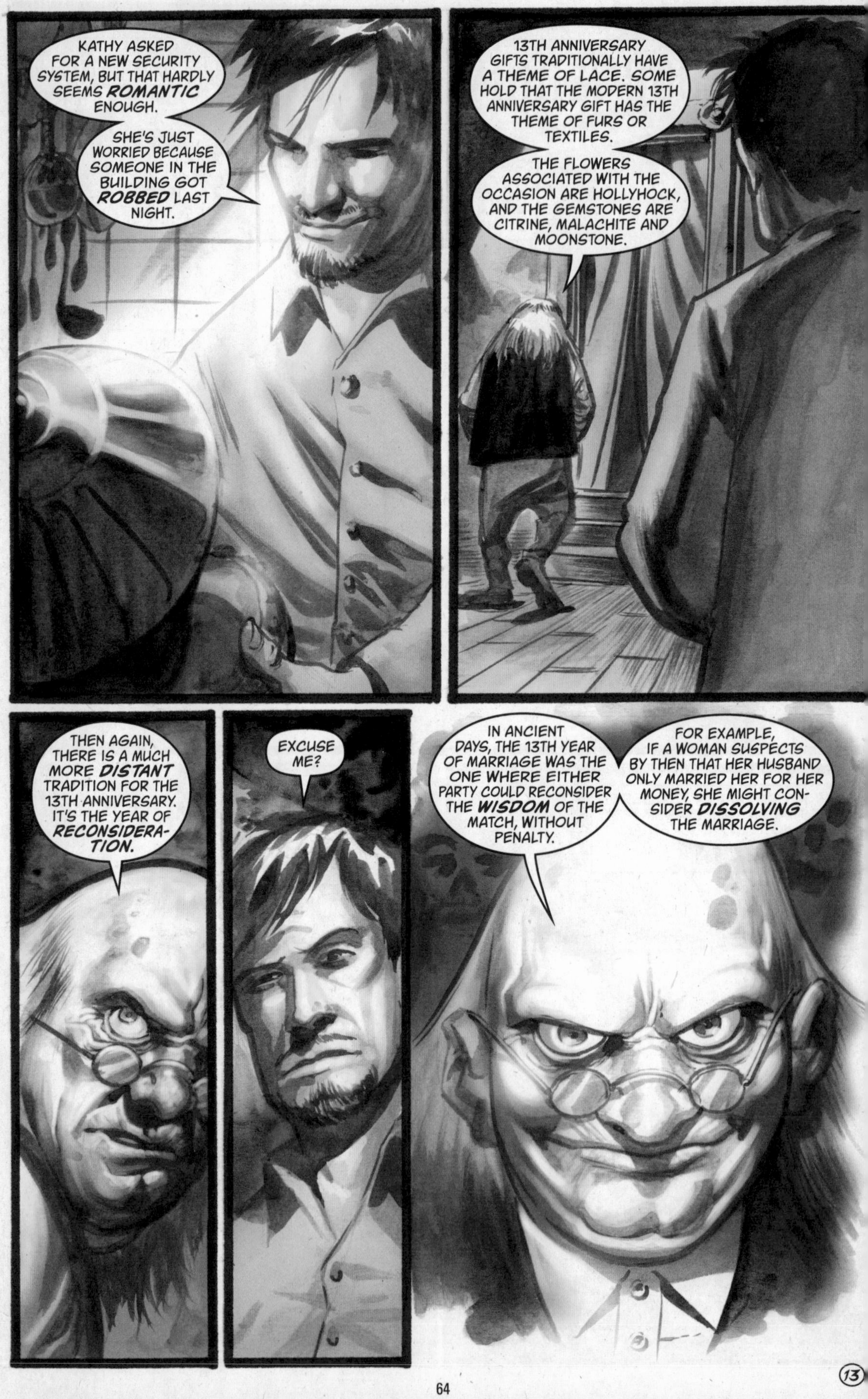

KATHY ASKED FOR A NEW SECURITY SYSTEM, BUT THAT HARDLY SEEMS ROMANTIC ENOUGH.
SHE'S JUST WORRIED BECAUSE SOMEONE IN THE BUILDING GOT ROBBED LAST NIGHT.
13TH ANNIVERSARY GIFTS TRADITIONALLY HAVE A THEME OF LACE. SOME HOLD THAT THE MODERN 13TH ANNIVERSARY GIFT HAS THE THEME OF FURS OR TEXTILES.
THE FLOWERS ASSOCIATED WITH THE OCCASION ARE HOLLYHOCK, AND THE GEMSTONES ARE CITRINE, MALACHITE AND MOONSTONE.
THEN AGAIN, THERE IS A MUCH MORE DISTANT TRADITION FOR THE 13TH ANNIVERSARY. IT'S THE YEAR OF RECONSIDERA-TION.
EXCUSE ME?
IN ANCIENT DAYS, THE 13TH YEAR OF MARRIAGE WAS THE ONE WHERE EITHER PARTY COULD RECONSIDER THE WISDOM OF THE MATCH, WITHOUT PENALTY.
FOR EXAMPLE, IF A WOMAN SUSPECTS BY THEN THAT HER HUSBAND ONLY MARRIED HER FOR HER MONEY, SHE MIGHT CON-SIDER DISSOLVING THE MARRIAGE.

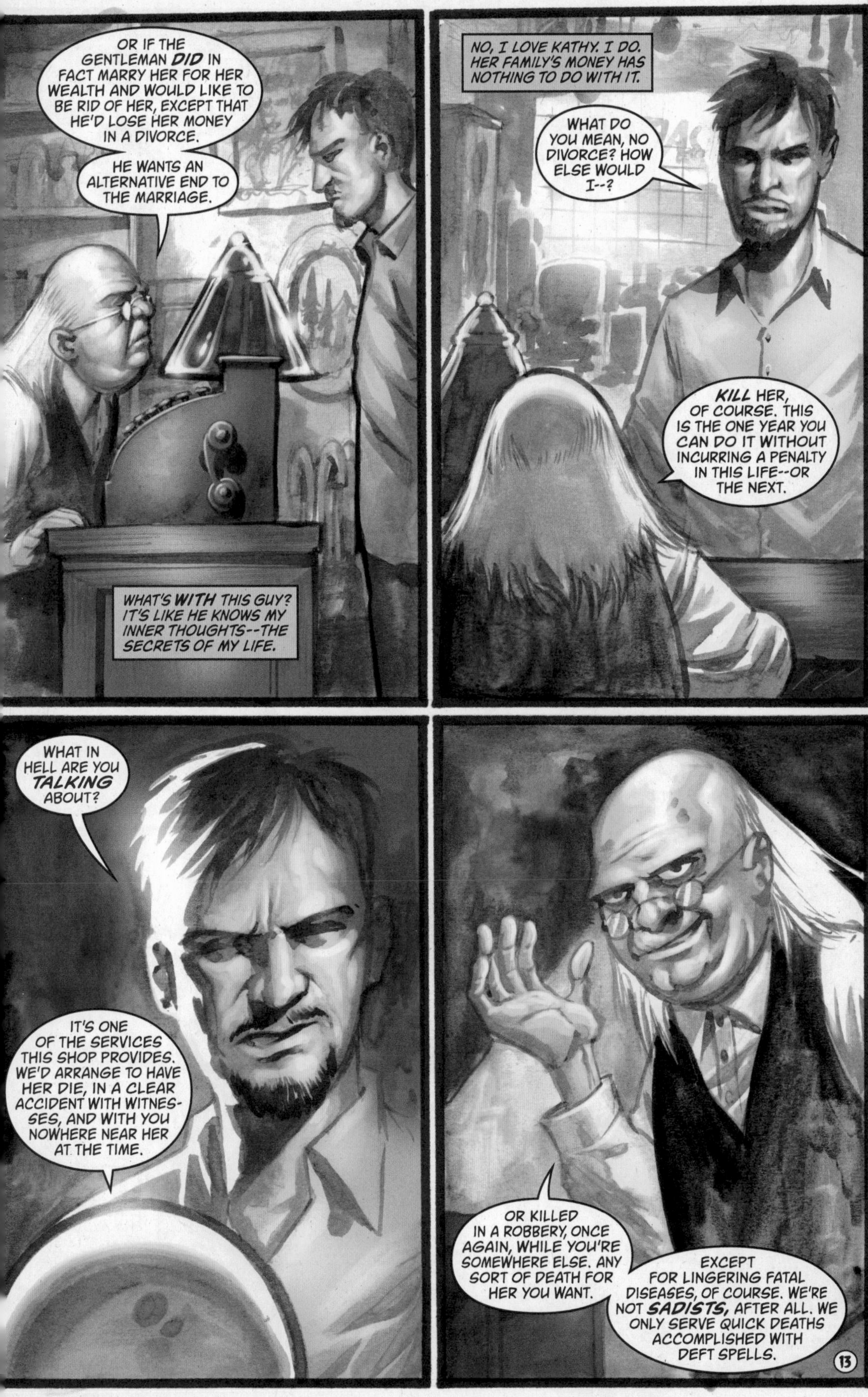
OR IF THE GENTLEMAN DID IN FACT MARRY HER FOR HER WEALTH AND WOULD LIKE TO BE RID OF HER, EXCEPT THAT HE'D LOSE HER MONEY IN A DIVORCE.
HE WANTS AN ALTERNATIVE END TO THE MARRIAGE.
WHAT'S WITH THIS GUY? IT'S LIKE HE KNOWS MY INNER THOUGHTS--THE SECRETS OF MY LIFE.
NO, I LOVE KATHY. I DO. HER FAMILY'S MONEY HAS NOTHING TO DO WITH IT.
WHAT DO YOU MEAN, NO DIVORCE? HOW ELSE WOULD I--?
KILL HER, OF COURSE. THIS IS THE ONE YEAR YOU CAN DO IT WITHOUT INCURRING A PENALTY IN THIS LIFE--OR THE NEXT.
WHAT IN HELL ARE YOU TALKING ABOUT?
IT'S ONE OF THE SERVICES THIS SHOP PROVIDES. WE'D ARRANGE TO HAVE HER DIE, IN A CLEAR ACCIDENT WITH WITNESSES, AND WITH YOU NOWHERE NEAR HER AT THE TIME.
OR KILLED IN A ROBBERY, ONCE AGAIN, WHILE YOU'RE SOMEWHERE ELSE. ANY SORT OF DEATH FOR HER YOU WANT.
EXCEPT FOR LINGERING FATAL DISEASES, OF COURSE. WE'RE NOT SADISTS, AFTER ALL. WE ONLY SERVE QUICK DEATHS ACCOMPLISHED WITH DEFT SPELLS.
13

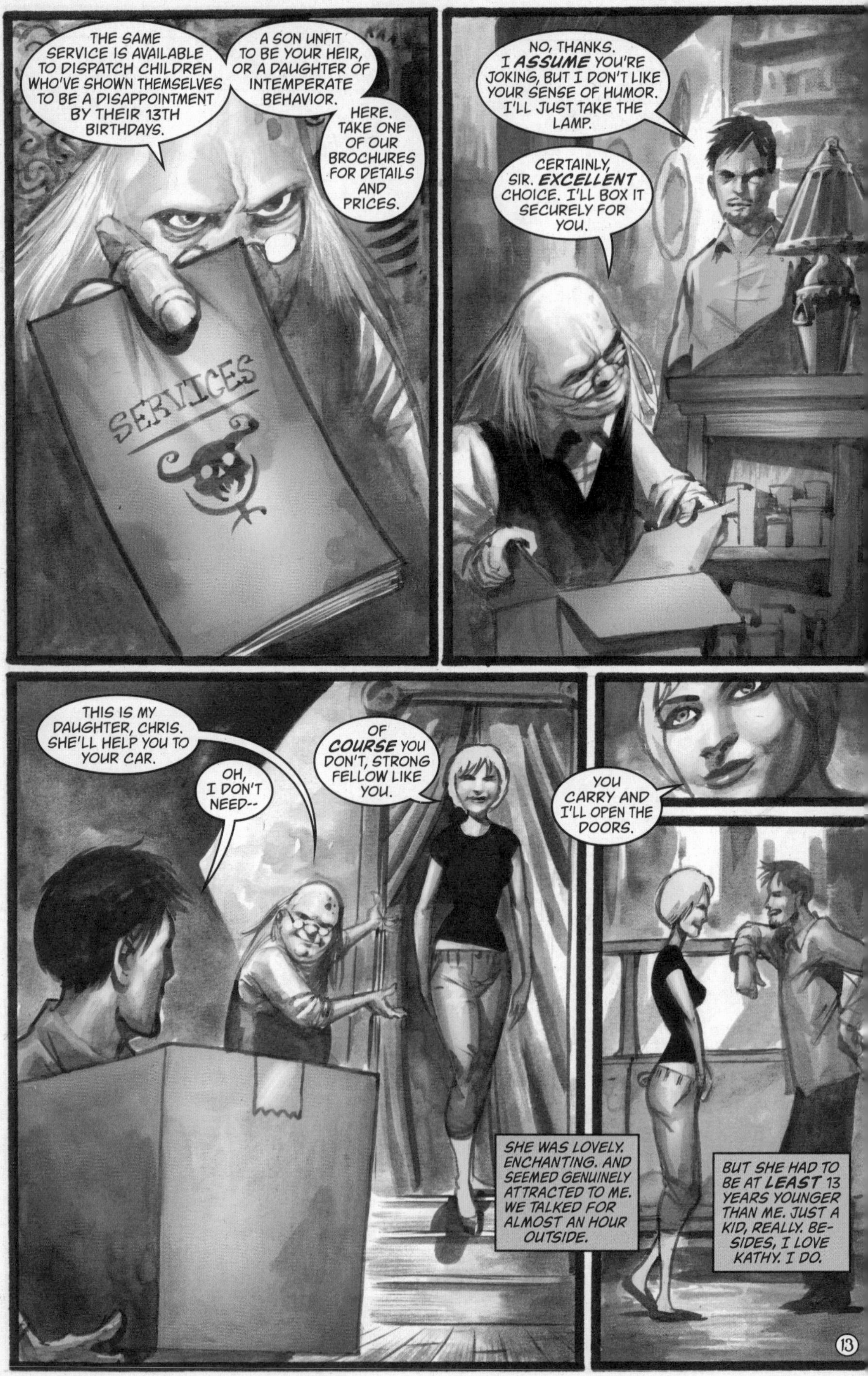
THE SAME SERVICE IS AVAILABLE TO DISPATCH CHILDREN WHO'VE SHOWN THEMSELVES TO BE A DISAPPOINTMENT BY THEIR 13TH BIRTHDAYS.
A SON UNFIT TO BE YOUR HEIR, OR A DAUGHTER OF INTEMPERATE BEHAVIOR.
HERE. TAKE ONE OF OUR BROCHURES FOR DETAILS AND PRICES.
SERVICES
NO, THANKS. I ASSUME YOU'RE JOKING, BUT I DON'T LIKE YOUR SENSE OF HUMOR. I'LL JUST TAKE THE LAMP.
CERTAINLY, SIR. EXCELLENT CHOICE. I'LL BOX IT SECURELY FOR YOU.
THIS IS MY DAUGHTER, CHRIS. SHE'LL HELP YOU TO YOUR CAR.
OH, I DON'T NEED--
OF COURSE YOU DON'T, STRONG FELLOW LIKE YOU.
SHE WAS LOVELY. ENCHANTING. AND SEEMED GENUINELY ATTRACTED TO ME. WE TALKED FOR ALMOST AN HOUR OUTSIDE.
YOU CARRY AND I'LL OPEN THE DOORS.
BUT SHE HAD TO BE AT LEAST 13 YEARS YOUNGER THAN ME. JUST A KID, REALLY. BESIDES, I LOVE KATHY. I DO.
13

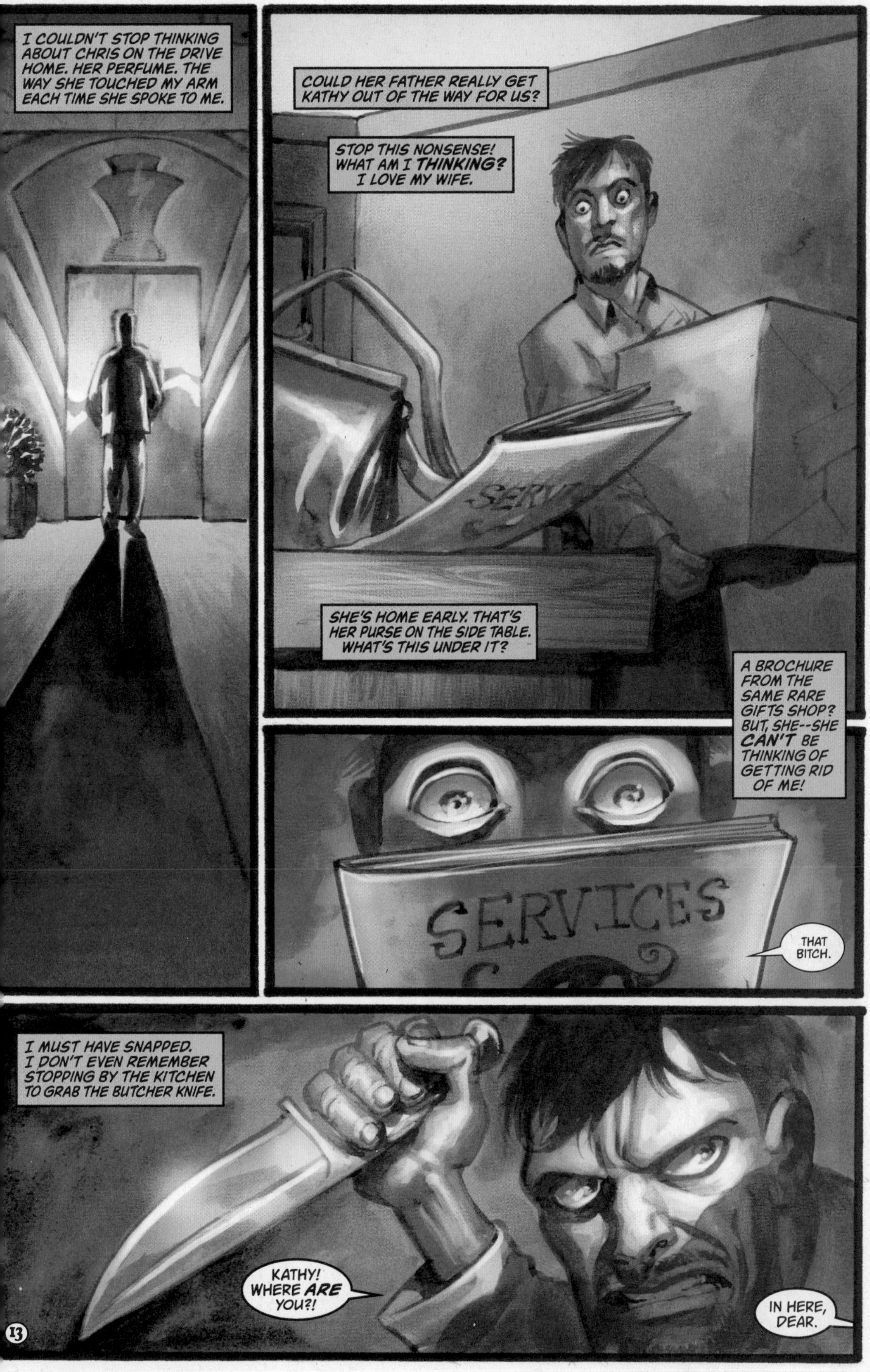
I COULDN'T STOP THINKING ABOUT CHRIS ON THE DRIVE HOME. HER PERFUME. THE WAY SHE TOUCHED MY ARM EACH TIME SHE SPOKE TO ME.
COULD HER FATHER REALLY GET KATHY OUT OF THE WAY FOR US?
STOP THIS NONSENSE! WHAT AM I THINKING? I LOVE MY WIFE.
SHE'S HOME EARLY. THAT'S HER PURSE ON THE SIDE TABLE. WHAT'S THIS UNDER IT?
A BROCHURE FROM THE SAME RARE GIFTS SHOP? BUT, SHE--SHE CAN'T BE THINKING OF GETTING RID OF ME!
SERVICES
THAT BITCH.
I MUST HAVE SNAPPED. I DON'T EVEN REMEMBER STOPPING BY THE KITCHEN TO GRAB THE BUTCHER KNIFE.
KATHY! WHERE ARE YOU?!
IN HERE, DEAR.
13

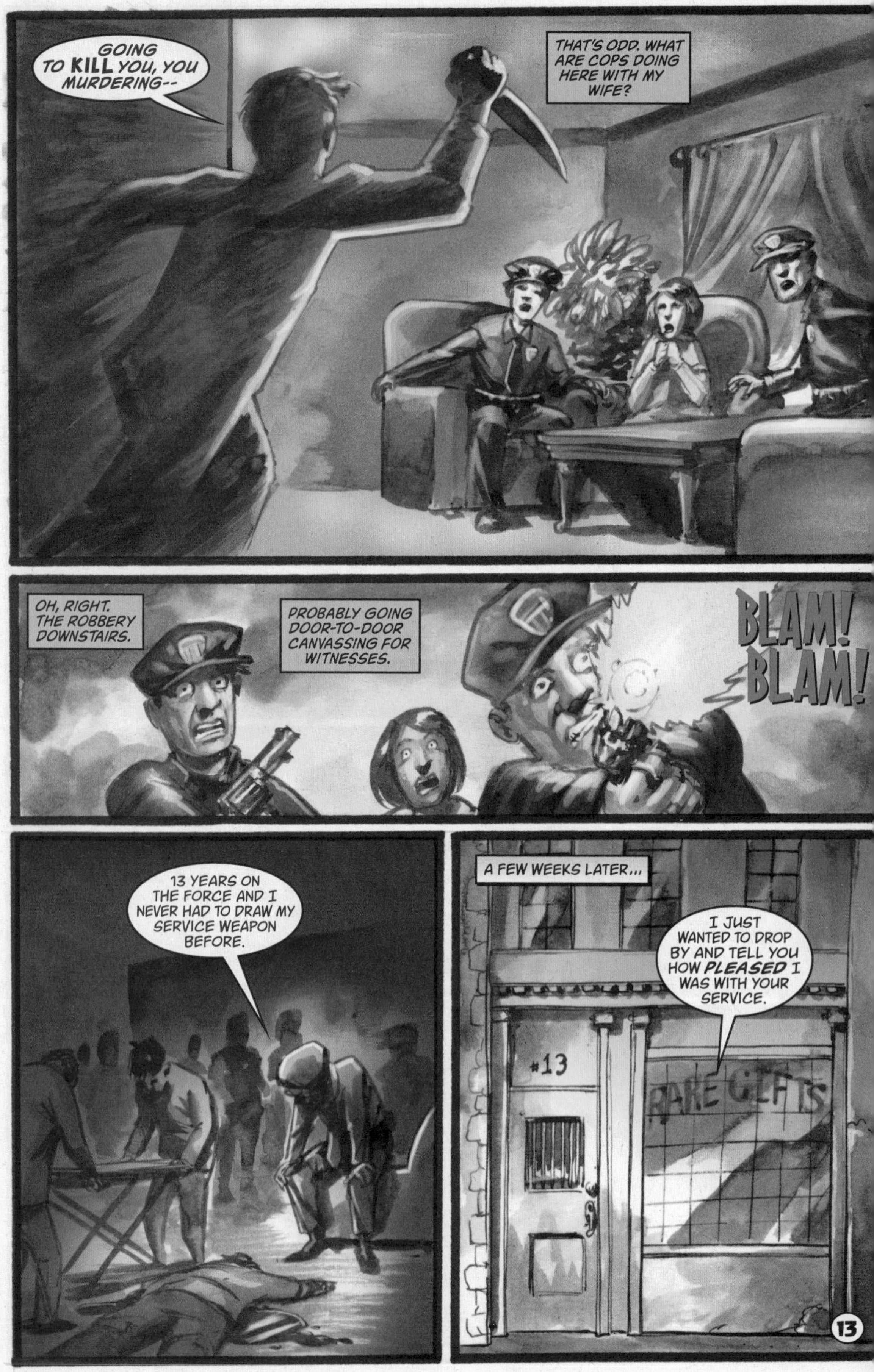
GOING TO KILL YOU, YOU MURDERING--
THAT'S ODD. WHAT ARE COPS DOING HERE WITH MY WIFE?
OH, RIGHT. THE ROBBERY DOWNSTAIRS.
PROBABLY GOING DOOR-TO-DOOR CANVASSING FOR WITNESSES.
BLAM! BLAM!
13 YEARS ON THE FORCE AND I NEVER HAD TO DRAW MY SERVICE WEAPON BEFORE.
A FEW WEEKS LATER...
I JUST WANTED TO DROP BY AND TELL YOU HOW PLEASED I WAS WITH YOUR SERVICE.
#13
13

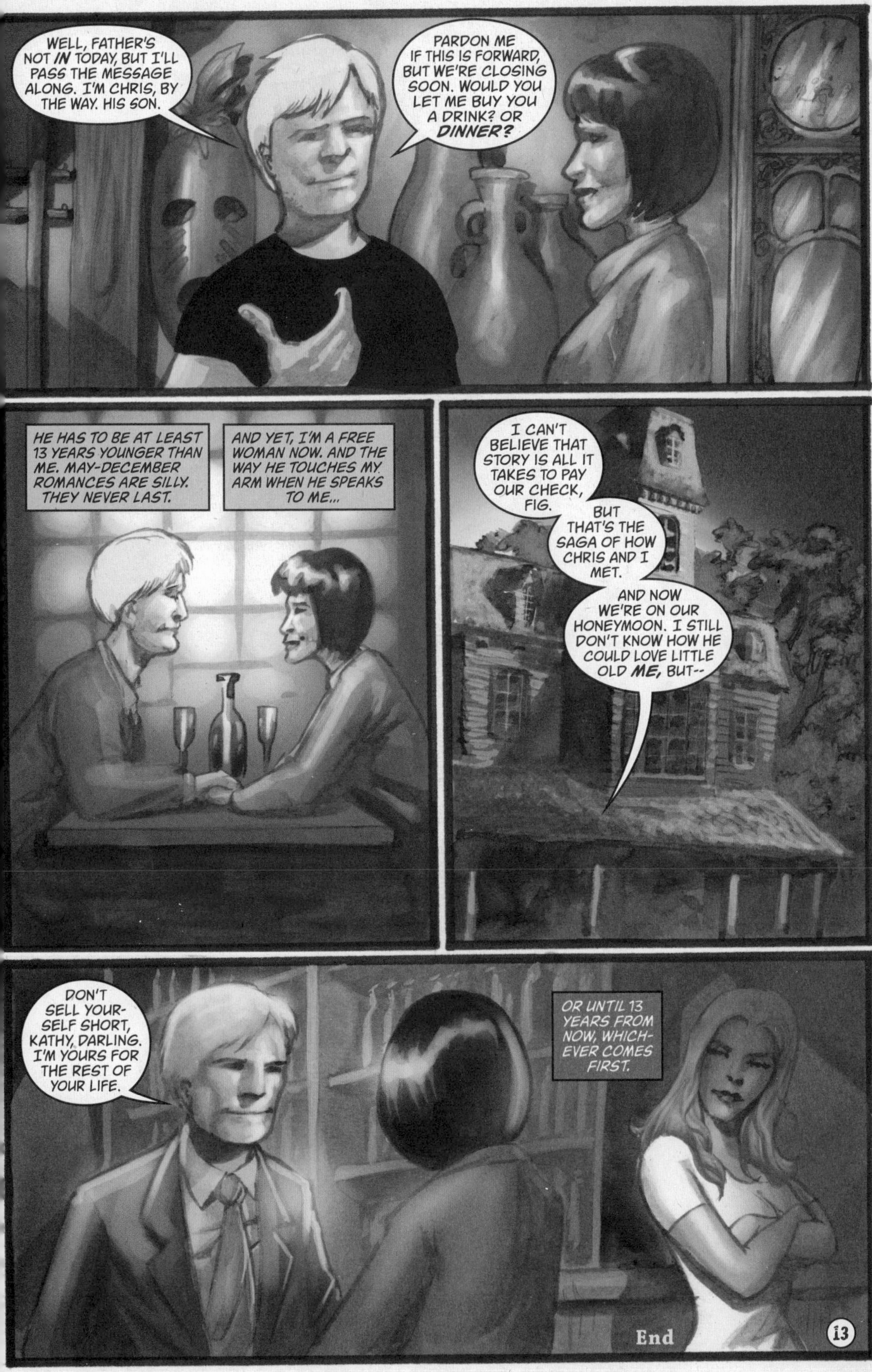
WELL, FATHER'S NOT *IN* TODAY, BUT I'LL PASS THE MESSAGE ALONG. I'M CHRIS, BY THE WAY. HIS SON.
PARDON ME IF THIS IS FORWARD, BUT WE'RE CLOSING SOON. WOULD YOU LET ME BUY YOU A DRINK? OR ***DINNER?***
HE HAS TO BE AT LEAST 13 YEARS YOUNGER THAN ME. MAY-DECEMBER ROMANCES ARE SILLY. THEY NEVER LAST.
AND YET, I'M A FREE WOMAN NOW. AND THE WAY HE TOUCHES MY ARM WHEN HE SPEAKS TO ME...
I CAN'T BELIEVE THAT STORY IS ALL IT TAKES TO PAY OUR CHECK, FIG.
BUT THAT'S THE SAGA OF HOW CHRIS AND I MET.
AND NOW WE'RE ON OUR HONEYMOON. I STILL DON'T KNOW HOW HE COULD LOVE LITTLE OLD ***ME,*** BUT--
DON'T SELL YOURSELF SHORT, KATHY, DARLING. I'M YOURS FOR THE REST OF YOUR LIFE.
OR UNTIL 13 YEARS FROM NOW, WHICHEVER COMES FIRST.
End
13

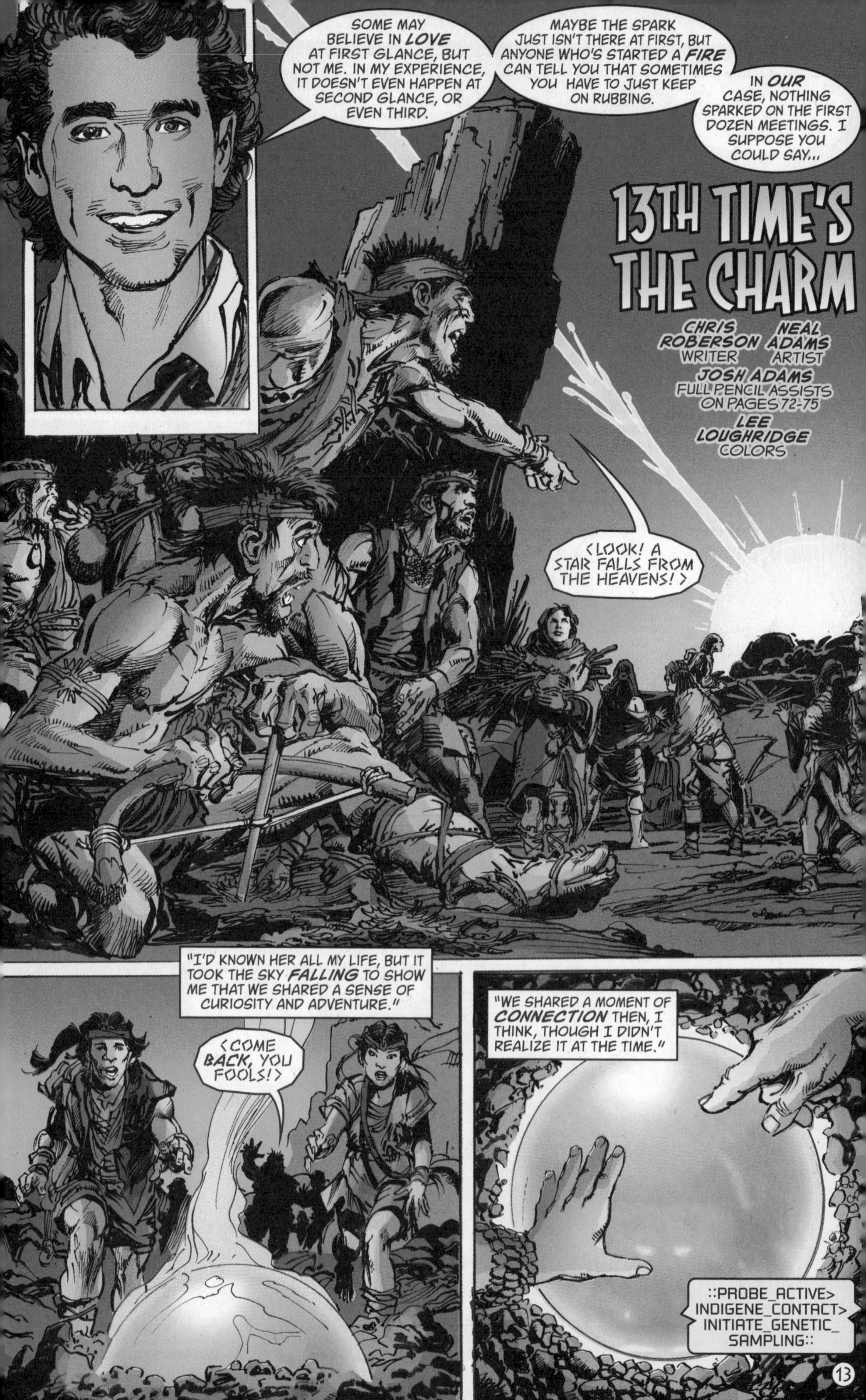
SOME MAY BELIEVE IN LOVE AT FIRST GLANCE, BUT NOT ME. IN MY EXPERIENCE, IT DOESN'T EVEN HAPPEN AT SECOND GLANCE, OR EVEN THIRD.
MAYBE THE SPARK JUST ISN'T THERE AT FIRST, BUT ANYONE WHO'S STARTED A FIRE CAN TELL YOU THAT SOMETIMES YOU HAVE TO JUST KEEP ON RUBBING.
IN OUR CASE, NOTHING SPARKED ON THE FIRST DOZEN MEETINGS. I SUPPOSE YOU COULD SAY...
13TH TIME'S THE CHARM
CHRIS ROBERSON WRITER
NEAL ADAMS ARTIST
JOSH ADAMS FULL PENCIL ASSISTS ON PAGES 72-75
LEE LOUGHRIDGE COLORS
<LOOK! A STAR FALLS FROM THE HEAVENS!>
"I'D KNOWN HER ALL MY LIFE, BUT IT TOOK THE SKY FALLING TO SHOW ME THAT WE SHARED A SENSE OF CURIOSITY AND ADVENTURE."
<COME BACK, YOU FOOLS!>
"WE SHARED A MOMENT OF CONNECTION THEN, I THINK, THOUGH I DIDN'T REALIZE IT AT THE TIME."
::PROBE_ACTIVE>
INDIGENE_CONTACT>
INITIATE_GENETIC_
SAMPLING::

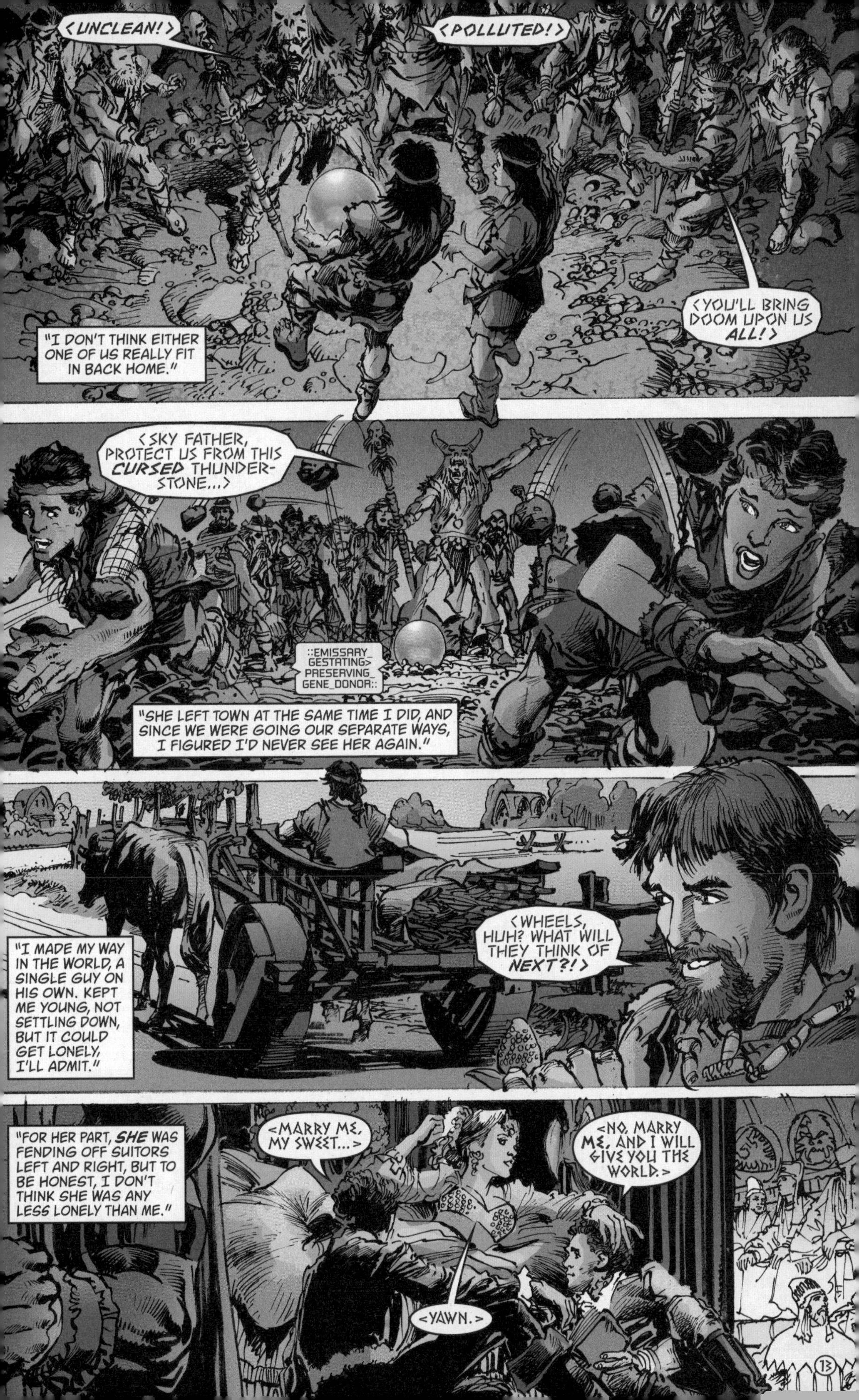

<UNCLEAN!>
<POLLUTED!>
<YOU'LL BRING DOOM UPON US ALL!>
"I DON'T THINK EITHER ONE OF US REALLY FIT IN BACK HOME."
<SKY FATHER, PROTECT US FROM THIS CURSED THUNDER-STONE...>
::EMISSARY_ GESTATING> PRESERVING_ GENE_DONOR::
"SHE LEFT TOWN AT THE SAME TIME I DID, AND SINCE WE WERE GOING OUR SEPARATE WAYS, I FIGURED I'D NEVER SEE HER AGAIN."
"I MADE MY WAY IN THE WORLD, A SINGLE GUY ON HIS OWN. KEPT ME YOUNG, NOT SETTLING DOWN, BUT IT COULD GET LONELY, I'LL ADMIT."
<WHEELS, HUH? WHAT WILL THEY THINK OF NEXT?!>
"FOR HER PART, SHE WAS FENDING OFF SUITORS LEFT AND RIGHT, BUT TO BE HONEST, I DON'T THINK SHE WAS ANY LESS LONELY THAN ME."
<MARRY ME, MY SWEET...>
<NO, MARRY ME, AND I WILL GIVE YOU THE WORLD.>
<YAWN.>
13

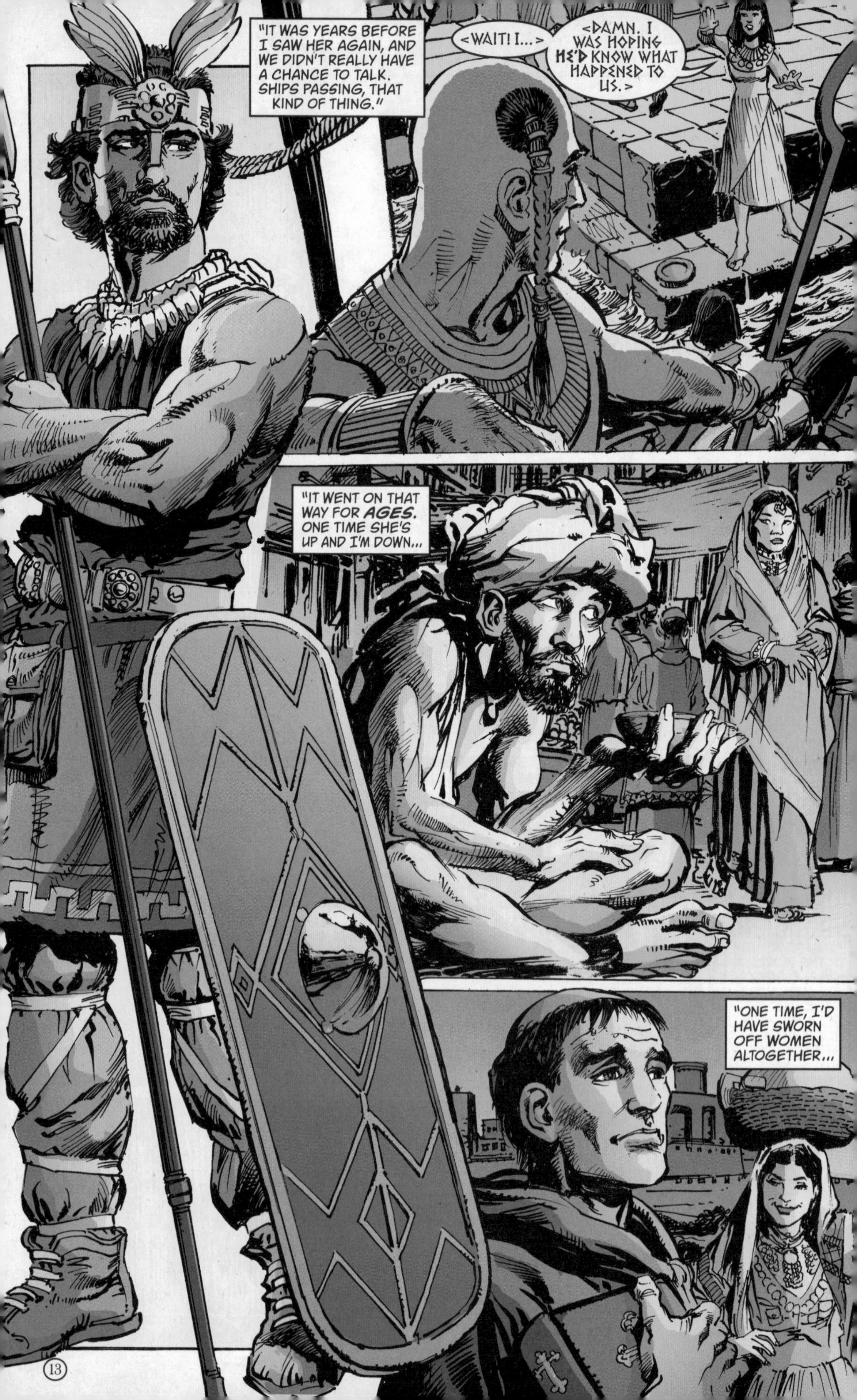
"IT WAS YEARS BEFORE I SAW HER AGAIN, AND WE DIDN'T REALLY HAVE A CHANCE TO TALK. SHIPS PASSING, THAT KIND OF THING."
<WAIT! I...>
<DAMN. I WAS HOPING HE'D KNOW WHAT HAPPENED TO US.>
"IT WENT ON THAT WAY FOR AGES. ONE TIME SHE'S UP AND I'M DOWN...
"ONE TIME, I'D HAVE SWORN OFF WOMEN ALTOGETHER...

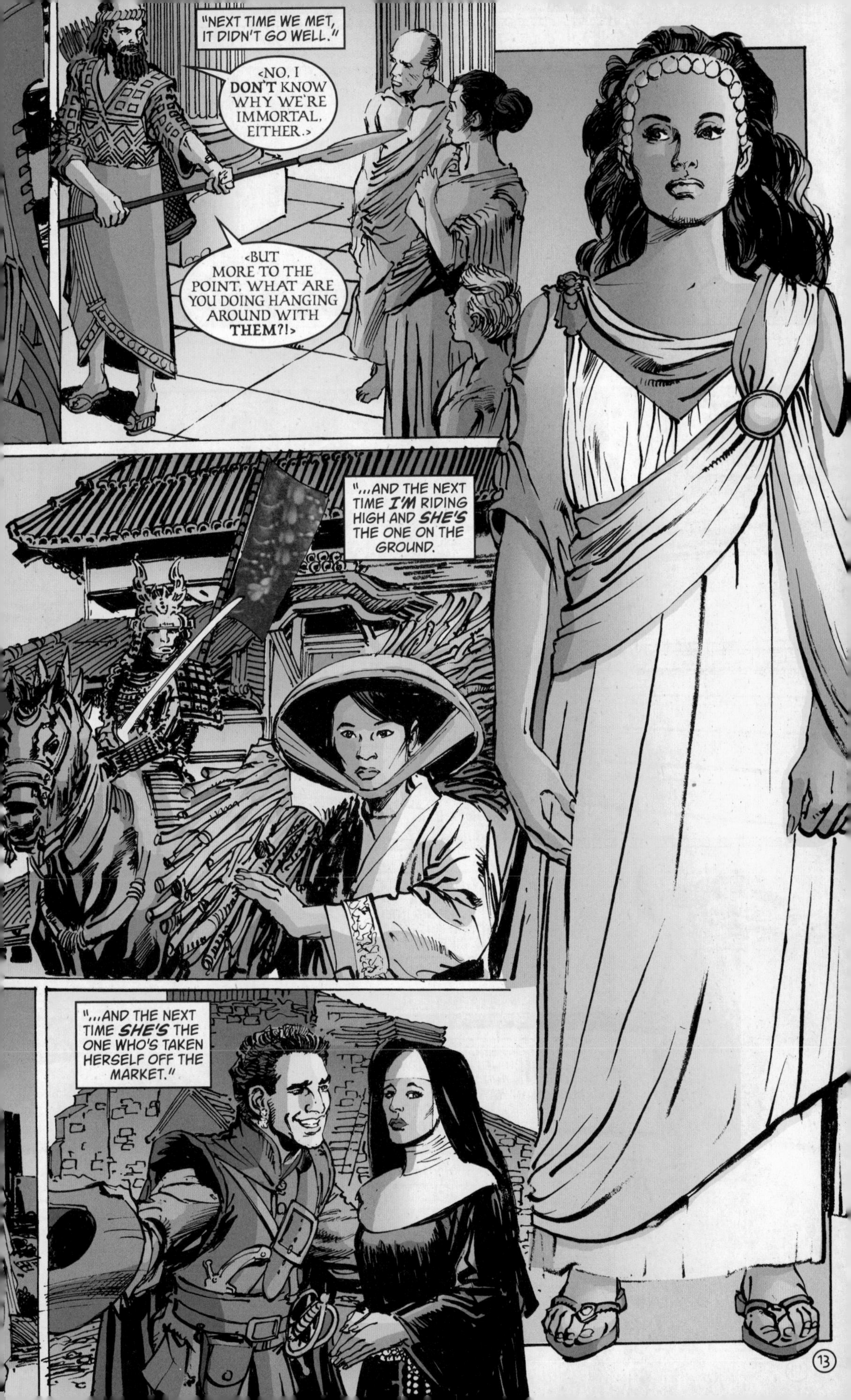
"NEXT TIME WE MET, IT DIDN'T GO WELL."
<NO, I DON'T KNOW WHY WE'RE IMMORTAL, EITHER.>
<BUT MORE TO THE POINT, WHAT ARE YOU DOING HANGING AROUND WITH THEM?!>
"...AND THE NEXT TIME I'M RIDING HIGH AND SHE'S THE ONE ON THE GROUND.
"...AND THE NEXT TIME SHE'S THE ONE WHO'S TAKEN HERSELF OFF THE MARKET."
13

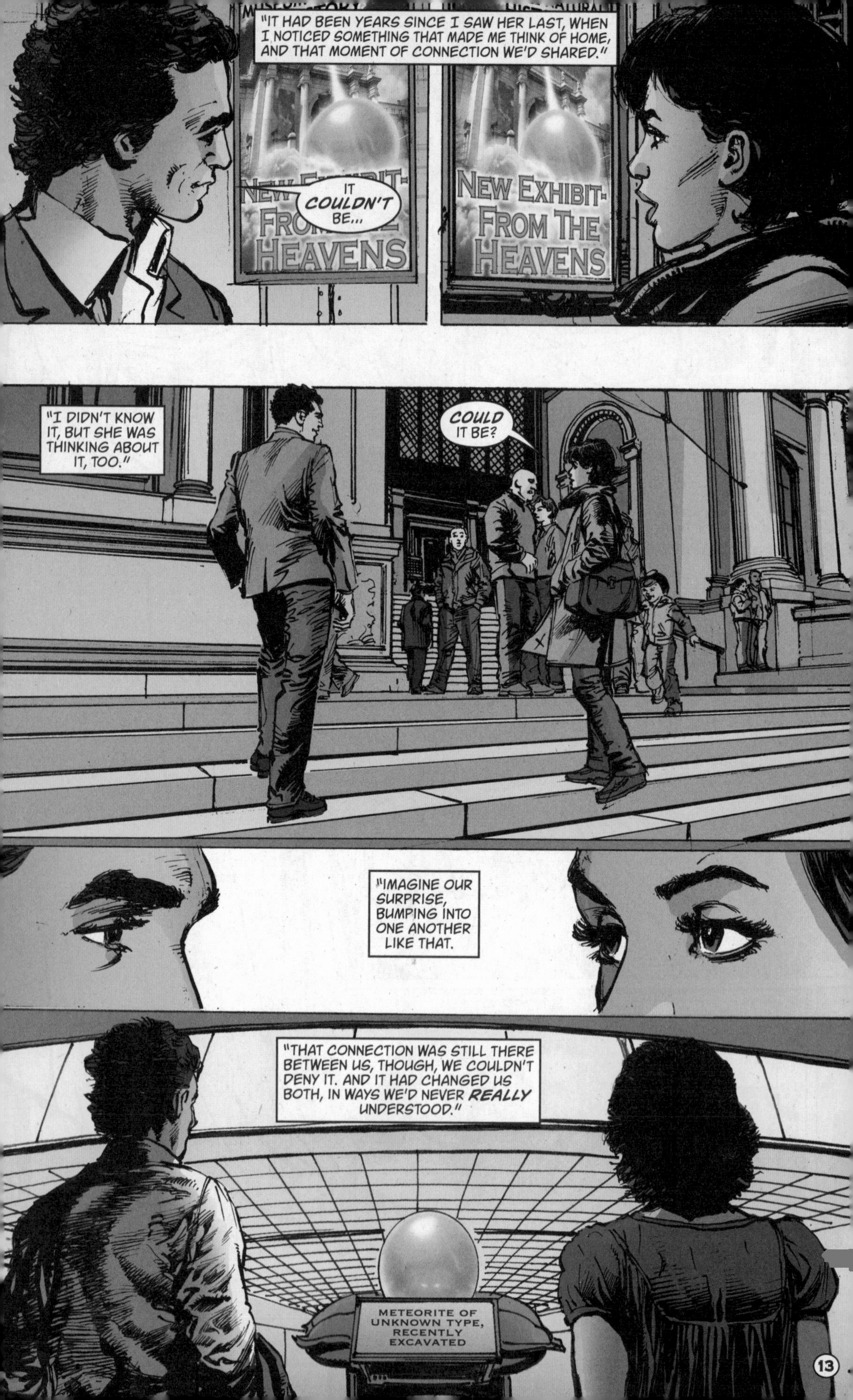

"IT HAD BEEN YEARS SINCE I SAW HER LAST, WHEN I NOTICED SOMETHING THAT MADE ME THINK OF HOME, AND THAT MOMENT OF CONNECTION WE'D SHARED."
NEW EXHIBIT- FROM THE HEAVENS
IT COULDN'T BE...
NEW EXHIBIT- FROM THE HEAVENS
"I DIDN'T KNOW IT, BUT SHE WAS THINKING ABOUT IT, TOO."
COULD IT BE?
"IMAGINE OUR SURPRISE, BUMPING INTO ONE ANOTHER LIKE THAT.
"THAT CONNECTION WAS STILL THERE BETWEEN US, THOUGH, WE COULDN'T DENY IT. AND IT HAD CHANGED US BOTH, IN WAYS WE'D NEVER REALLY UNDERSTOOD."
METEORITE OF UNKNOWN TYPE, RECENTLY EXCAVATED

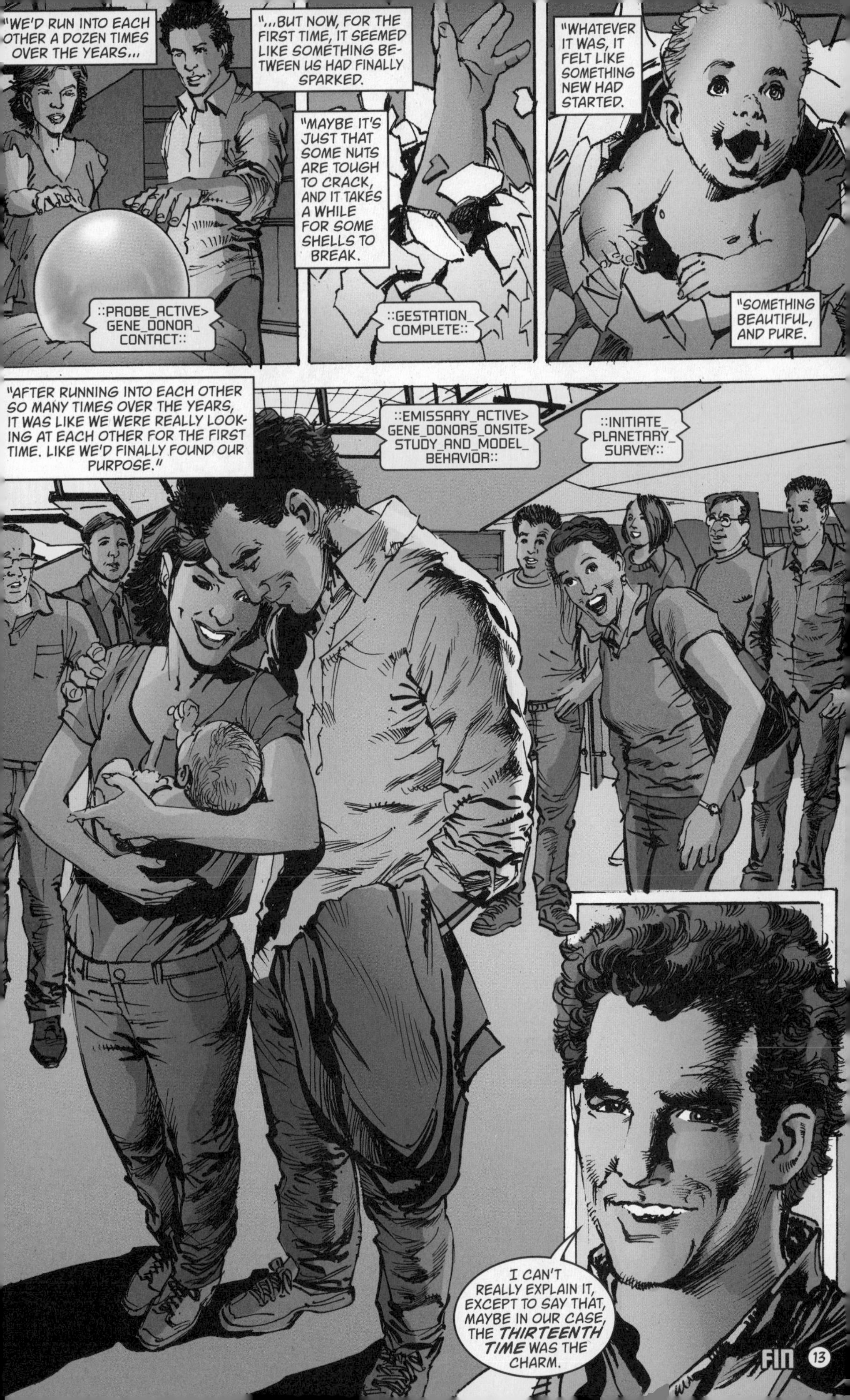

"WE'D RUN INTO EACH OTHER A DOZEN TIMES OVER THE YEARS...
"...BUT NOW, FOR THE FIRST TIME, IT SEEMED LIKE SOMETHING BETWEEN US HAD FINALLY SPARKED.
::PROBE_ACTIVE> GENE_DONOR_ CONTACT::
"MAYBE IT'S JUST THAT SOME NUTS ARE TOUGH TO CRACK, AND IT TAKES A WHILE FOR SOME SHELLS TO BREAK.
::GESTATION_ COMPLETE::
"WHATEVER IT WAS, IT FELT LIKE SOMETHING NEW HAD STARTED.
"SOMETHING BEAUTIFUL, AND PURE.
"AFTER RUNNING INTO EACH OTHER SO MANY TIMES OVER THE YEARS, IT WAS LIKE WE WERE REALLY LOOKING AT EACH OTHER FOR THE FIRST TIME. LIKE WE'D FINALLY FOUND OUR PURPOSE."
::EMISSARY_ACTIVE> GENE_DONORS_ONSITE> STUDY_AND_MODEL_ BEHAVIOR::
::INITIATE_ PLANETARY_ SURVEY::
I CAN'T REALLY EXPLAIN IT, EXCEPT TO SAY THAT, MAYBE IN OUR CASE, THE *THIRTEENTH TIME* WAS THE CHARM.
FIN

ISSUE #14 COVER ART BY ESAO ANDREWS.

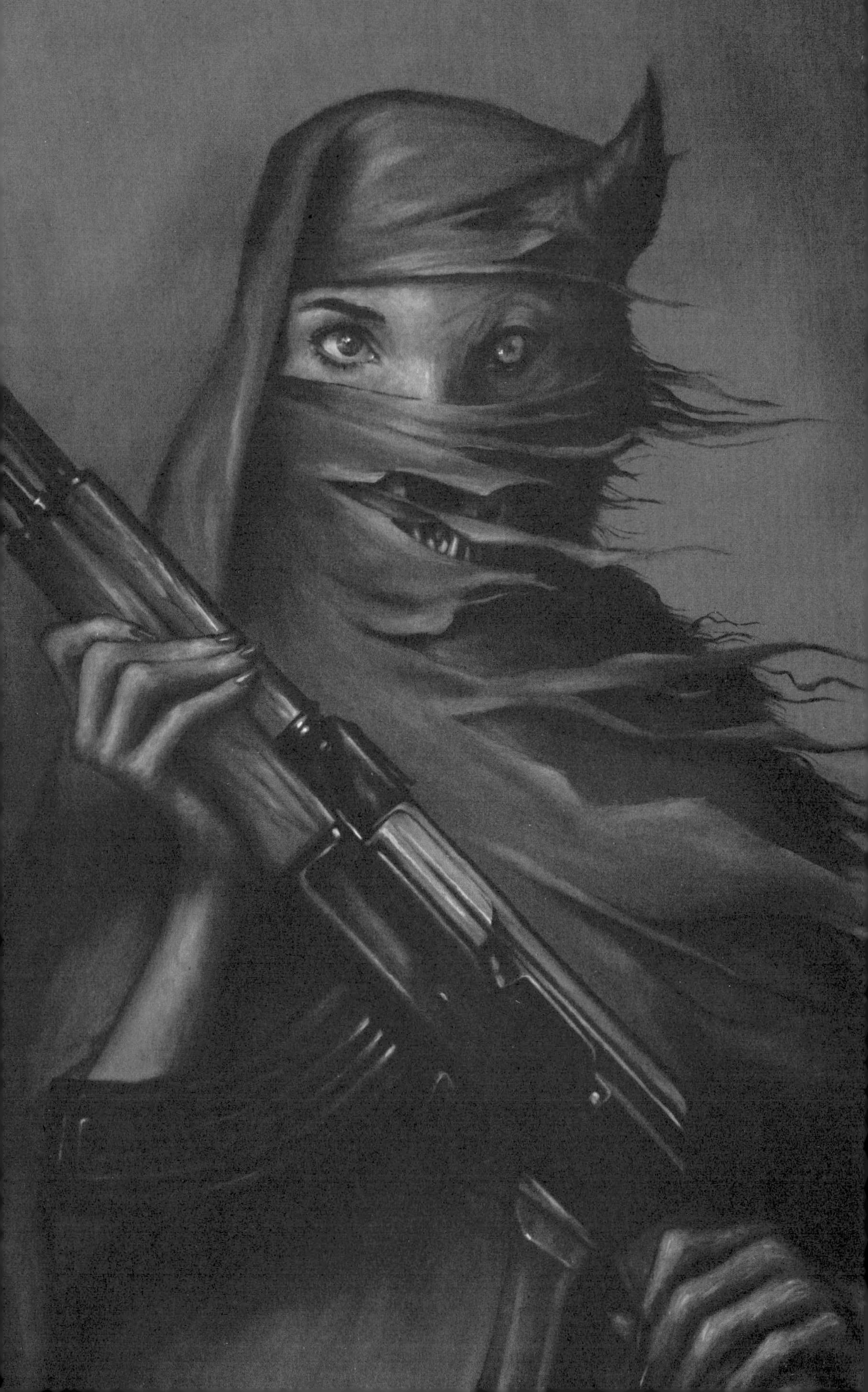

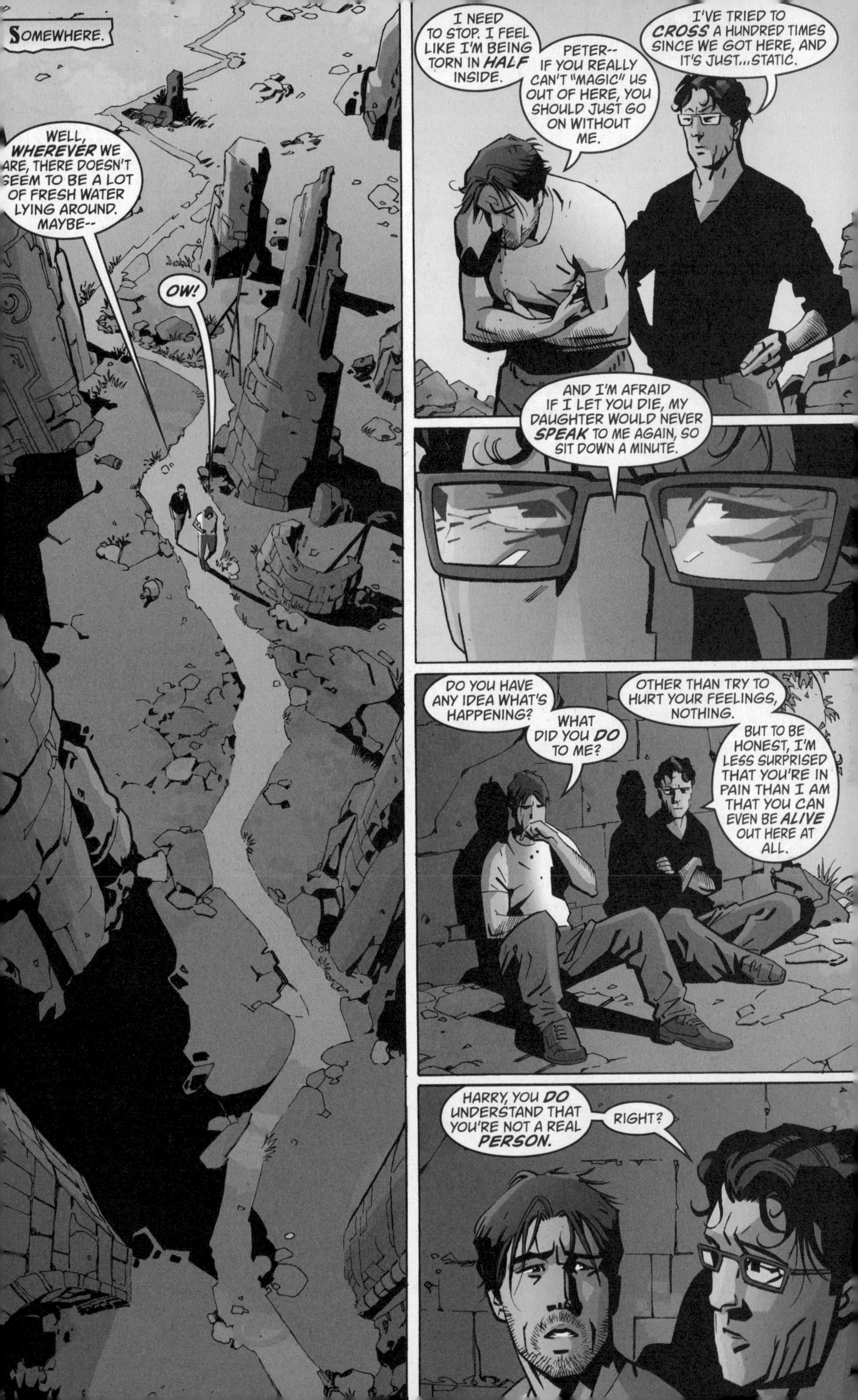
SOMEWHERE.
WELL, WHEREVER WE ARE, THERE DOESN'T SEEM TO BE A LOT OF FRESH WATER LYING AROUND. MAYBE--
OW!
I NEED TO STOP. I FEEL LIKE I'M BEING TORN IN HALF INSIDE.
PETER-- IF YOU REALLY CAN'T "MAGIC" US OUT OF HERE, YOU SHOULD JUST GO ON WITHOUT ME.
I'VE TRIED TO CROSS A HUNDRED TIMES SINCE WE GOT HERE, AND IT'S JUST...STATIC.
AND I'M AFRAID IF I LET YOU DIE, MY DAUGHTER WOULD NEVER SPEAK TO ME AGAIN, SO SIT DOWN A MINUTE.
DO YOU HAVE ANY IDEA WHAT'S HAPPENING?
WHAT DID YOU DO TO ME?
OTHER THAN TRY TO HURT YOUR FEELINGS, NOTHING.
BUT TO BE HONEST, I'M LESS SURPRISED THAT YOU'RE IN PAIN THAN I AM THAT YOU CAN EVEN BE ALIVE OUT HERE AT ALL.
HARRY, YOU DO UNDERSTAND THAT YOU'RE NOT A REAL PERSON.
RIGHT?

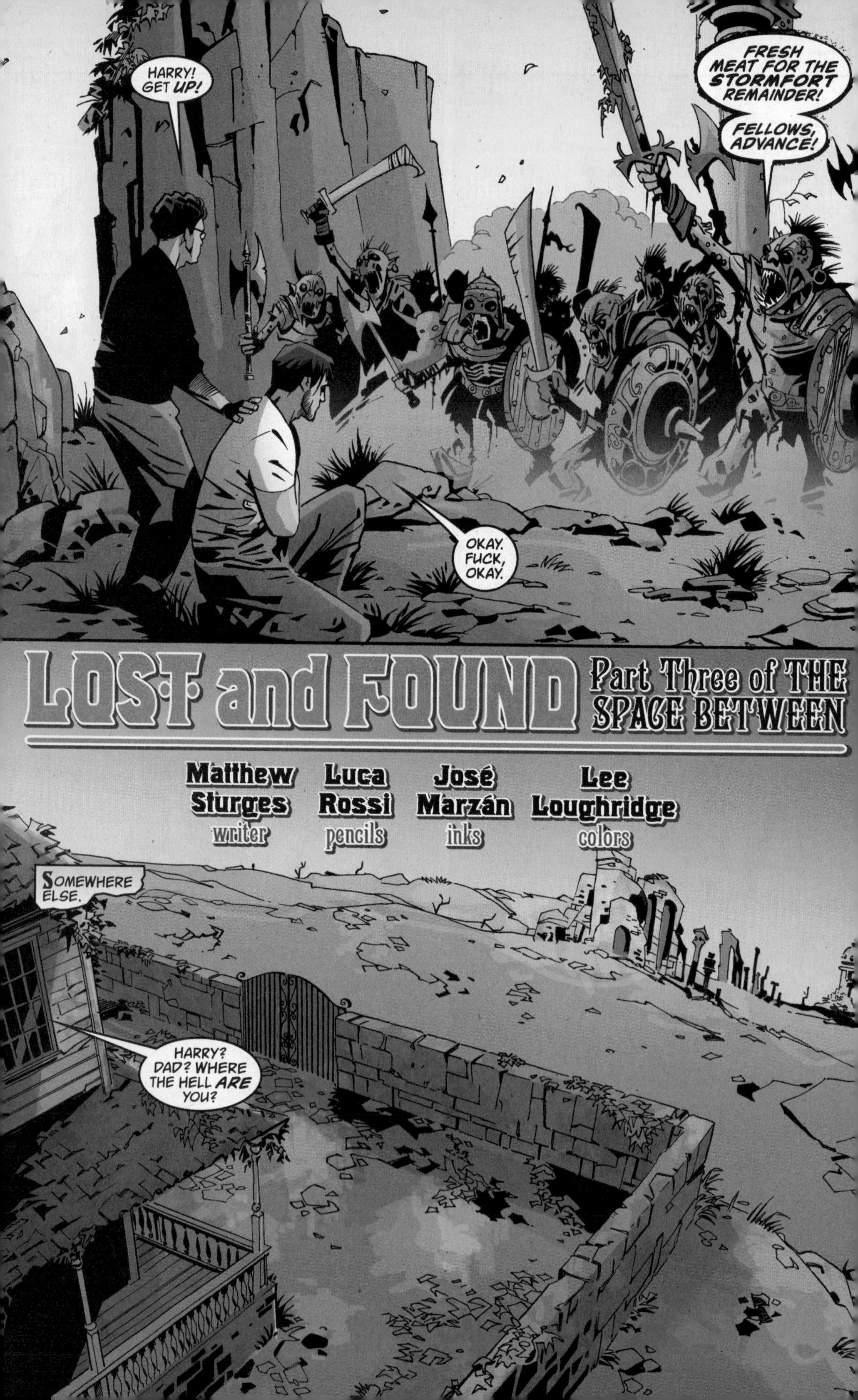
HARRY! GET UP!
FRESH MEAT FOR THE STORMFORT REMAINDER!
FELLOWS, ADVANCE!
OKAY. FUCK, OKAY.
LOST and FOUND
Part Three of THE SPACE BETWEEN
Matthew Sturges writer
Luca Rossi pencils
José Marzán inks
Lee Loughridge colors
SOMEWHERE ELSE.
HARRY? DAD? WHERE THE HELL ARE YOU?

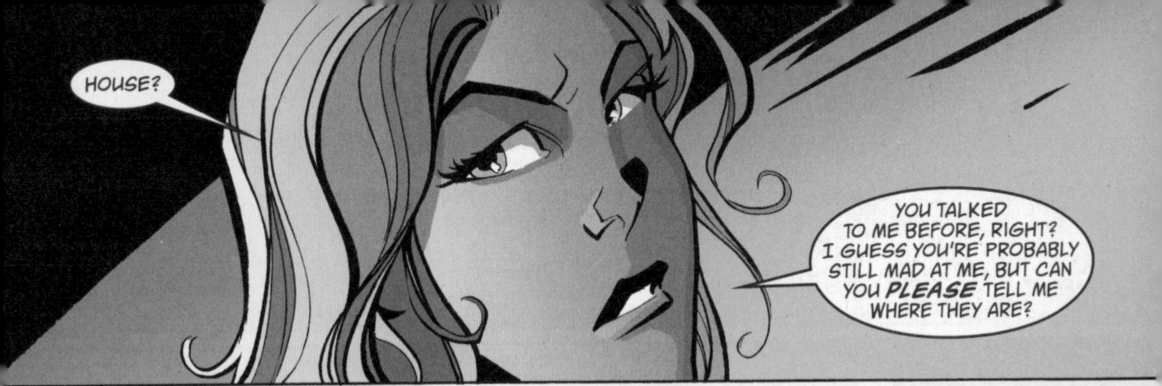
HOUSE?
YOU TALKED TO ME BEFORE, RIGHT? I GUESS YOU'RE PROBABLY STILL MAD AT ME, BUT CAN YOU PLEASE TELL ME WHERE THEY ARE?

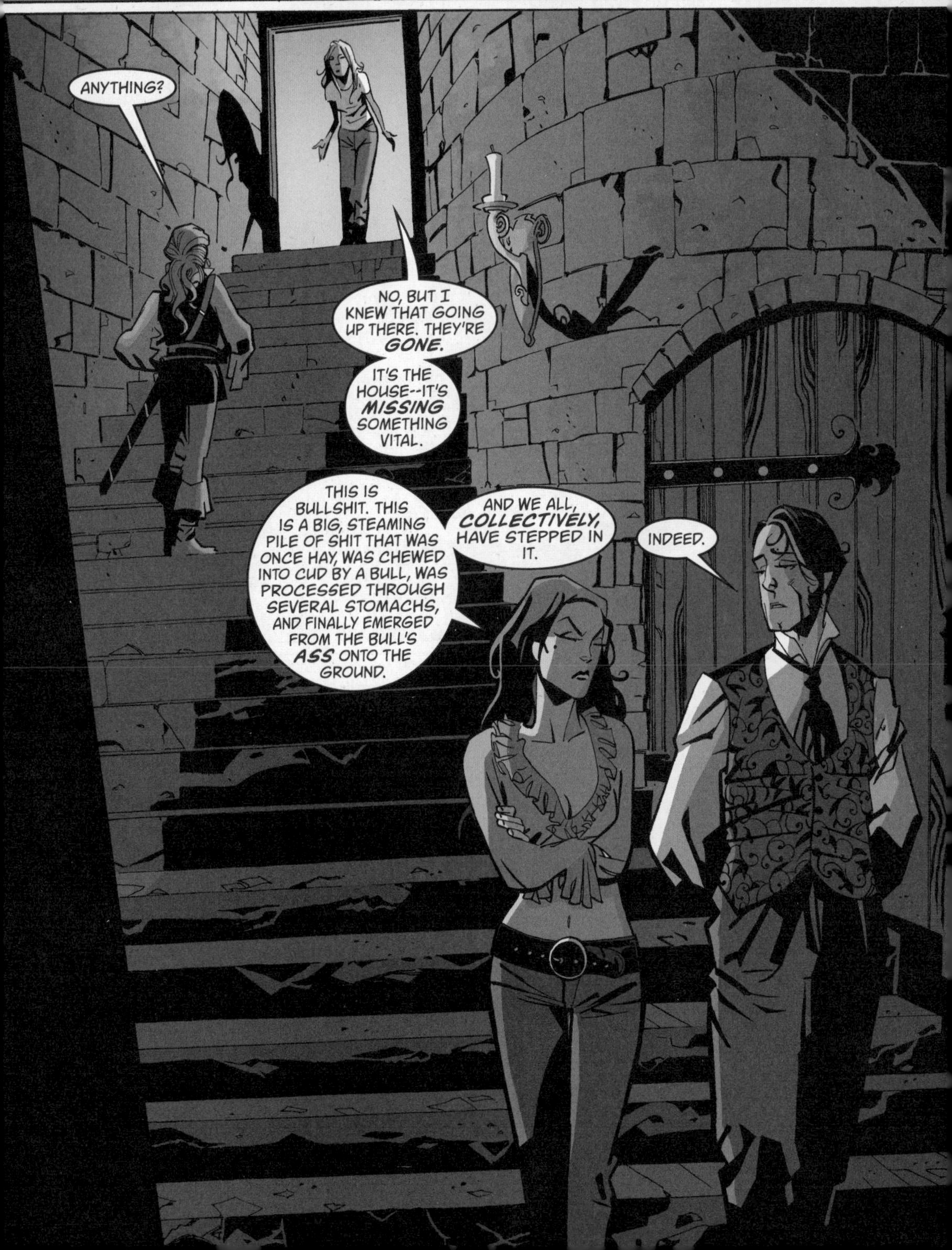
ANYTHING?
NO, BUT I KNEW THAT GOING UP THERE. THEY'RE GONE.
IT'S THE HOUSE--IT'S MISSING SOMETHING VITAL.
THIS IS BULLSHIT. THIS IS A BIG, STEAMING PILE OF SHIT THAT WAS ONCE HAY, WAS CHEWED INTO CUD BY A BULL, WAS PROCESSED THROUGH SEVERAL STOMACHS, AND FINALLY EMERGED FROM THE BULL'S ASS ONTO THE GROUND.
AND WE ALL, COLLECTIVELY, HAVE STEPPED IN IT.
INDEED.

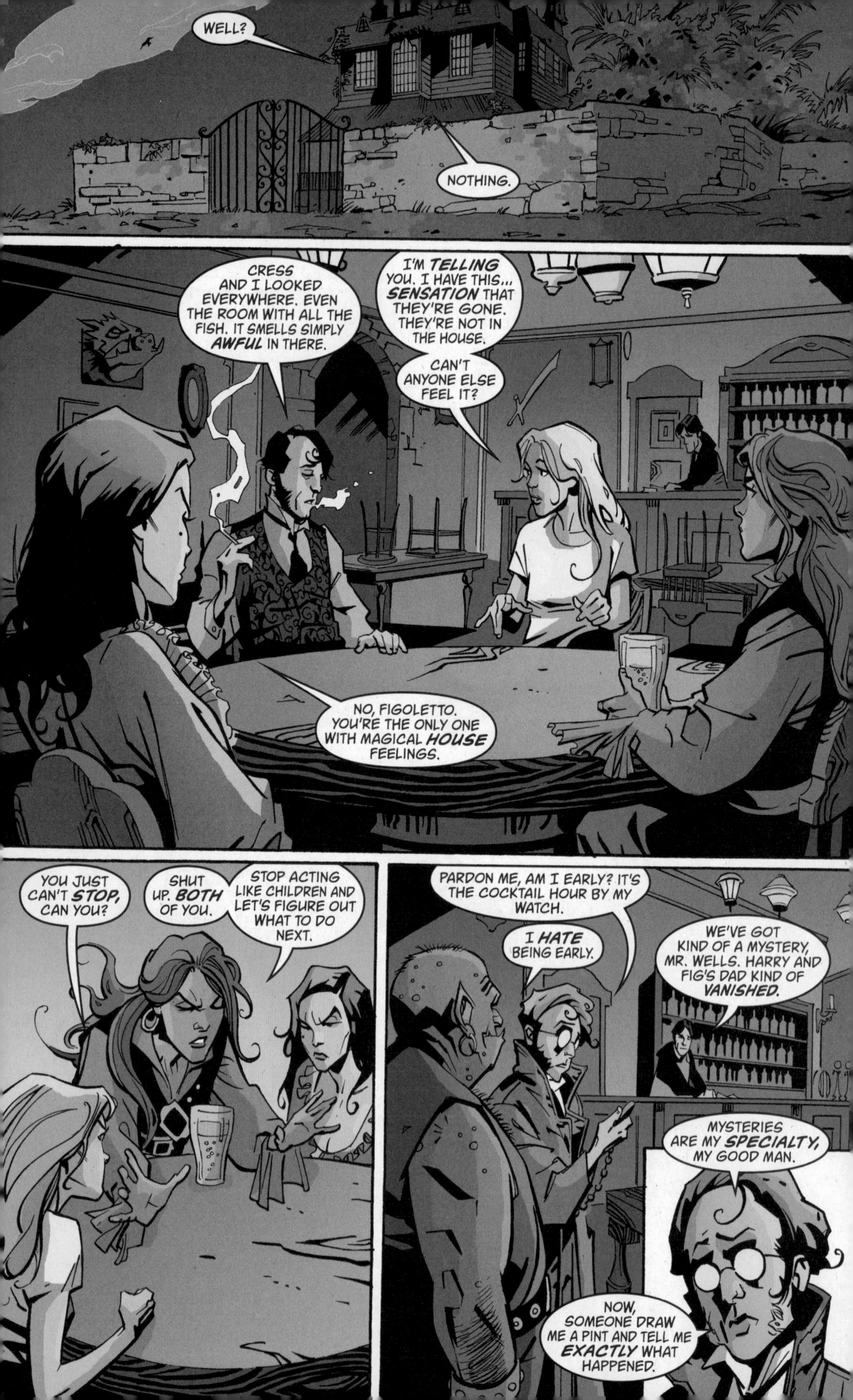
WELL?
NOTHING.
CRESS AND I LOOKED EVERYWHERE. EVEN THE ROOM WITH ALL THE FISH. IT SMELLS SIMPLY AWFUL IN THERE.
I'M TELLING YOU. I HAVE THIS... SENSATION THAT THEY'RE GONE. THEY'RE NOT IN THE HOUSE.
CAN'T ANYONE ELSE FEEL IT?
NO, FIGOLETTO. YOU'RE THE ONLY ONE WITH MAGICAL HOUSE FEELINGS.
YOU JUST CAN'T STOP, CAN YOU?
SHUT UP. BOTH OF YOU.
STOP ACTING LIKE CHILDREN AND LET'S FIGURE OUT WHAT TO DO NEXT.
PARDON ME, AM I EARLY? IT'S THE COCKTAIL HOUR BY MY WATCH.
I HATE BEING EARLY.
WE'VE GOT KIND OF A MYSTERY, MR. WELLS. HARRY AND FIG'S DAD KIND OF VANISHED.
MYSTERIES ARE MY SPECIALTY, MY GOOD MAN.
NOW, SOMEONE DRAW ME A PINT AND TELL ME EXACTLY WHAT HAPPENED.

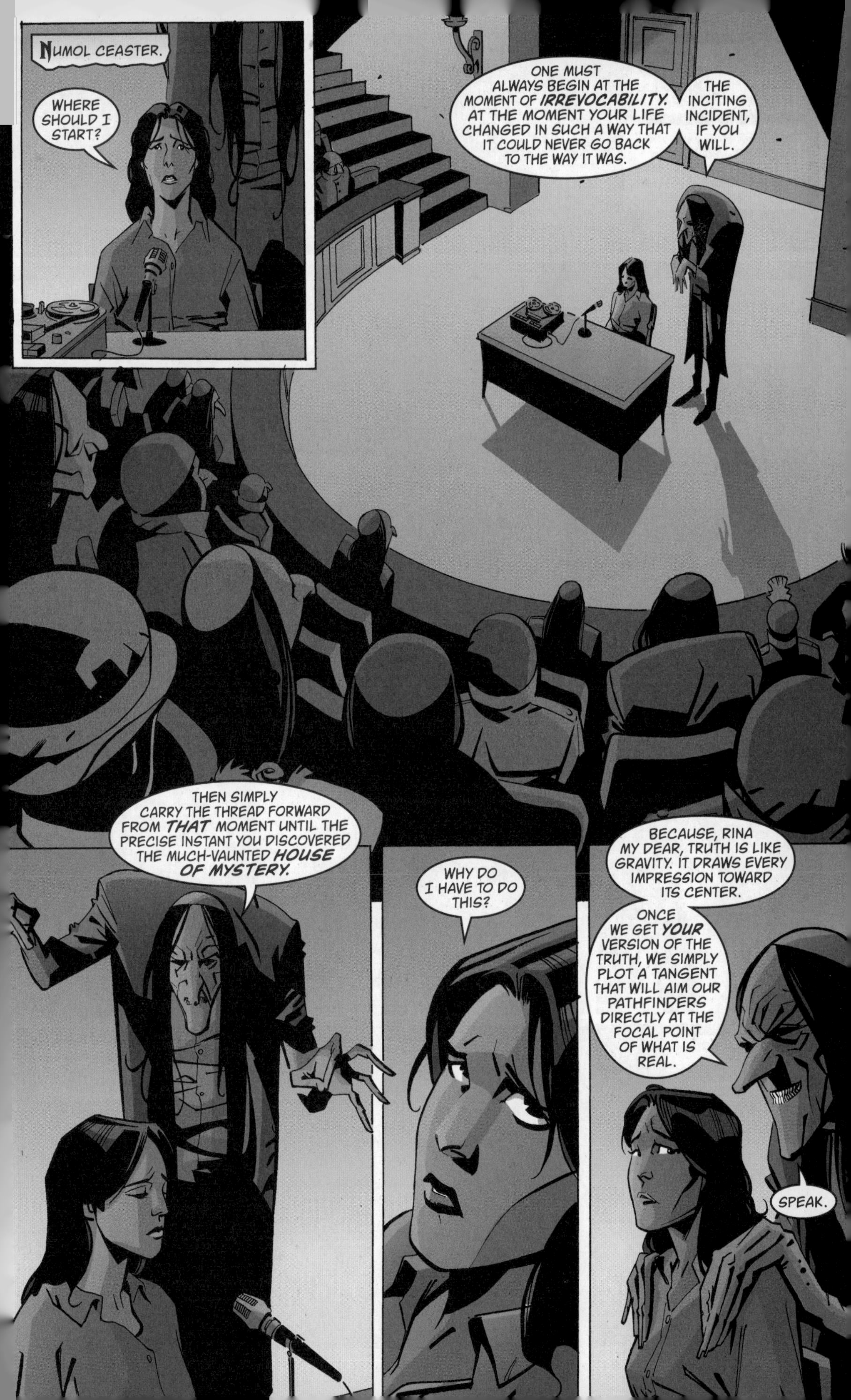
NUMOL CEASTER.
WHERE SHOULD I START?
ONE MUST ALWAYS BEGIN AT THE MOMENT OF IRREVOCABILITY. AT THE MOMENT YOUR LIFE CHANGED IN SUCH A WAY THAT IT COULD NEVER GO BACK TO THE WAY IT WAS.
THE INCITING INCIDENT, IF YOU WILL.
THEN SIMPLY CARRY THE THREAD FORWARD FROM THAT MOMENT UNTIL THE PRECISE INSTANT YOU DISCOVERED THE MUCH-VAUNTED HOUSE OF MYSTERY.
WHY DO I HAVE TO DO THIS?
BECAUSE, RINA MY DEAR, TRUTH IS LIKE GRAVITY. IT DRAWS EVERY IMPRESSION TOWARD ITS CENTER.
ONCE WE GET YOUR VERSION OF THE TRUTH, WE SIMPLY PLOT A TANGENT THAT WILL AIM OUR PATHFINDERS DIRECTLY AT THE FOCAL POINT OF WHAT IS REAL.
SPEAK.

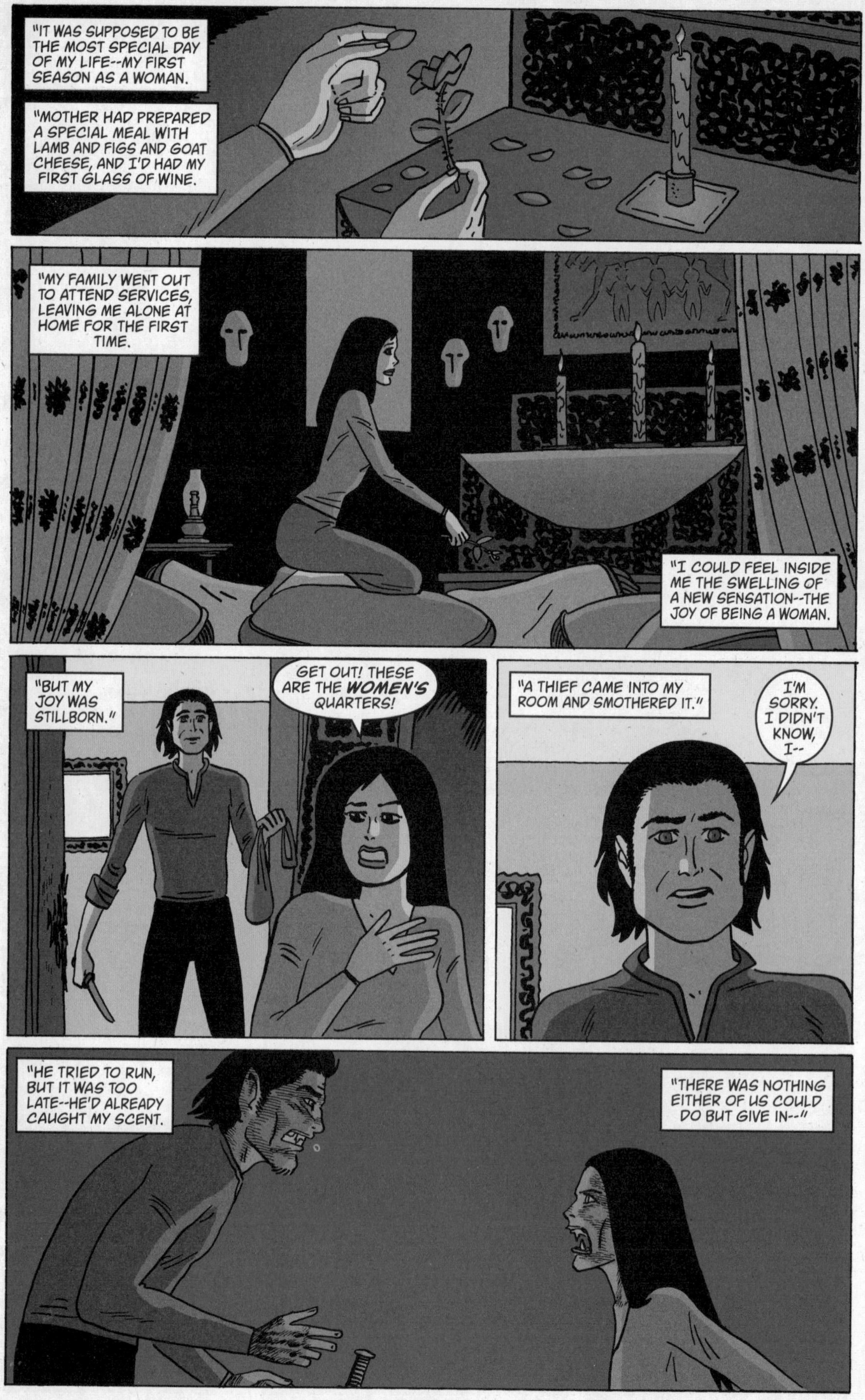
"IT WAS SUPPOSED TO BE THE MOST SPECIAL DAY OF MY LIFE--MY FIRST SEASON AS A WOMAN.
"MOTHER HAD PREPARED A SPECIAL MEAL WITH LAMB AND FIGS AND GOAT CHEESE, AND I'D HAD MY FIRST GLASS OF WINE.
"MY FAMILY WENT OUT TO ATTEND SERVICES, LEAVING ME ALONE AT HOME FOR THE FIRST TIME.
"I COULD FEEL INSIDE ME THE SWELLING OF A NEW SENSATION--THE JOY OF BEING A WOMAN.
"BUT MY JOY WAS STILLBORN."
GET OUT! THESE ARE THE WOMEN'S QUARTERS!
"A THIEF CAME INTO MY ROOM AND SMOTHERED IT."
I'M SORRY. I DIDN'T KNOW, I--
"HE TRIED TO RUN, BUT IT WAS TOO LATE--HE'D ALREADY CAUGHT MY SCENT.
"THERE WAS NOTHING EITHER OF US COULD DO BUT GIVE IN--"

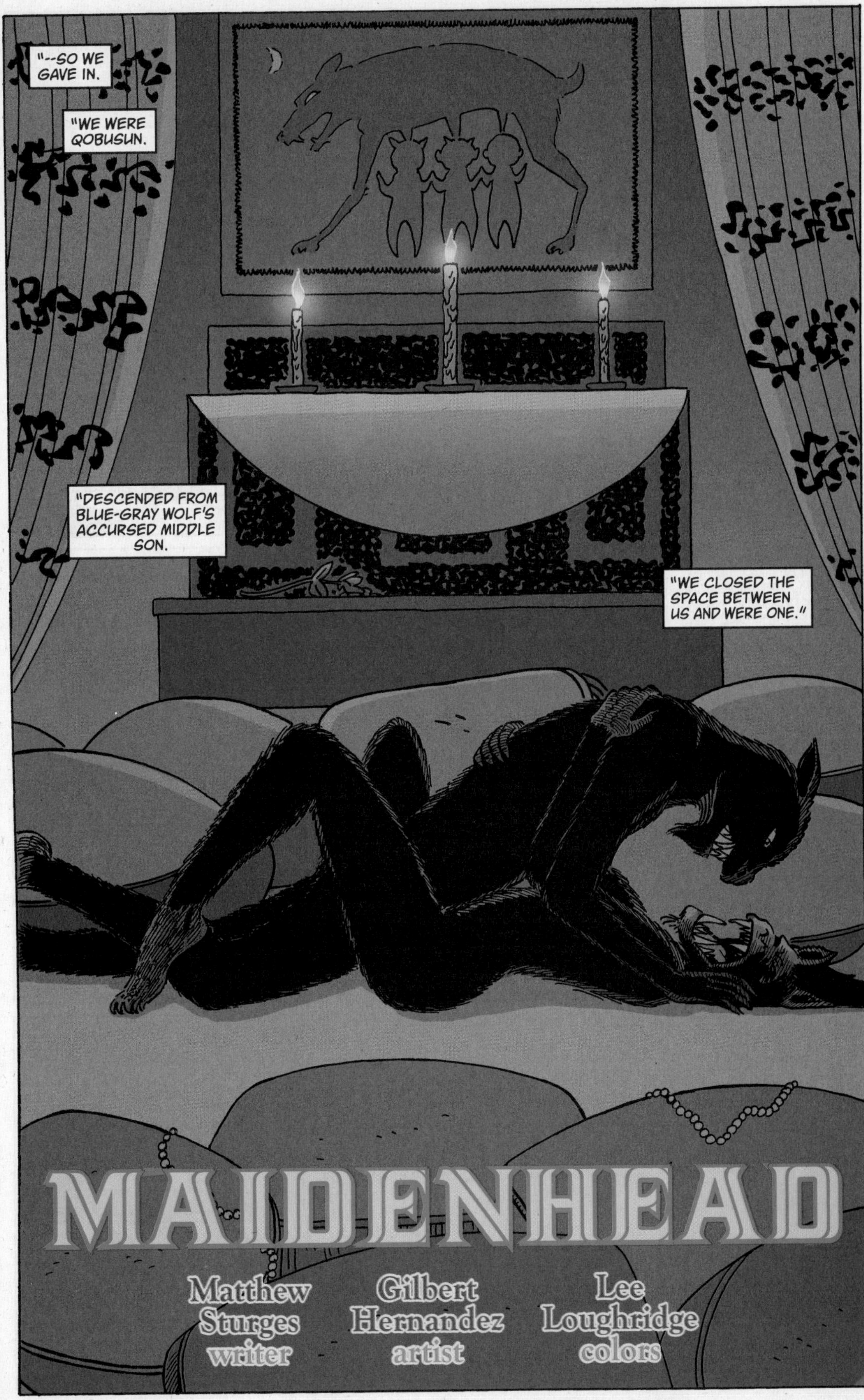
"--SO WE GAVE IN.
"WE WERE QOBUSUN.
"DESCENDED FROM BLUE-GRAY WOLF'S ACCURSED MIDDLE SON.
"WE CLOSED THE SPACE BETWEEN US AND WERE ONE."
MAIDENHEAD
Matthew Sturges writer
Gilbert Hernandez artist
Lee Loughridge colors

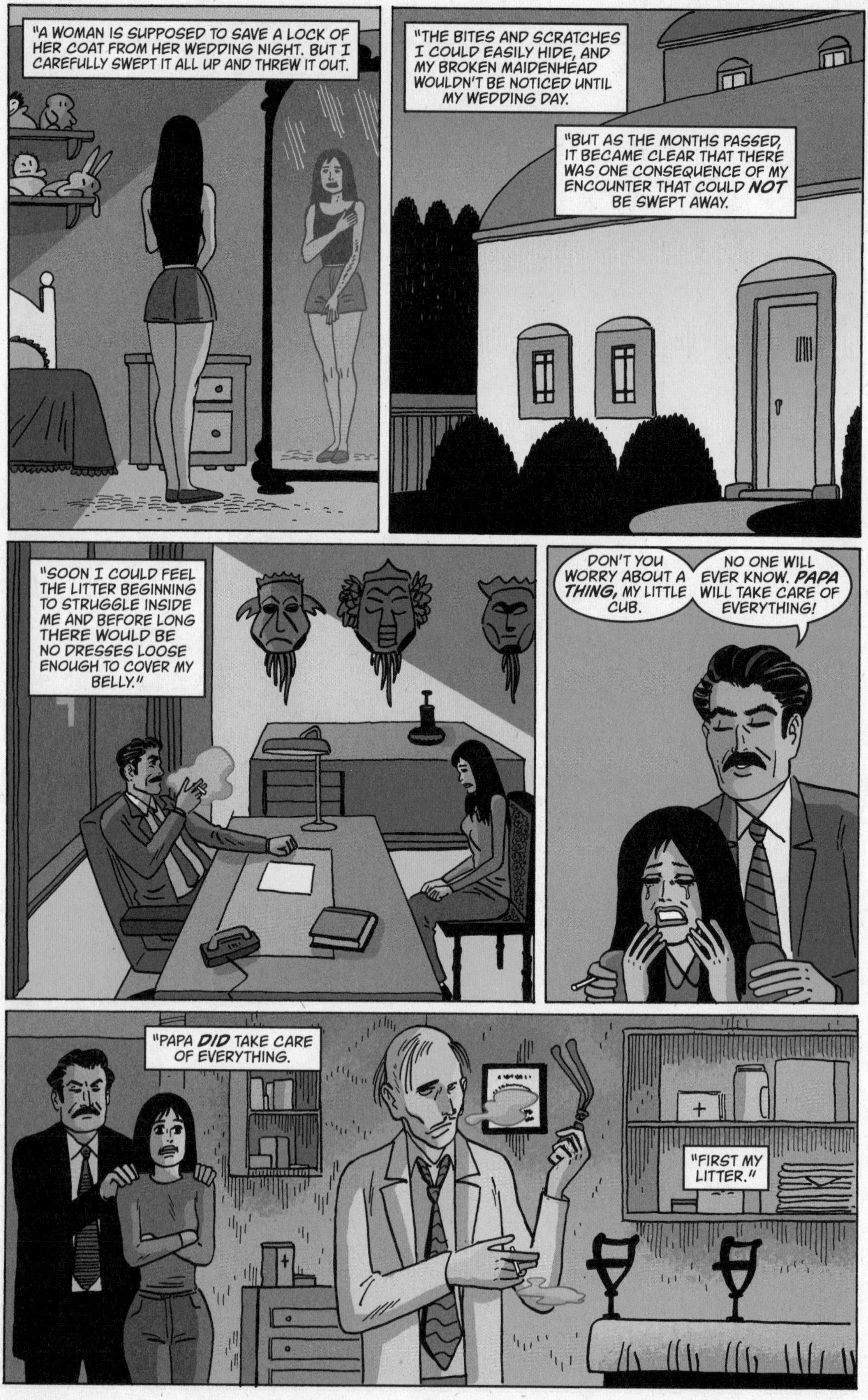
"A WOMAN IS SUPPOSED TO SAVE A LOCK OF HER COAT FROM HER WEDDING NIGHT. BUT I CAREFULLY SWEPT IT ALL UP AND THREW IT OUT.
"THE BITES AND SCRATCHES I COULD EASILY HIDE, AND MY BROKEN MAIDENHEAD WOULDN'T BE NOTICED UNTIL MY WEDDING DAY.
"BUT AS THE MONTHS PASSED, IT BECAME CLEAR THAT THERE WAS ONE CONSEQUENCE OF MY ENCOUNTER THAT COULD NOT BE SWEPT AWAY.
"SOON I COULD FEEL THE LITTER BEGINNING TO STRUGGLE INSIDE ME AND BEFORE LONG THERE WOULD BE NO DRESSES LOOSE ENOUGH TO COVER MY BELLY."
DON'T YOU WORRY ABOUT A THING, MY LITTLE CUB.
NO ONE WILL EVER KNOW. PAPA WILL TAKE CARE OF EVERYTHING!
"PAPA DID TAKE CARE OF EVERYTHING.
"FIRST MY LITTER."

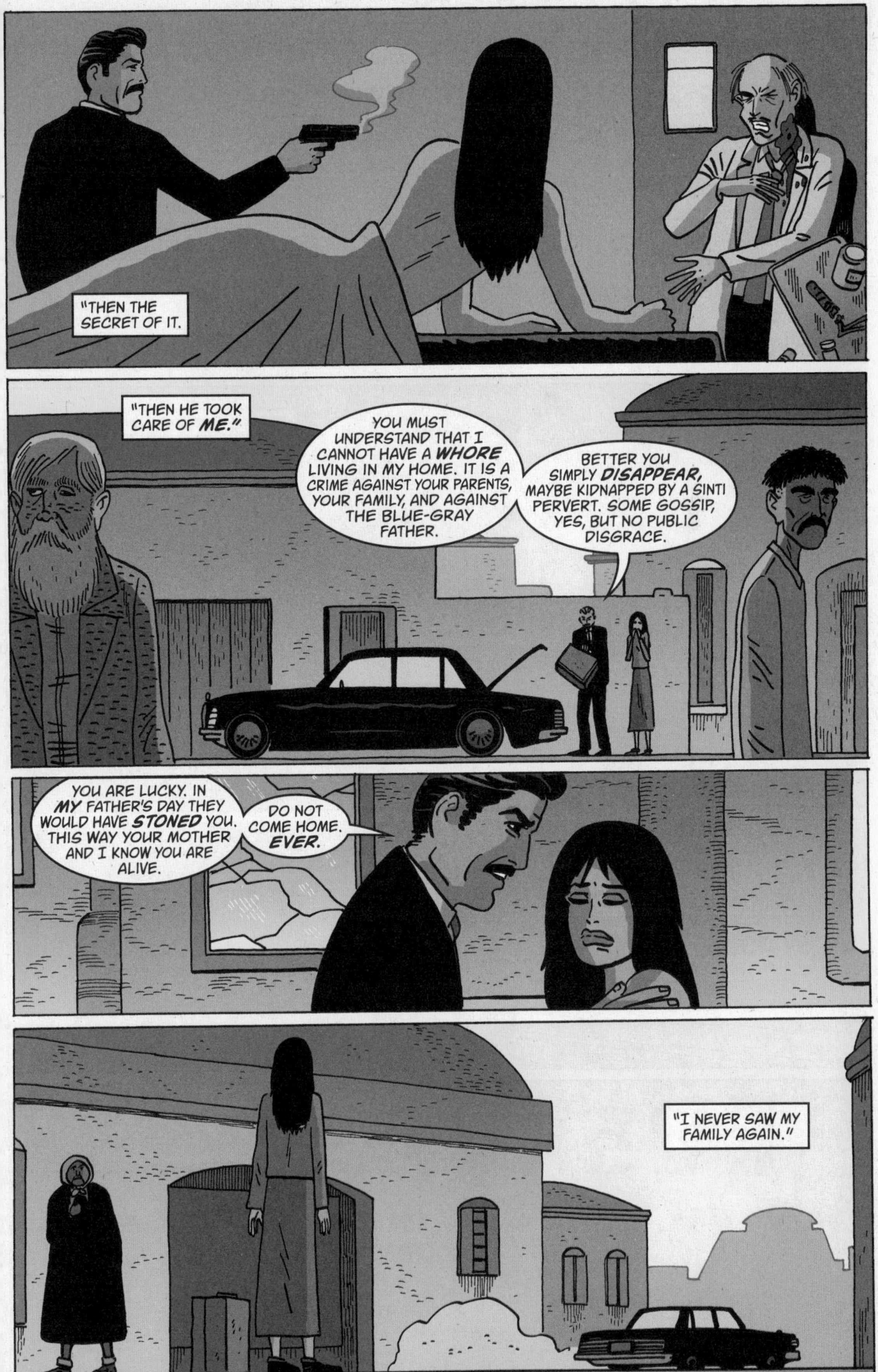
"THEN THE SECRET OF IT.
"THEN HE TOOK CARE OF ME."
YOU MUST UNDERSTAND THAT I CANNOT HAVE A WHORE LIVING IN MY HOME. IT IS A CRIME AGAINST YOUR PARENTS, YOUR FAMILY, AND AGAINST THE BLUE-GRAY FATHER.
BETTER YOU SIMPLY DISAPPEAR, MAYBE KIDNAPPED BY A SINTI PERVERT. SOME GOSSIP, YES, BUT NO PUBLIC DISGRACE.
YOU ARE LUCKY. IN MY FATHER'S DAY THEY WOULD HAVE STONED YOU. THIS WAY YOUR MOTHER AND I KNOW YOU ARE ALIVE.
DO NOT COME HOME. EVER.
"I NEVER SAW MY FAMILY AGAIN."

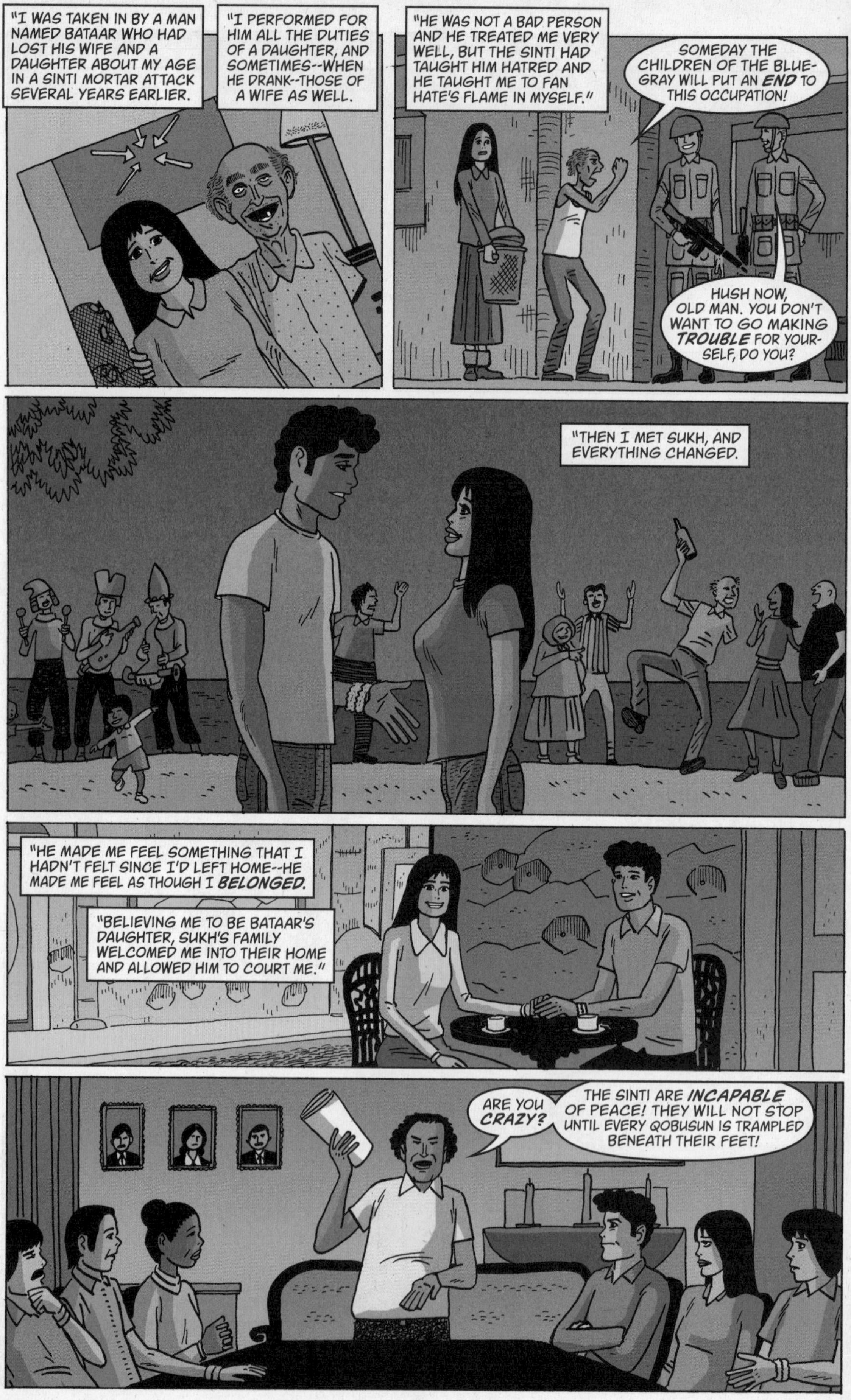
"I WAS TAKEN IN BY A MAN NAMED BATAAR WHO HAD LOST HIS WIFE AND A DAUGHTER ABOUT MY AGE IN A SINTI MORTAR ATTACK SEVERAL YEARS EARLIER.
"I PERFORMED FOR HIM ALL THE DUTIES OF A DAUGHTER, AND SOMETIMES--WHEN HE DRANK--THOSE OF A WIFE AS WELL.
"HE WAS NOT A BAD PERSON AND HE TREATED ME VERY WELL, BUT THE SINTI HAD TAUGHT HIM HATRED AND HE TAUGHT ME TO FAN HATE'S FLAME IN MYSELF."
SOMEDAY THE CHILDREN OF THE BLUE-GRAY WILL PUT AN END TO THIS OCCUPATION!
HUSH NOW, OLD MAN. YOU DON'T WANT TO GO MAKING TROUBLE FOR YOURSELF, DO YOU?
"THEN I MET SUKH, AND EVERYTHING CHANGED.
"HE MADE ME FEEL SOMETHING THAT I HADN'T FELT SINCE I'D LEFT HOME--HE MADE ME FEEL AS THOUGH I BELONGED.
"BELIEVING ME TO BE BATAAR'S DAUGHTER, SUKH'S FAMILY WELCOMED ME INTO THEIR HOME AND ALLOWED HIM TO COURT ME."
ARE YOU CRAZY?
THE SINTI ARE INCAPABLE OF PEACE! THEY WILL NOT STOP UNTIL EVERY QOBUSUN IS TRAMPLED BENEATH THEIR FEET!

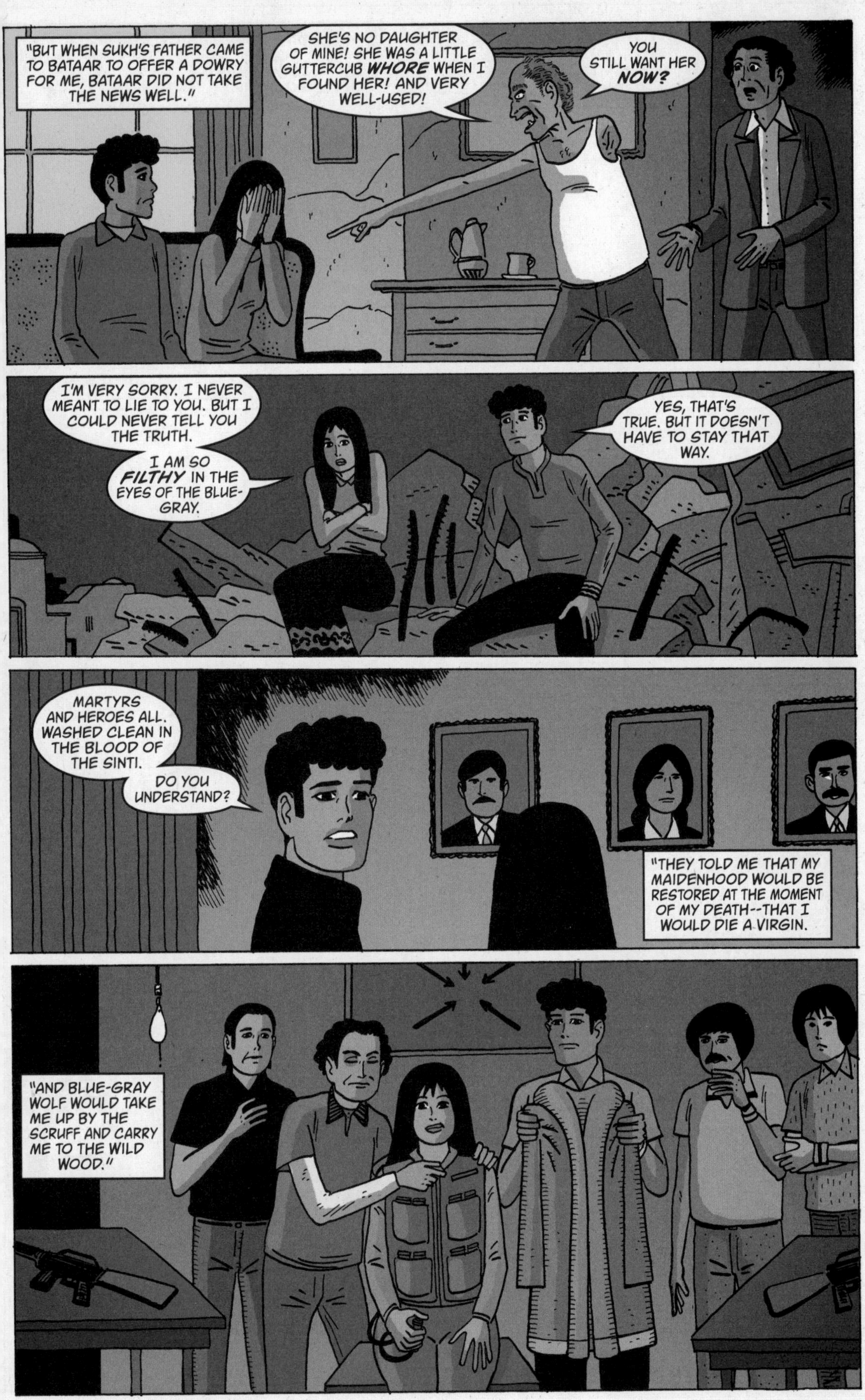
"BUT WHEN SUKH'S FATHER CAME TO BATAAR TO OFFER A DOWRY FOR ME, BATAAR DID NOT TAKE THE NEWS WELL."
SHE'S NO DAUGHTER OF MINE! SHE WAS A LITTLE GUTTERCUB WHORE WHEN I FOUND HER! AND VERY WELL-USED!
YOU STILL WANT HER NOW?
I'M VERY SORRY. I NEVER MEANT TO LIE TO YOU. BUT I COULD NEVER TELL YOU THE TRUTH.
I AM SO FILTHY IN THE EYES OF THE BLUE-GRAY.
YES, THAT'S TRUE. BUT IT DOESN'T HAVE TO STAY THAT WAY.
MARTYRS AND HEROES ALL. WASHED CLEAN IN THE BLOOD OF THE SINTI.
DO YOU UNDERSTAND?
"THEY TOLD ME THAT MY MAIDENHOOD WOULD BE RESTORED AT THE MOMENT OF MY DEATH--THAT I WOULD DIE A VIRGIN.
"AND BLUE-GRAY WOLF WOULD TAKE ME UP BY THE SCRUFF AND CARRY ME TO THE WILD WOOD."

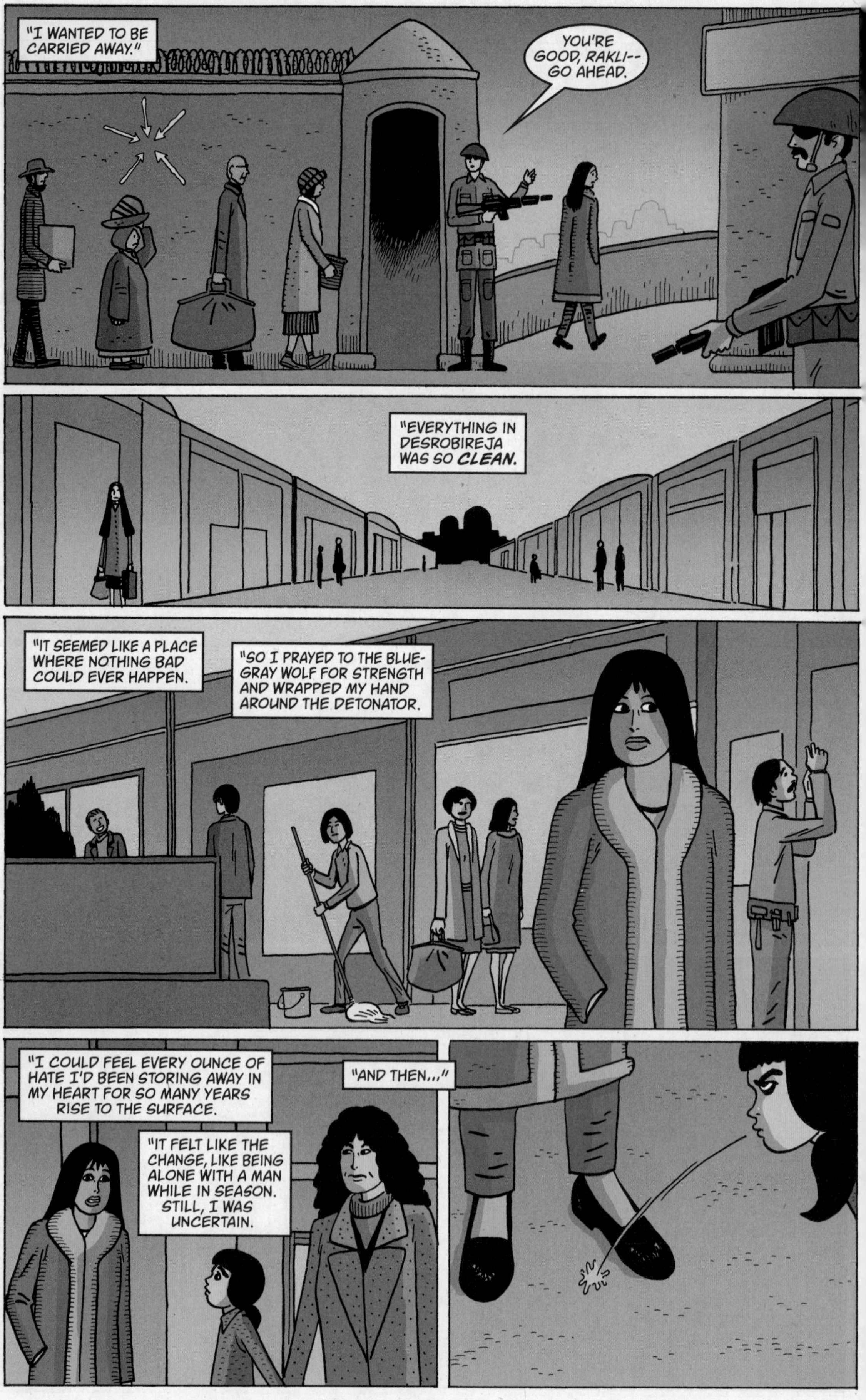
"I WANTED TO BE CARRIED AWAY."
YOU'RE GOOD, RAKLI-- GO AHEAD.
"EVERYTHING IN DESROBIREJA WAS SO CLEAN.
"IT SEEMED LIKE A PLACE WHERE NOTHING BAD COULD EVER HAPPEN.
"SO I PRAYED TO THE BLUE-GRAY WOLF FOR STRENGTH AND WRAPPED MY HAND AROUND THE DETONATOR.
"I COULD FEEL EVERY OUNCE OF HATE I'D BEEN STORING AWAY IN MY HEART FOR SO MANY YEARS RISE TO THE SURFACE.
"IT FELT LIKE THE CHANGE, LIKE BEING ALONE WITH A MAN WHILE IN SEASON. STILL, I WAS UNCERTAIN.
"AND THEN..."

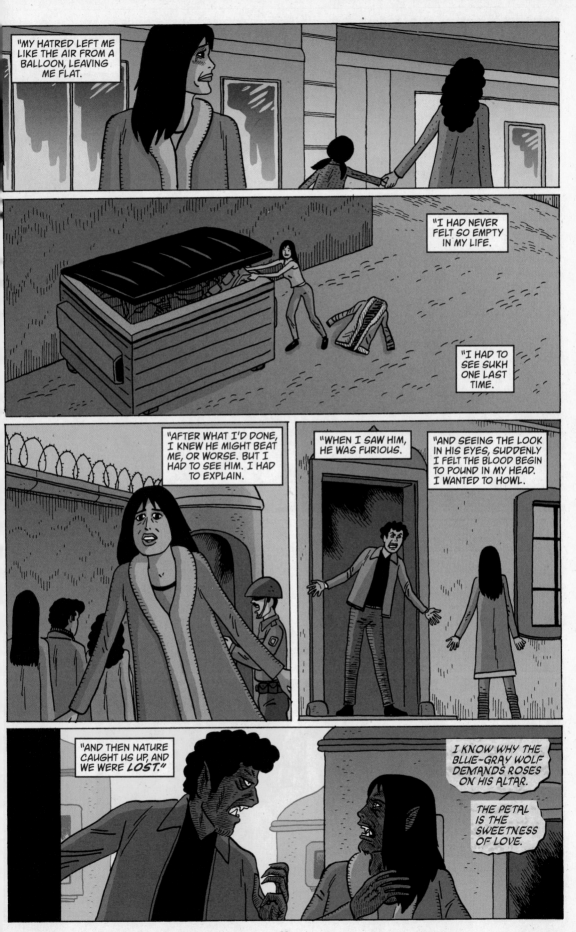

"MY HATRED LEFT ME LIKE THE AIR FROM A BALLOON, LEAVING ME FLAT."

"I HAD NEVER FELT SO EMPTY IN MY LIFE.

"I HAD TO SEE SUKH ONE LAST TIME.

"AFTER WHAT I'D DONE, I KNEW HE MIGHT BEAT ME, OR WORSE. BUT I HAD TO SEE HIM. I HAD TO EXPLAIN.

"WHEN I SAW HIM, HE WAS FURIOUS.

"AND SEEING THE LOOK IN HIS EYES, SUDDENLY I FELT THE BLOOD BEGIN TO POUND IN MY HEAD. I WANTED TO HOWL.

"AND THEN NATURE CAUGHT US UP, AND WE WERE *LOST*."

I KNOW WHY THE BLUE-GRAY WOLF DEMANDS ROSES ON HIS ALTAR.

THE PETAL IS THE SWEETNESS OF LOVE.

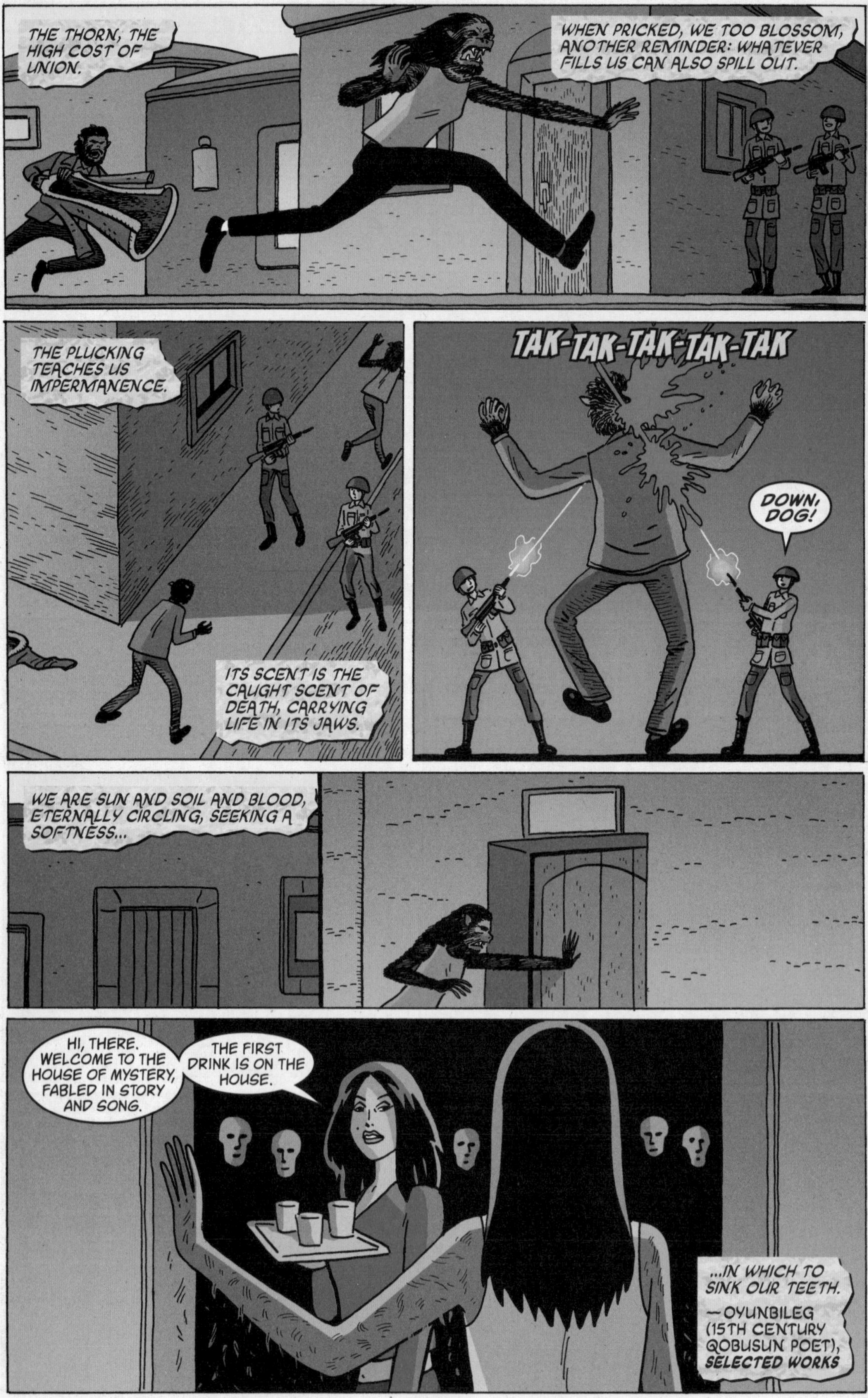
THE THORN, THE HIGH COST OF UNION.
WHEN PRICKED, WE TOO BLOSSOM, ANOTHER REMINDER: WHATEVER FILLS US CAN ALSO SPILL OUT.
THE PLUCKING TEACHES US IMPERMANENCE.
ITS SCENT IS THE CAUGHT SCENT OF DEATH, CARRYING LIFE IN ITS JAWS.
TAK-TAK-TAK-TAK-TAK
DOWN, DOG!
WE ARE SUN AND SOIL AND BLOOD, ETERNALLY CIRCLING, SEEKING A SOFTNESS...
HI, THERE. WELCOME TO THE HOUSE OF MYSTERY, FABLED IN STORY AND SONG.
THE FIRST DRINK IS ON THE HOUSE.
...IN WHICH TO SINK OUR TEETH.
—OYUNBILEG (15TH CENTURY QOBUSUN POET), SELECTED WORKS

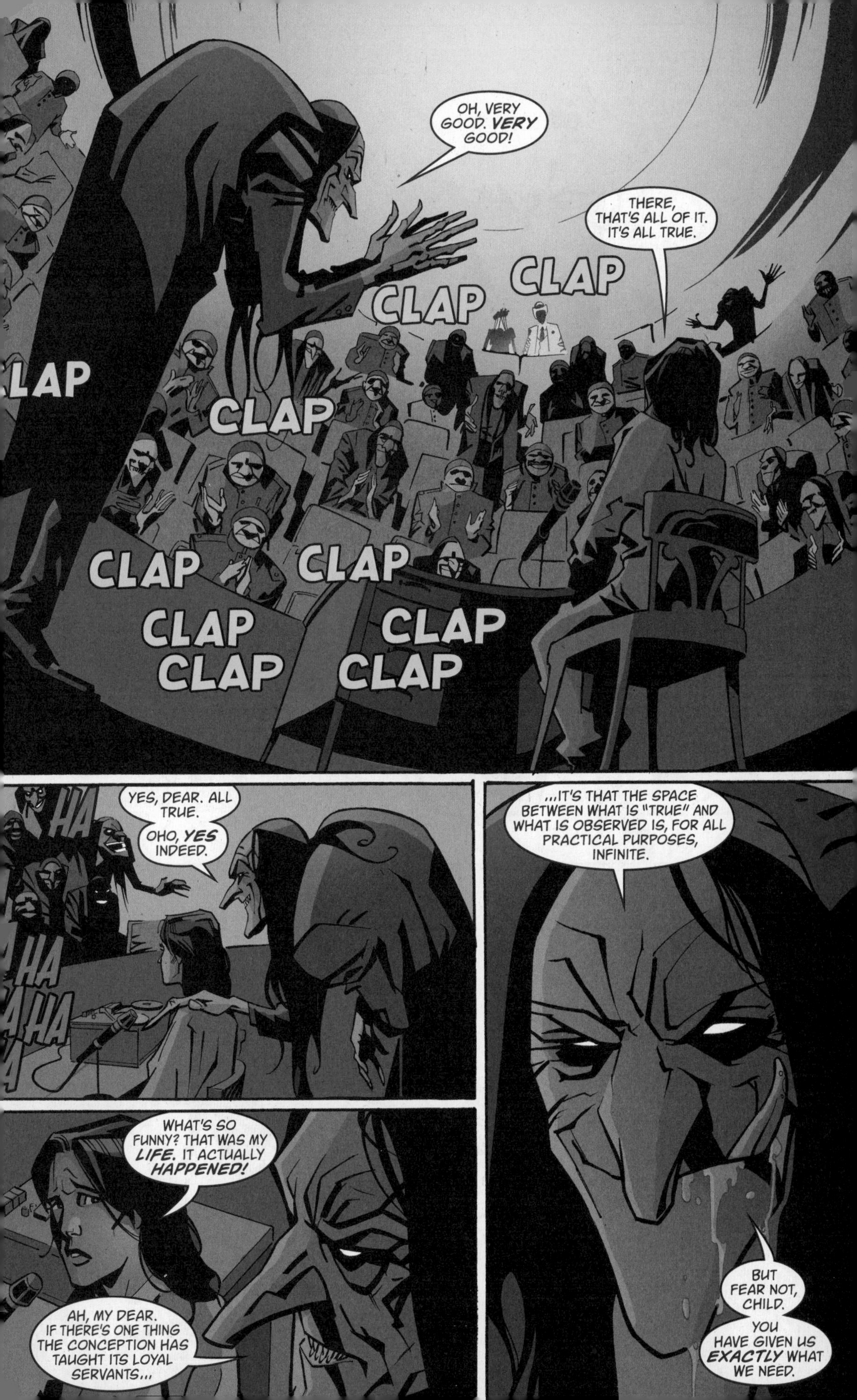
OH, VERY GOOD. VERY GOOD!
THERE, THAT'S ALL OF IT. IT'S ALL TRUE.
CLAP
CLAP
LAP
CLAP
CLAP
CLAP
CLAP
CLAP
CLAP
CLAP
YES, DEAR. ALL TRUE.
OHO, YES INDEED.
HA
HA
HA HA
WHAT'S SO FUNNY? THAT WAS MY LIFE. IT ACTUALLY HAPPENED!
AH, MY DEAR. IF THERE'S ONE THING THE CONCEPTION HAS TAUGHT ITS LOYAL SERVANTS...
...IT'S THAT THE SPACE BETWEEN WHAT IS "TRUE" AND WHAT IS OBSERVED IS, FOR ALL PRACTICAL PURPOSES, INFINITE.
BUT FEAR NOT, CHILD.
YOU HAVE GIVEN US EXACTLY WHAT WE NEED.

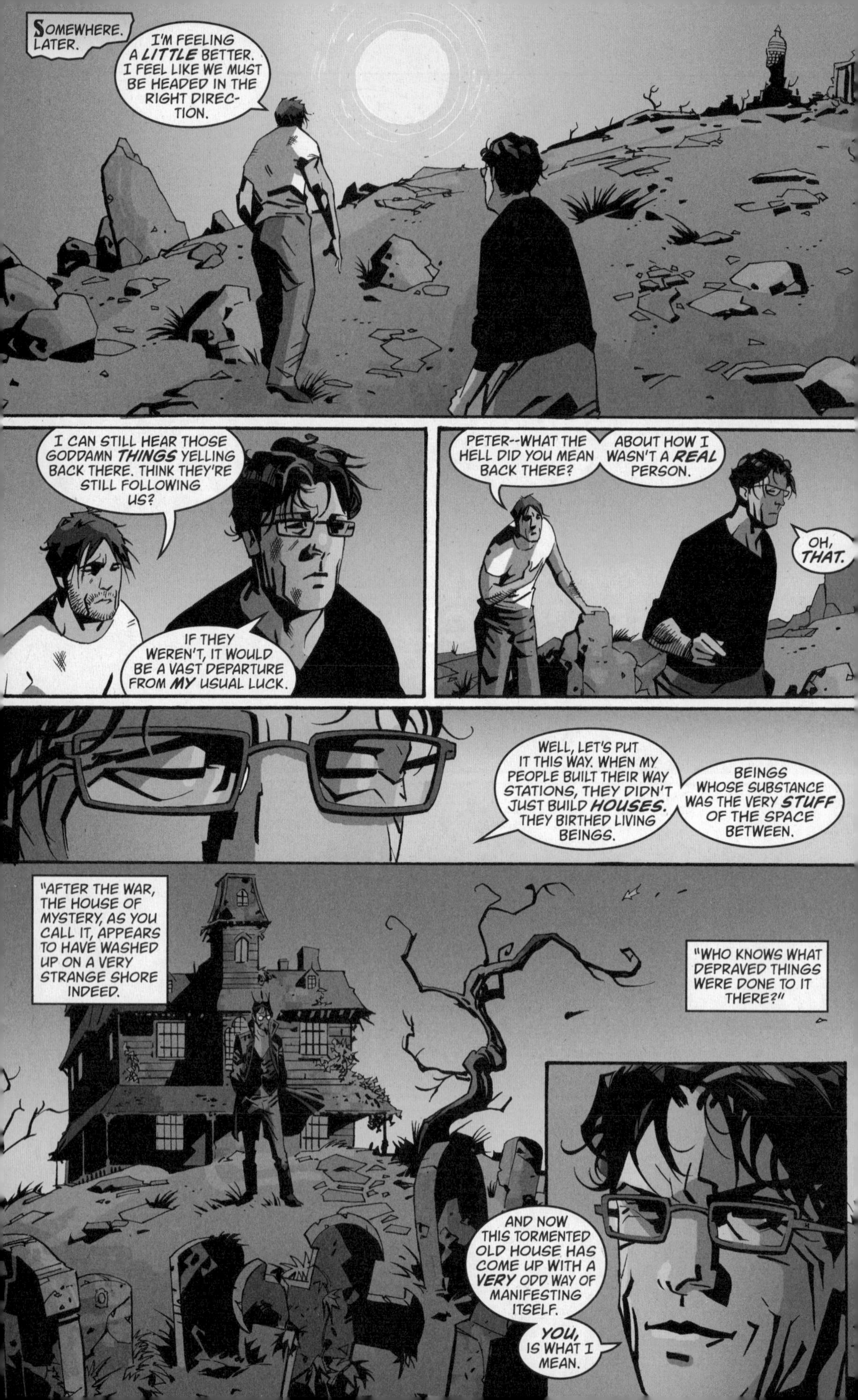

SOMEWHERE. LATER.
I'M FEELING A LITTLE BETTER. I FEEL LIKE WE MUST BE HEADED IN THE RIGHT DIREC-TION.
I CAN STILL HEAR THOSE GODDAMN THINGS YELLING BACK THERE. THINK THEY'RE STILL FOLLOWING US?
IF THEY WEREN'T, IT WOULD BE A VAST DEPARTURE FROM MY USUAL LUCK.
PETER--WHAT THE HELL DID YOU MEAN BACK THERE?
ABOUT HOW I WASN'T A REAL PERSON.
OH, THAT.
WELL, LET'S PUT IT THIS WAY. WHEN MY PEOPLE BUILT THEIR WAY STATIONS, THEY DIDN'T JUST BUILD HOUSES. THEY BIRTHED LIVING BEINGS.
BEINGS WHOSE SUBSTANCE WAS THE VERY STUFF OF THE SPACE BETWEEN.
"AFTER THE WAR, THE HOUSE OF MYSTERY, AS YOU CALL IT, APPEARS TO HAVE WASHED UP ON A VERY STRANGE SHORE INDEED.
"WHO KNOWS WHAT DEPRAVED THINGS WERE DONE TO IT THERE?"
AND NOW THIS TORMENTED OLD HOUSE HAS COME UP WITH A VERY ODD WAY OF MANIFESTING ITSELF.
YOU, IS WHAT I MEAN.

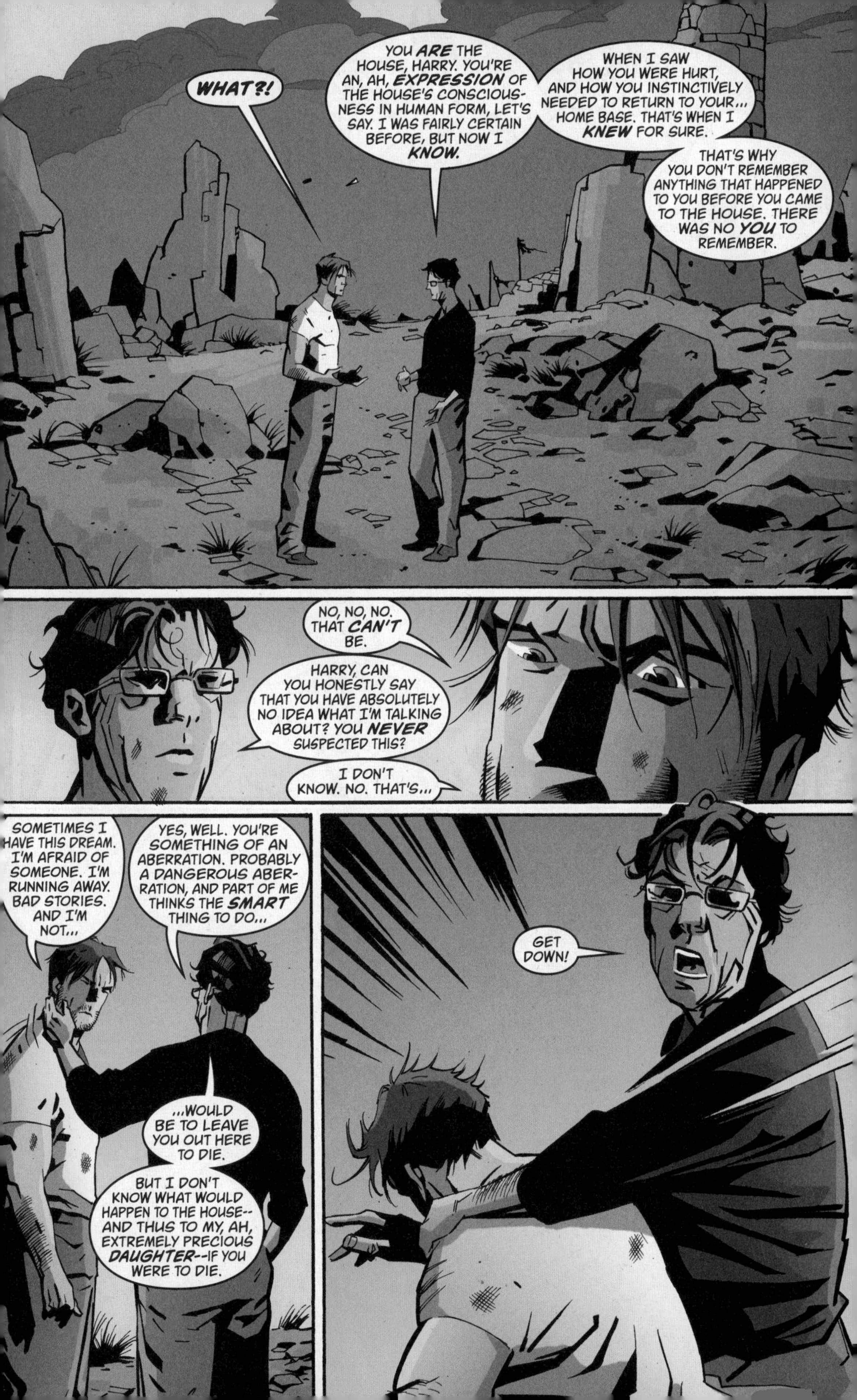
WHAT?!
YOU ARE THE HOUSE, HARRY. YOU'RE AN, AH, EXPRESSION OF THE HOUSE'S CONSCIOUSNESS IN HUMAN FORM, LET'S SAY. I WAS FAIRLY CERTAIN BEFORE, BUT NOW I KNOW.
WHEN I SAW HOW YOU WERE HURT, AND HOW YOU INSTINCTIVELY NEEDED TO RETURN TO YOUR... HOME BASE. THAT'S WHEN I KNEW FOR SURE.
THAT'S WHY YOU DON'T REMEMBER ANYTHING THAT HAPPENED TO YOU BEFORE YOU CAME TO THE HOUSE. THERE WAS NO YOU TO REMEMBER.
NO, NO, NO. THAT CAN'T BE.
HARRY, CAN YOU HONESTLY SAY THAT YOU HAVE ABSOLUTELY NO IDEA WHAT I'M TALKING ABOUT? YOU NEVER SUSPECTED THIS?
I DON'T KNOW. NO. THAT'S...
SOMETIMES I HAVE THIS DREAM. I'M AFRAID OF SOMEONE. I'M RUNNING AWAY. BAD STORIES. AND I'M NOT...
YES, WELL. YOU'RE SOMETHING OF AN ABERRATION. PROBABLY A DANGEROUS ABERRATION, AND PART OF ME THINKS THE SMART THING TO DO...
...WOULD BE TO LEAVE YOU OUT HERE TO DIE.
BUT I DON'T KNOW WHAT WOULD HAPPEN TO THE HOUSE-- AND THUS TO MY, AH, EXTREMELY PRECIOUS DAUGHTER--IF YOU WERE TO DIE.
GET DOWN!

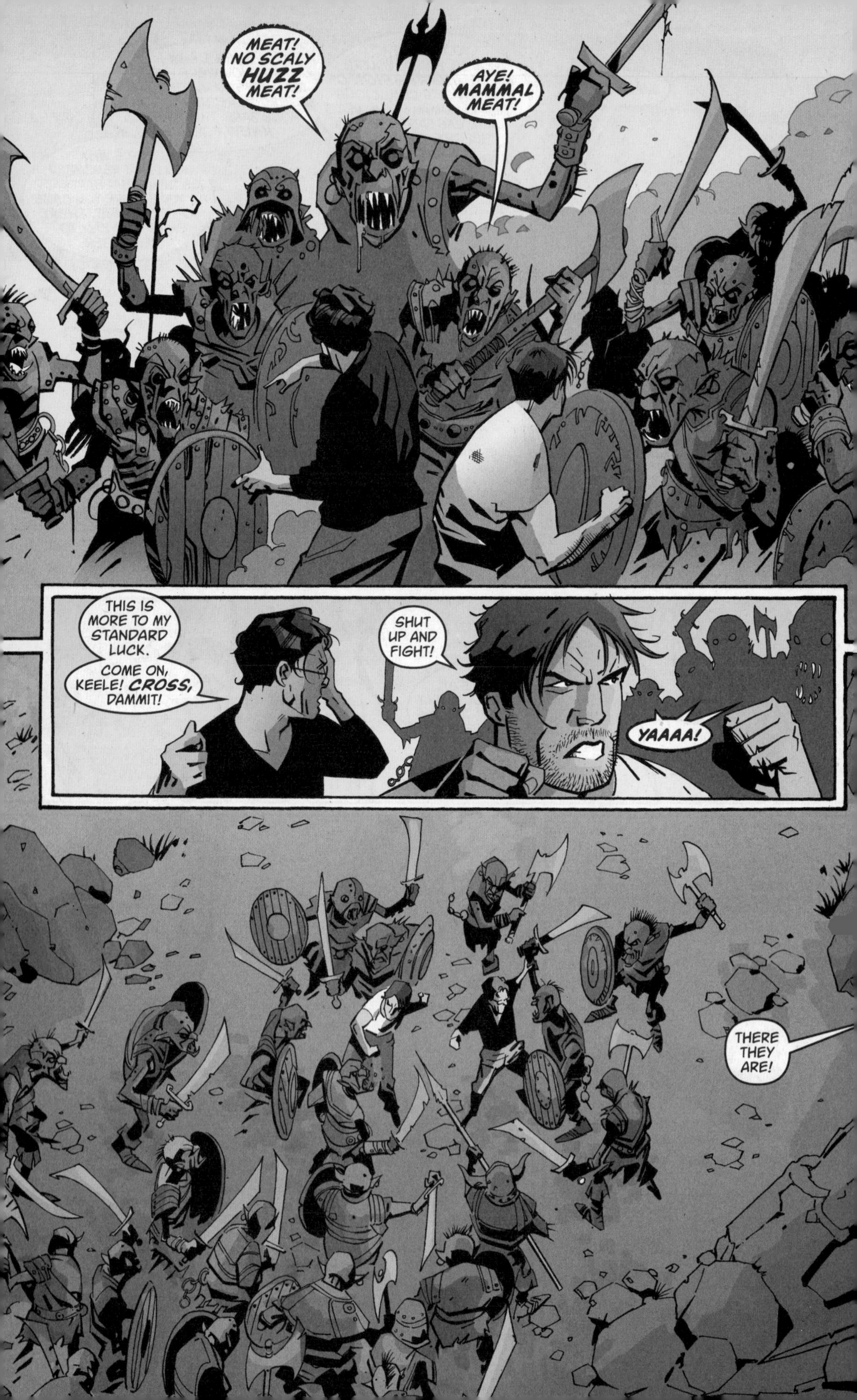
MEAT! NO SCALY HUZZ MEAT!
AYE! MAMMAL MEAT!
THIS IS MORE TO MY STANDARD LUCK.
COME ON, KEELE! CROSS, DAMMIT!
SHUT UP AND FIGHT!
YAAAA!
THERE THEY ARE!

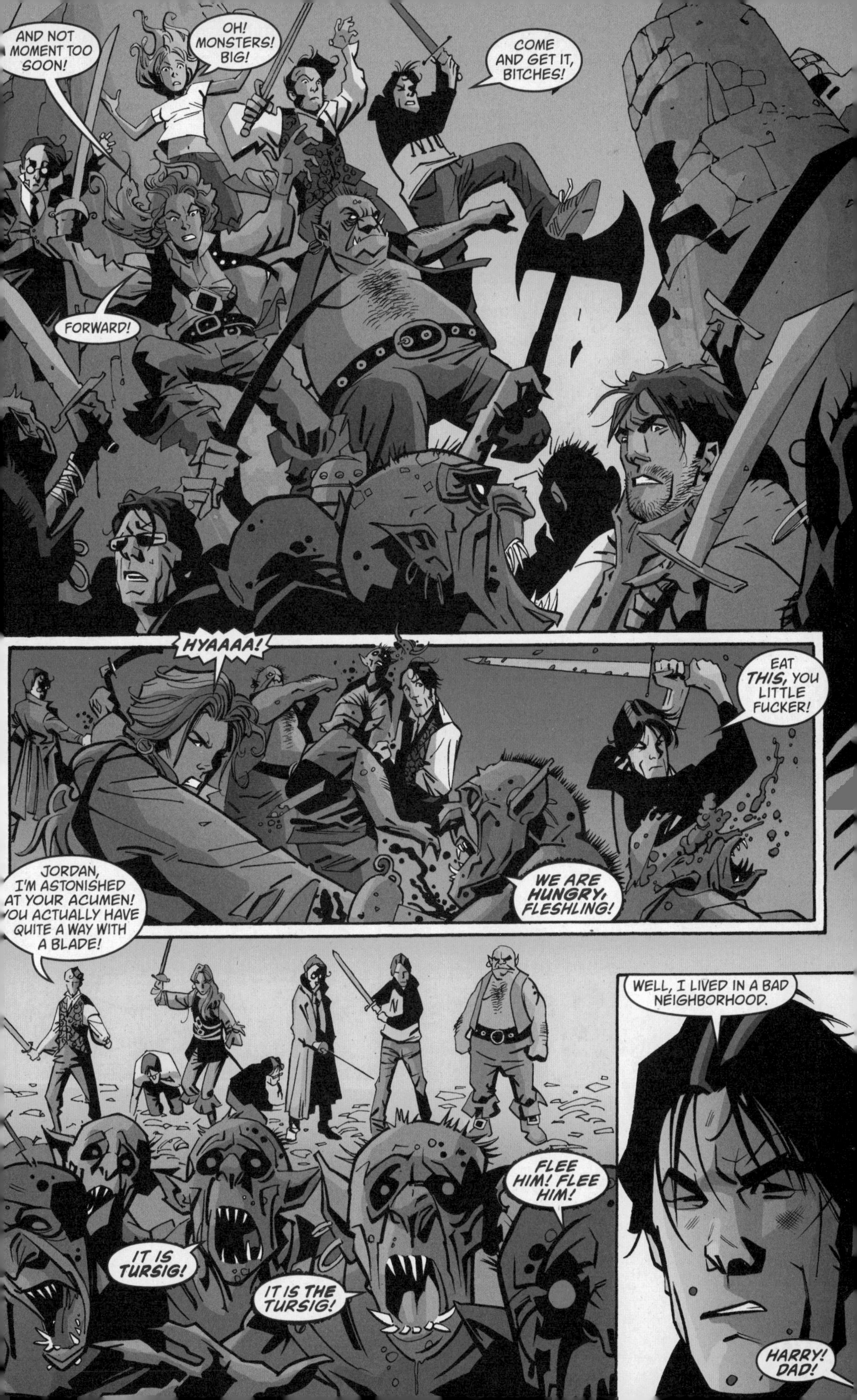
AND NOT MOMENT TOO SOON!
OH! MONSTERS! BIG!
COME AND GET IT, BITCHES!
FORWARD!
HYAAAA!
EAT THIS, YOU LITTLE FUCKER!
WE ARE HUNGRY, FLESHLING!
JORDAN, I'M ASTONISHED AT YOUR ACUMEN! YOU ACTUALLY HAVE QUITE A WAY WITH A BLADE!
IT IS TURSIG!
IT IS THE TURSIG!
FLEE HIM! FLEE HIM!
WELL, I LIVED IN A BAD NEIGHBORHOOD.
HARRY! DAD!

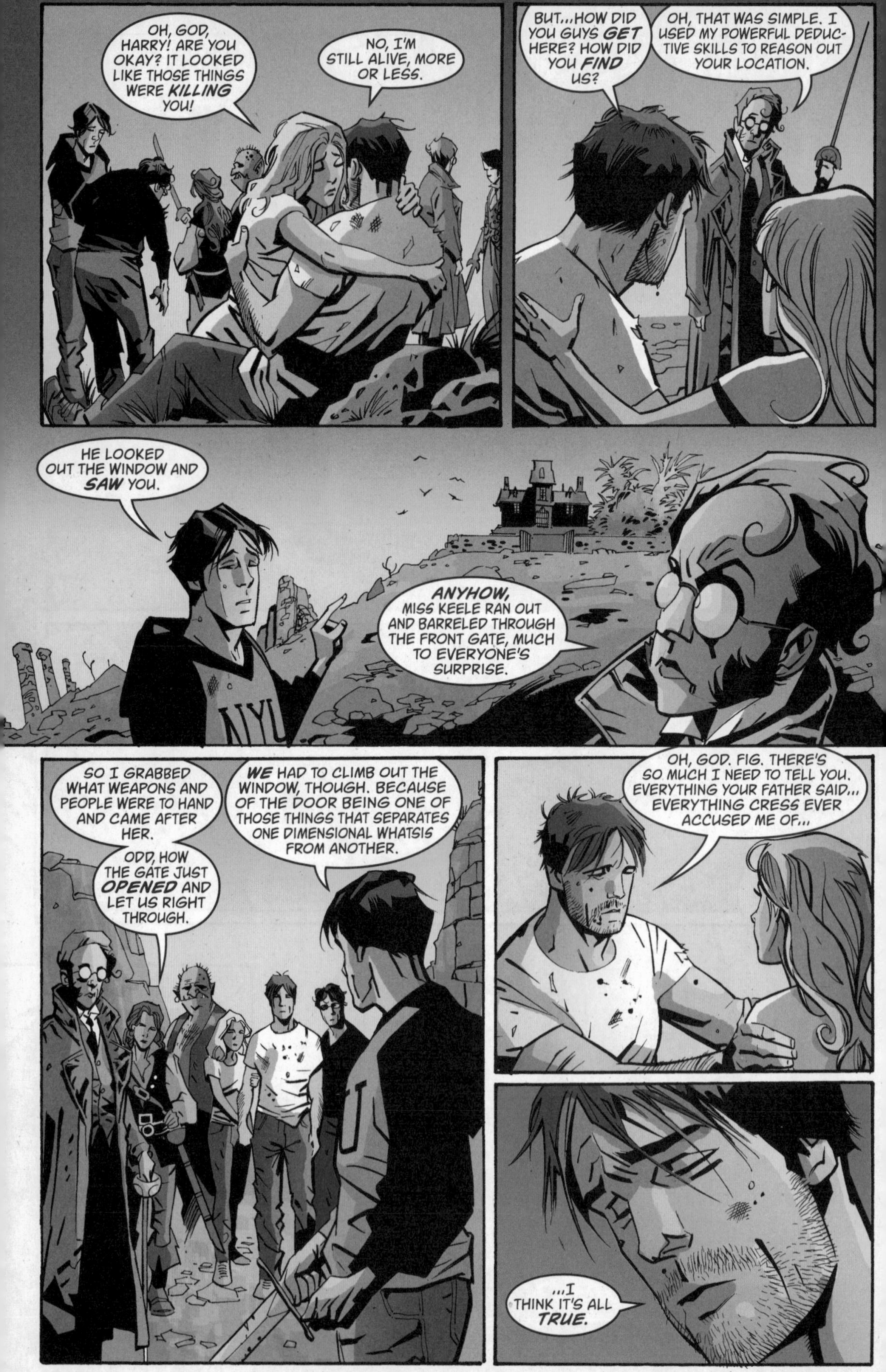
OH, GOD, HARRY! ARE YOU OKAY? IT LOOKED LIKE THOSE THINGS WERE KILLING YOU!
NO, I'M STILL ALIVE, MORE OR LESS.
BUT...HOW DID YOU GUYS GET HERE? HOW DID YOU FIND US?
OH, THAT WAS SIMPLE. I USED MY POWERFUL DEDUCTIVE SKILLS TO REASON OUT YOUR LOCATION.
HE LOOKED OUT THE WINDOW AND SAW YOU.
ANYHOW, MISS KEELE RAN OUT AND BARRELED THROUGH THE FRONT GATE, MUCH TO EVERYONE'S SURPRISE.
SO I GRABBED WHAT WEAPONS AND PEOPLE WERE TO HAND AND CAME AFTER HER.
ODD, HOW THE GATE JUST OPENED AND LET US RIGHT THROUGH.
WE HAD TO CLIMB OUT THE WINDOW, THOUGH. BECAUSE OF THE DOOR BEING ONE OF THOSE THINGS THAT SEPARATES ONE DIMENSIONAL WHATSIS FROM ANOTHER.
OH, GOD. FIG. THERE'S SO MUCH I NEED TO TELL YOU. EVERYTHING YOUR FATHER SAID... EVERYTHING CRESS EVER ACCUSED ME OF...
...I THINK IT'S ALL TRUE.

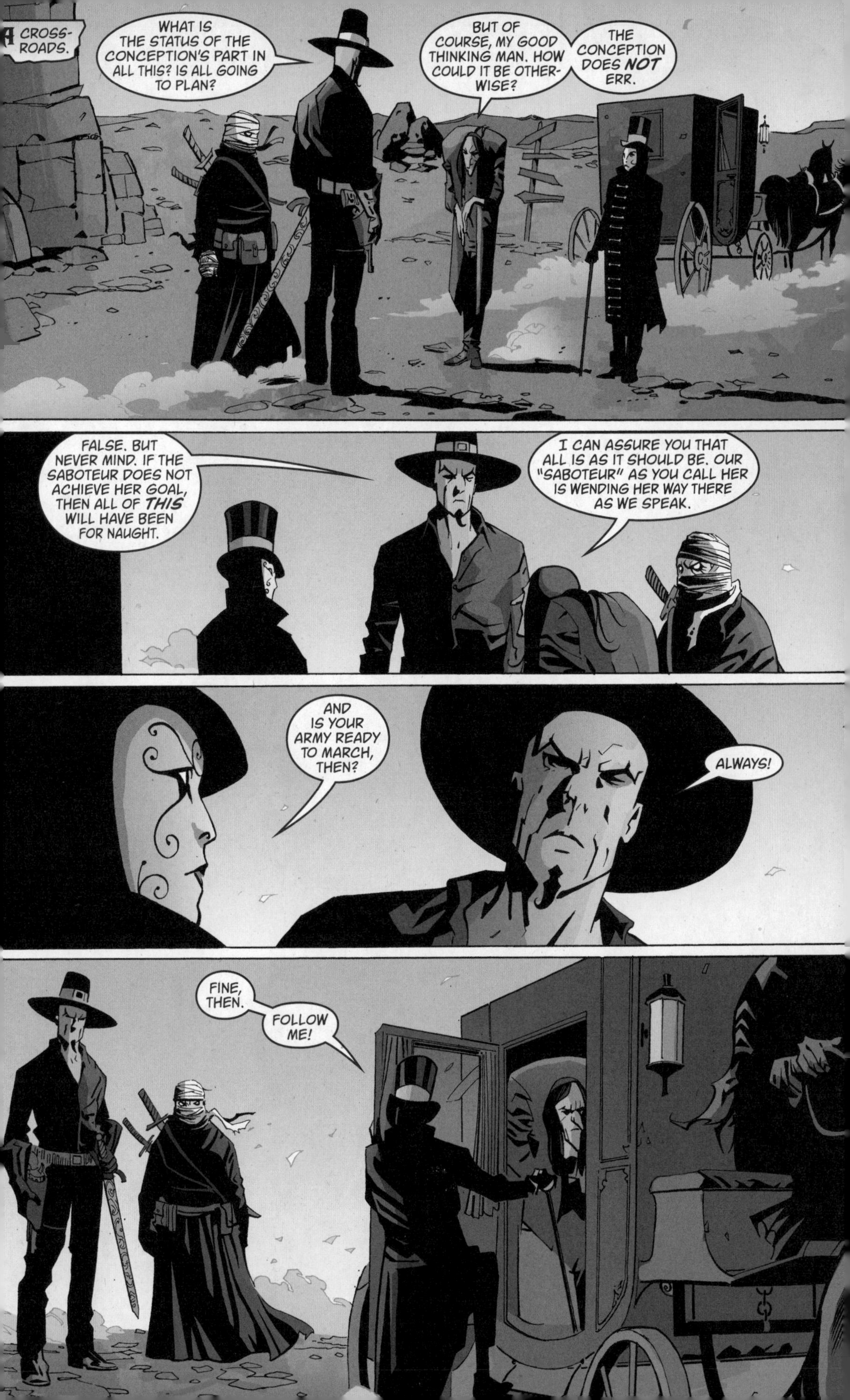
A CROSS-ROADS.
WHAT IS THE STATUS OF THE CONCEPTION'S PART IN ALL THIS? IS ALL GOING TO PLAN?
BUT OF COURSE, MY GOOD THINKING MAN. HOW COULD IT BE OTHER-WISE?
THE CONCEPTION DOES NOT ERR.
FALSE. BUT NEVER MIND. IF THE SABOTEUR DOES NOT ACHIEVE HER GOAL, THEN ALL OF THIS WILL HAVE BEEN FOR NAUGHT.
I CAN ASSURE YOU THAT ALL IS AS IT SHOULD BE. OUR "SABOTEUR" AS YOU CALL HER IS WENDING HER WAY THERE AS WE SPEAK.
AND IS YOUR ARMY READY TO MARCH, THEN?
ALWAYS!
FINE, THEN.
FOLLOW ME!

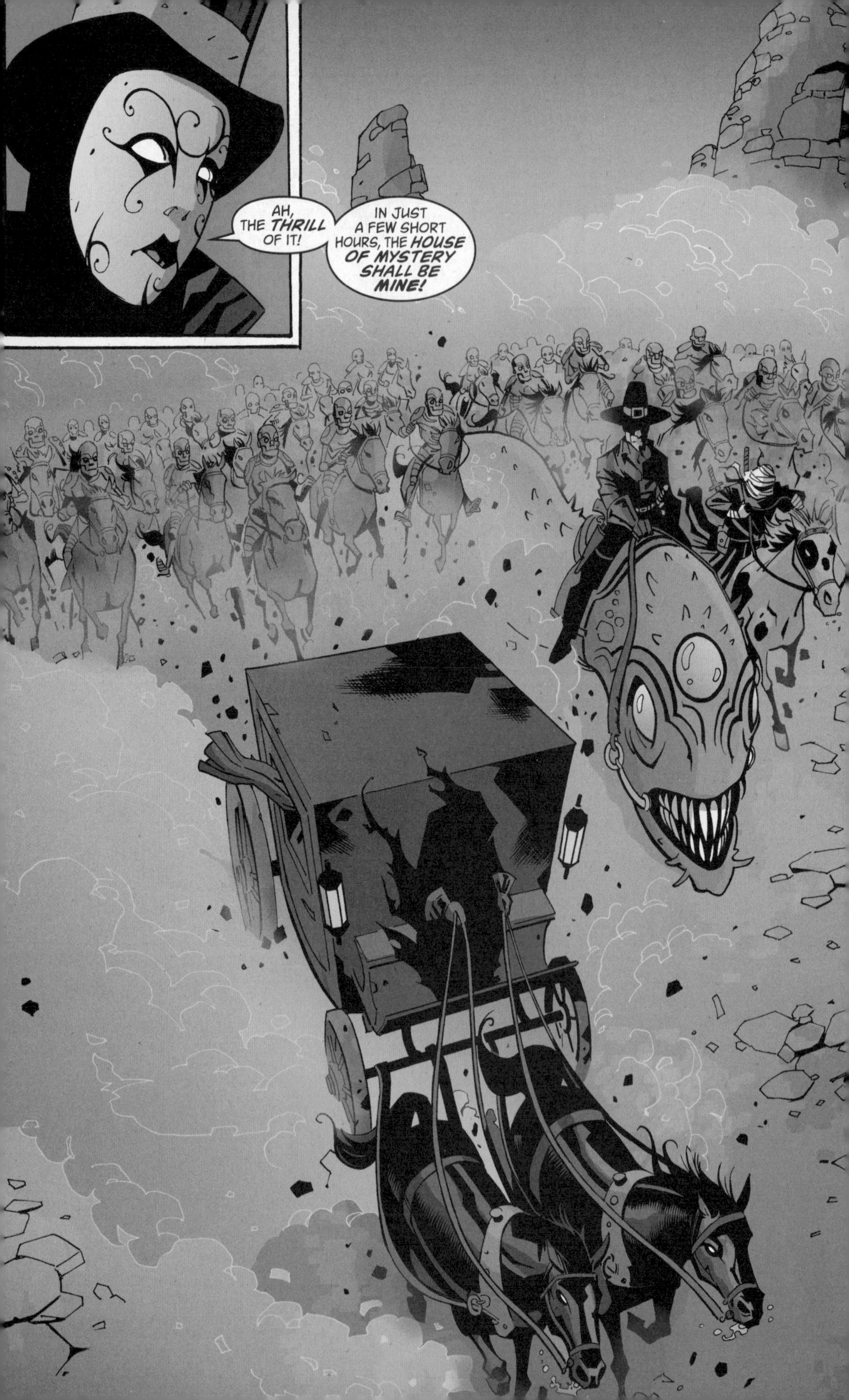
AH, THE THRILL OF IT!
IN JUST A FEW SHORT HOURS, THE HOUSE OF MYSTERY SHALL BE MINE!

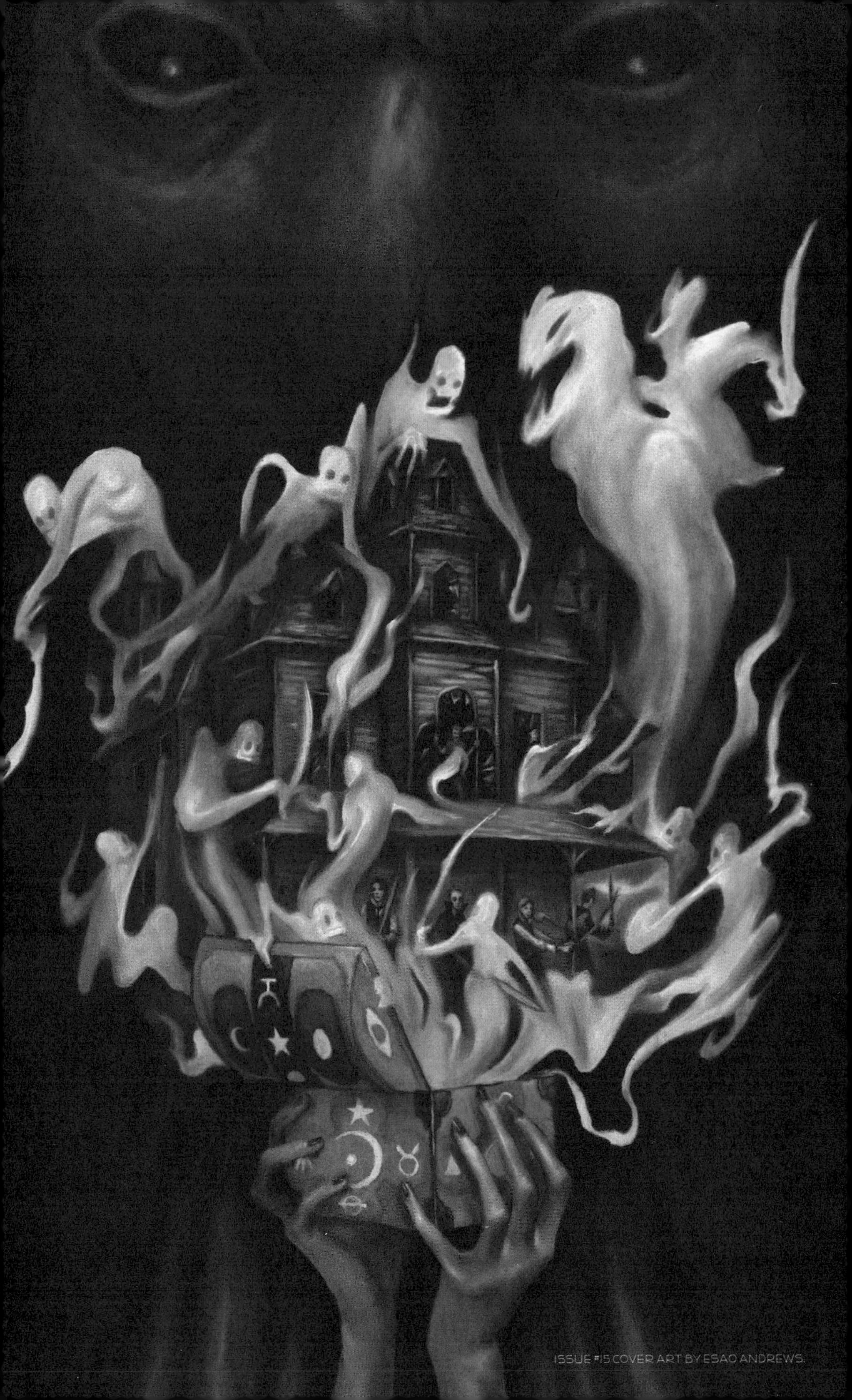

ISSUE #15 COVER ART BY ESAO ANDREWS.

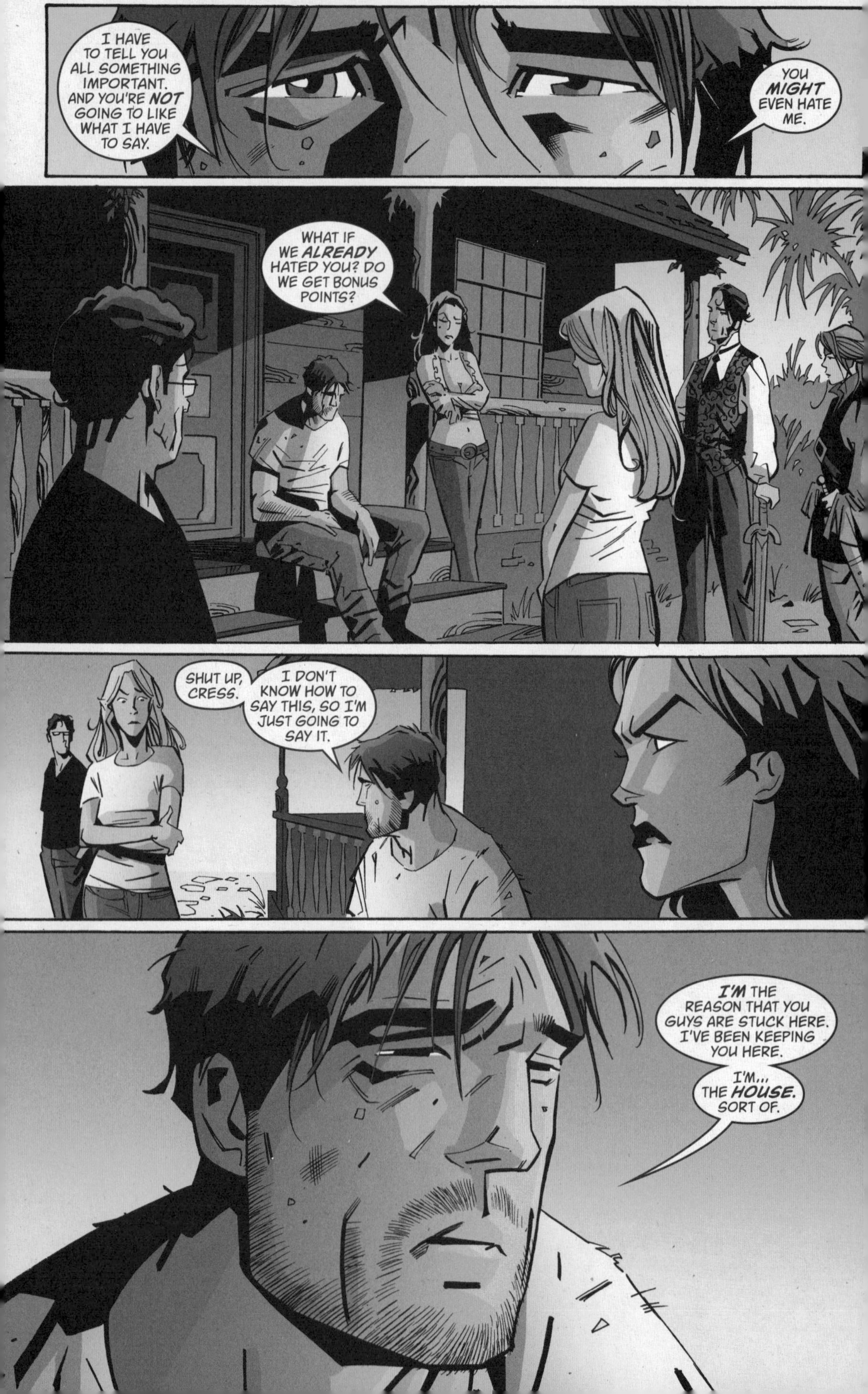
I HAVE TO TELL YOU ALL SOMETHING IMPORTANT. AND YOU'RE NOT GOING TO LIKE WHAT I HAVE TO SAY.
YOU MIGHT EVEN HATE ME.
WHAT IF WE ALREADY HATED YOU? DO WE GET BONUS POINTS?
SHUT UP, CRESS.
I DON'T KNOW HOW TO SAY THIS, SO I'M JUST GOING TO SAY IT.
I'M THE REASON THAT YOU GUYS ARE STUCK HERE. I'VE BEEN KEEPING YOU HERE.
I'M... THE HOUSE. SORT OF.

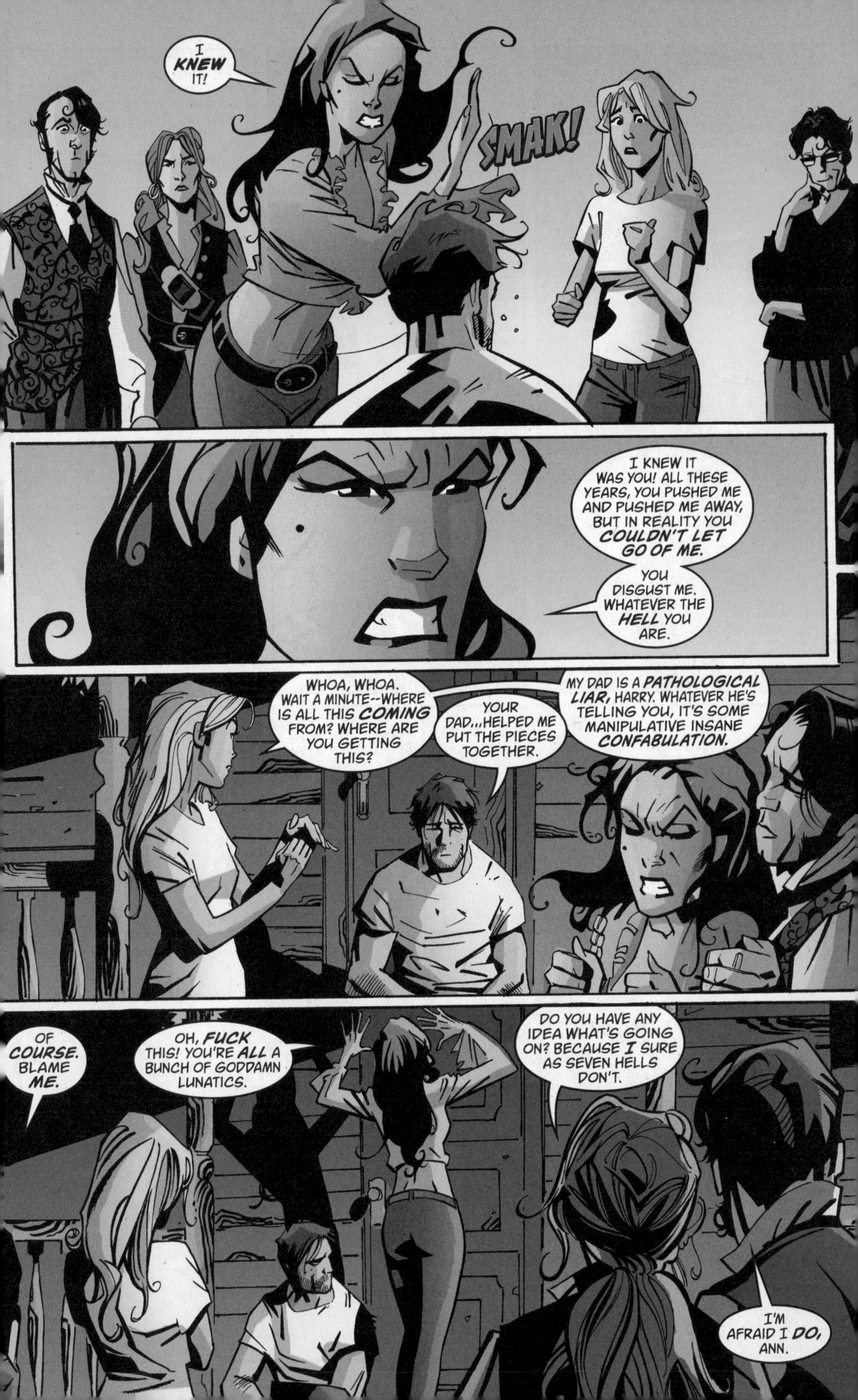
I KNEW IT!
SMAK!
I KNEW IT WAS YOU! ALL THESE YEARS, YOU PUSHED ME AND PUSHED ME AWAY, BUT IN REALITY YOU COULDN'T LET GO OF ME.
YOU DISGUST ME. WHATEVER THE HELL YOU ARE.
WHOA, WHOA. WAIT A MINUTE--WHERE IS ALL THIS COMING FROM? WHERE ARE YOU GETTING THIS?
YOUR DAD...HELPED ME PUT THE PIECES TOGETHER.
MY DAD IS A PATHOLOGICAL LIAR, HARRY. WHATEVER HE'S TELLING YOU, IT'S SOME MANIPULATIVE INSANE CONFABULATION.
OF COURSE. BLAME ME.
OH, FUCK THIS! YOU'RE ALL A BUNCH OF GODDAMN LUNATICS.
DO YOU HAVE ANY IDEA WHAT'S GOING ON? BECAUSE I SURE AS SEVEN HELLS DON'T.
I'M AFRAID I DO, ANN.

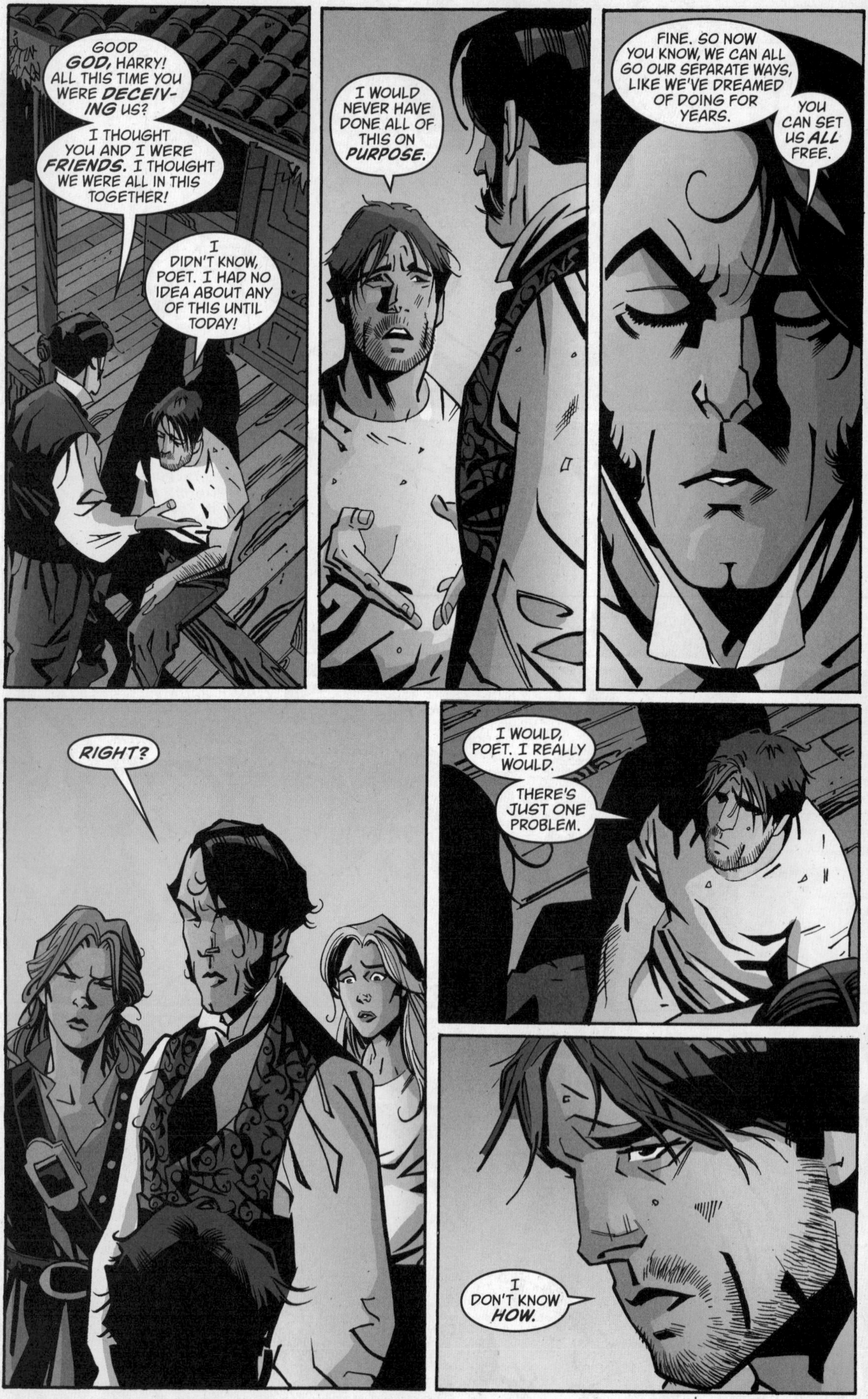
GOOD GOD, HARRY! ALL THIS TIME YOU WERE DECEIVING US?
I THOUGHT YOU AND I WERE FRIENDS. I THOUGHT WE WERE ALL IN THIS TOGETHER!
I DIDN'T KNOW, POET. I HAD NO IDEA ABOUT ANY OF THIS UNTIL TODAY!
I WOULD NEVER HAVE DONE ALL OF THIS ON PURPOSE.
FINE. SO NOW YOU KNOW, WE CAN ALL GO OUR SEPARATE WAYS, LIKE WE'VE DREAMED OF DOING FOR YEARS.
YOU CAN SET US ALL FREE.
RIGHT?
I WOULD, POET. I REALLY WOULD.
THERE'S JUST ONE PROBLEM.
I DON'T KNOW HOW.

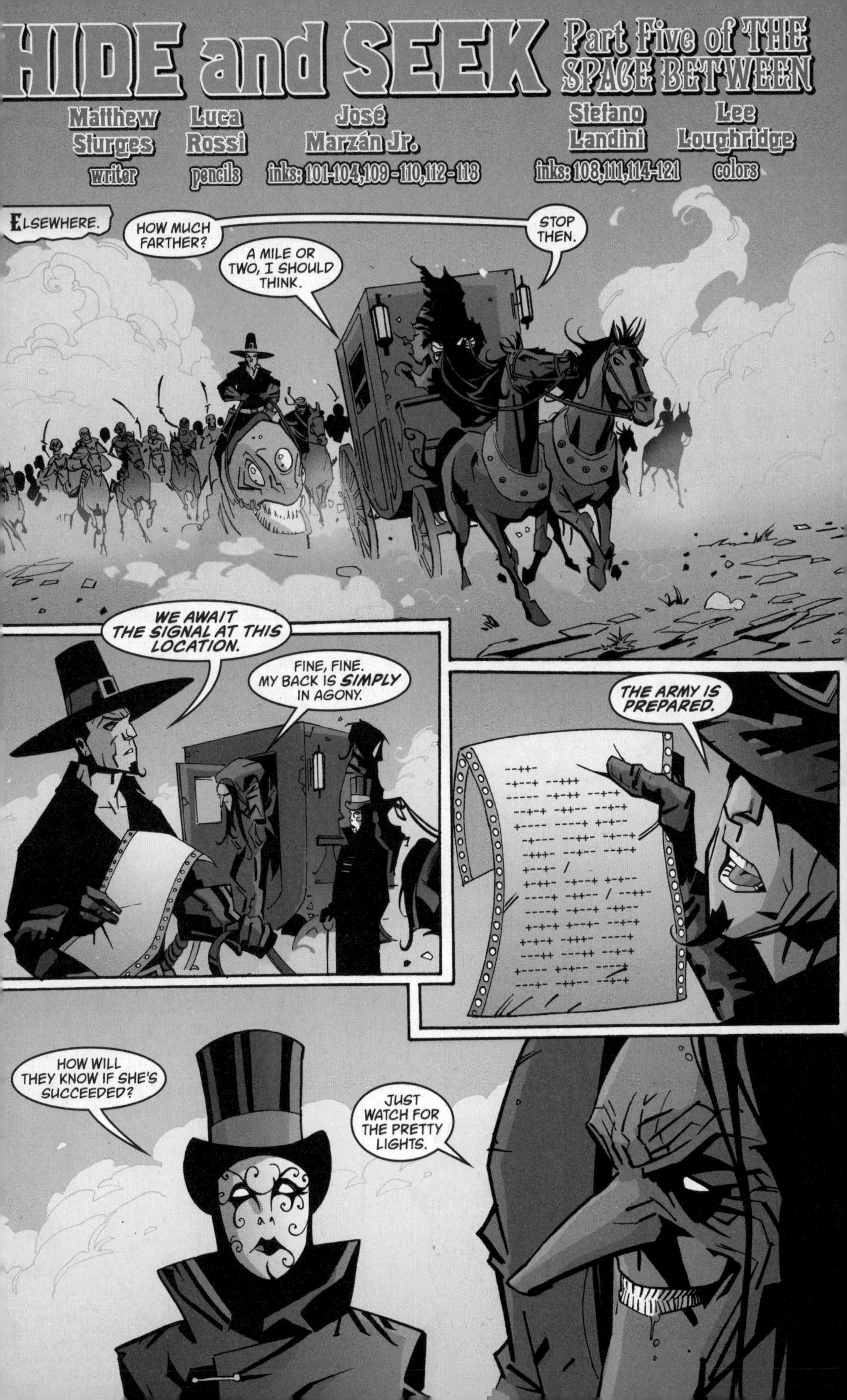
HIDE and SEEK
Part Five of THE SPACE BETWEEN
Matthew Sturges writer
Luca Rossi pencils
José Marzán Jr. inks: 101-104,109-110,112-113
Stefano Landini inks: 108,111,114-121
Lee Loughridge colors
ELSEWHERE.
HOW MUCH FARTHER?
A MILE OR TWO, I SHOULD THINK.
STOP THEN.
WE AWAIT THE SIGNAL AT THIS LOCATION.
FINE, FINE. MY BACK IS SIMPLY IN AGONY.
THE ARMY IS PREPARED.
HOW WILL THEY KNOW IF SHE'S SUCCEEDED?
JUST WATCH FOR THE PRETTY LIGHTS.

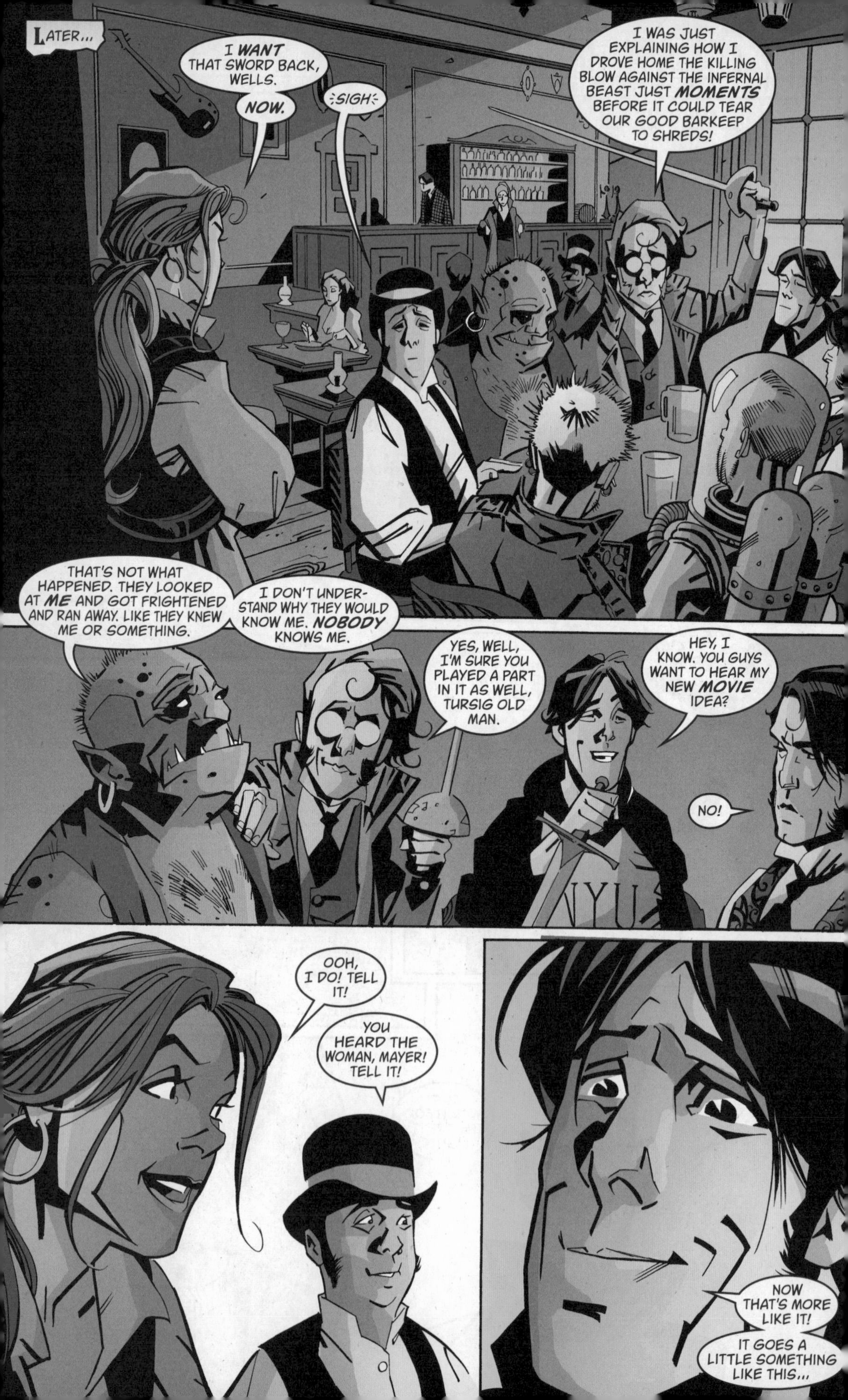
LATER...
I WANT THAT SWORD BACK, WELLS.
NOW.
SIGH
I WAS JUST EXPLAINING HOW I DROVE HOME THE KILLING BLOW AGAINST THE INFERNAL BEAST JUST MOMENTS BEFORE IT COULD TEAR OUR GOOD BARKEEP TO SHREDS!
THAT'S NOT WHAT HAPPENED. THEY LOOKED AT ME AND GOT FRIGHTENED AND RAN AWAY. LIKE THEY KNEW ME OR SOMETHING.
I DON'T UNDERSTAND WHY THEY WOULD KNOW ME. NOBODY KNOWS ME.
YES, WELL, I'M SURE YOU PLAYED A PART IN IT AS WELL, TURSIG OLD MAN.
HEY, I KNOW. YOU GUYS WANT TO HEAR MY NEW MOVIE IDEA?
NO!
NYU
OOH, I DO! TELL IT!
YOU HEARD THE WOMAN, MAYER! TELL IT!
NOW THAT'S MORE LIKE IT!
IT GOES A LITTLE SOMETHING LIKE THIS...

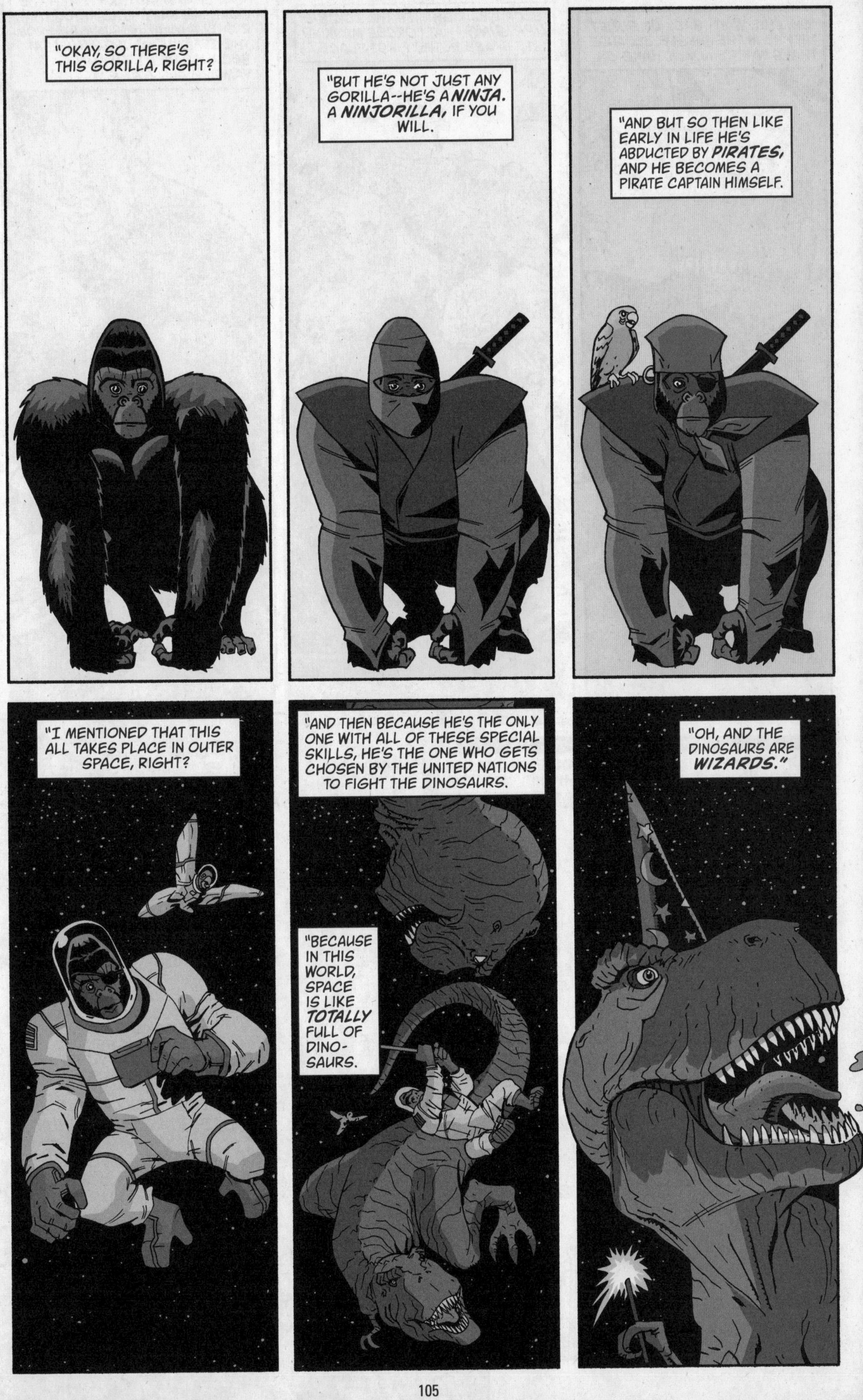
"OKAY, SO THERE'S THIS GORILLA, RIGHT?
"BUT HE'S NOT JUST ANY GORILLA--HE'S A NINJA. A NINJORILLA, IF YOU WILL.
"AND BUT SO THEN LIKE EARLY IN LIFE HE'S ABDUCTED BY PIRATES, AND HE BECOMES A PIRATE CAPTAIN HIMSELF.
"I MENTIONED THAT THIS ALL TAKES PLACE IN OUTER SPACE, RIGHT?
"AND THEN BECAUSE HE'S THE ONLY ONE WITH ALL OF THESE SPECIAL SKILLS, HE'S THE ONE WHO GETS CHOSEN BY THE UNITED NATIONS TO FIGHT THE DINOSAURS.
"BECAUSE IN THIS WORLD, SPACE IS LIKE TOTALLY FULL OF DINOSAURS.
"OH, AND THE DINOSAURS ARE WIZARDS."

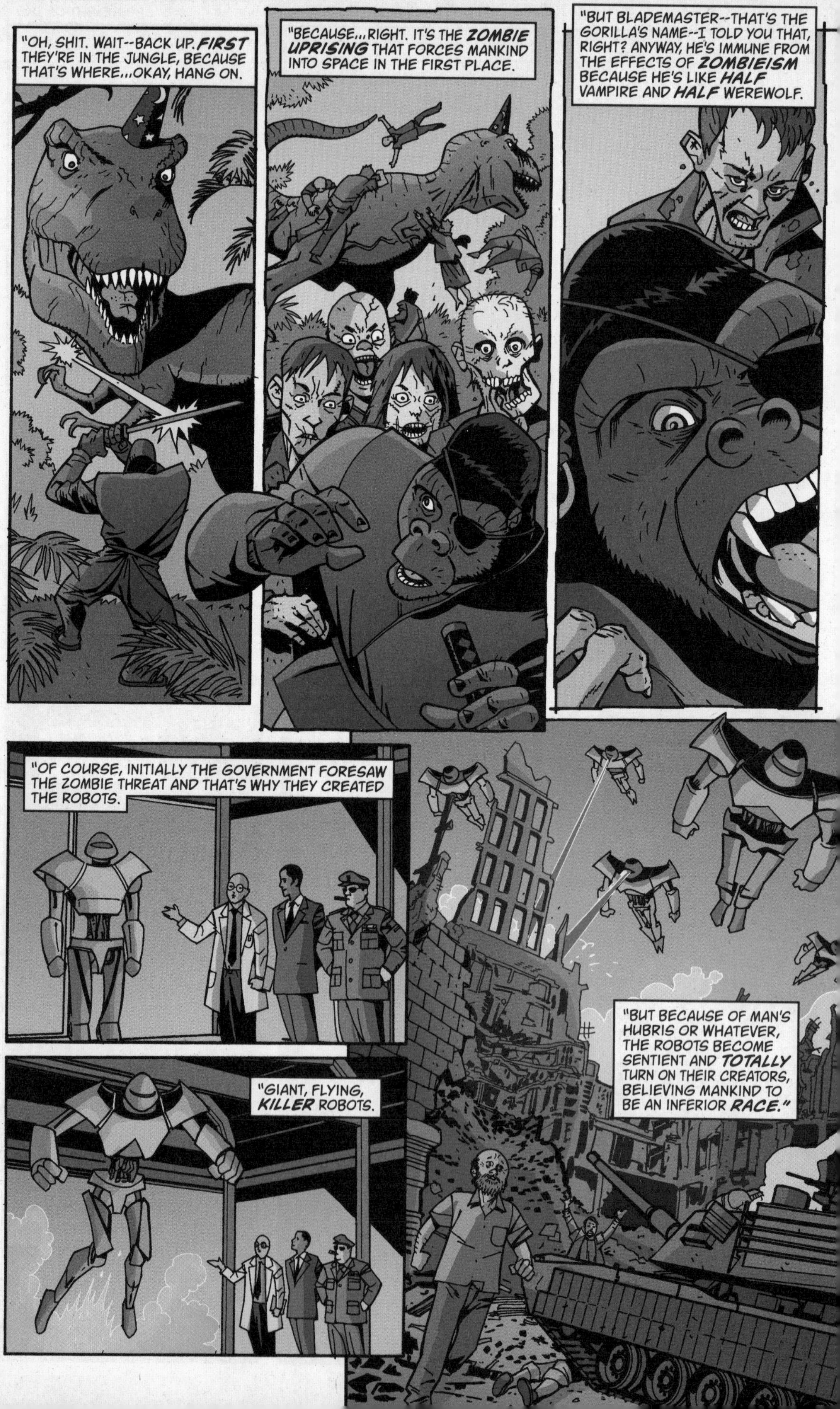
"OH, SHIT. WAIT--BACK UP. FIRST THEY'RE IN THE JUNGLE, BECAUSE THAT'S WHERE...OKAY, HANG ON.
"BECAUSE... RIGHT. IT'S THE ZOMBIE UPRISING THAT FORCES MANKIND INTO SPACE IN THE FIRST PLACE.
"BUT BLADEMASTER--THAT'S THE GORILLA'S NAME--I TOLD YOU THAT, RIGHT? ANYWAY, HE'S IMMUNE FROM THE EFFECTS OF ZOMBIEISM BECAUSE HE'S LIKE HALF VAMPIRE AND HALF WEREWOLF.
"OF COURSE, INITIALLY THE GOVERNMENT FORESAW THE ZOMBIE THREAT AND THAT'S WHY THEY CREATED THE ROBOTS.
"GIANT, FLYING, KILLER ROBOTS.
"BUT BECAUSE OF MAN'S HUBRIS OR WHATEVER, THE ROBOTS BECOME SENTIENT AND TOTALLY TURN ON THEIR CREATORS, BELIEVING MANKIND TO BE AN INFERIOR RACE."

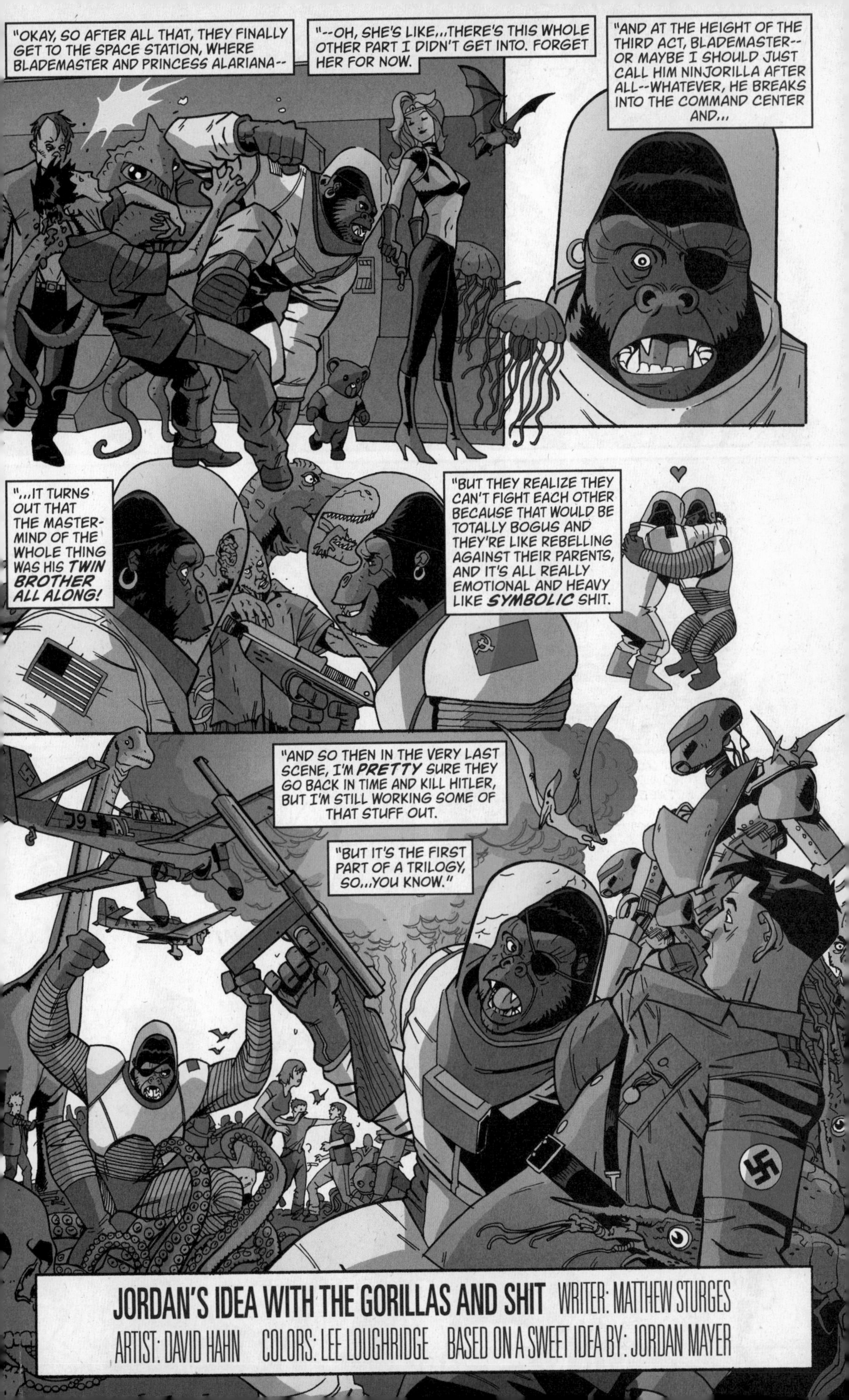
"OKAY, SO AFTER ALL THAT, THEY FINALLY GET TO THE SPACE STATION, WHERE BLADEMASTER AND PRINCESS ALARIANA--
"--OH, SHE'S LIKE,..THERE'S THIS WHOLE OTHER PART I DIDN'T GET INTO. FORGET HER FOR NOW.
"AND AT THE HEIGHT OF THE THIRD ACT, BLADEMASTER--OR MAYBE I SHOULD JUST CALL HIM NINJORILLA AFTER ALL--WHATEVER, HE BREAKS INTO THE COMMAND CENTER AND...
"...IT TURNS OUT THAT THE MASTERMIND OF THE WHOLE THING WAS HIS TWIN BROTHER ALL ALONG!
"BUT THEY REALIZE THEY CAN'T FIGHT EACH OTHER BECAUSE THAT WOULD BE TOTALLY BOGUS AND THEY'RE LIKE REBELLING AGAINST THEIR PARENTS, AND IT'S ALL REALLY EMOTIONAL AND HEAVY LIKE SYMBOLIC SHIT.
"AND SO THEN IN THE VERY LAST SCENE, I'M PRETTY SURE THEY GO BACK IN TIME AND KILL HITLER, BUT I'M STILL WORKING SOME OF THAT STUFF OUT.
"BUT IT'S THE FIRST PART OF A TRILOGY, SO...YOU KNOW."
JORDAN'S IDEA WITH THE GORILLAS AND SHIT
WRITER: MATTHEW STURGES
ARTIST: DAVID HAHN
COLORS: LEE LOUGHRIDGE
BASED ON A SWEET IDEA BY: JORDAN MAYER

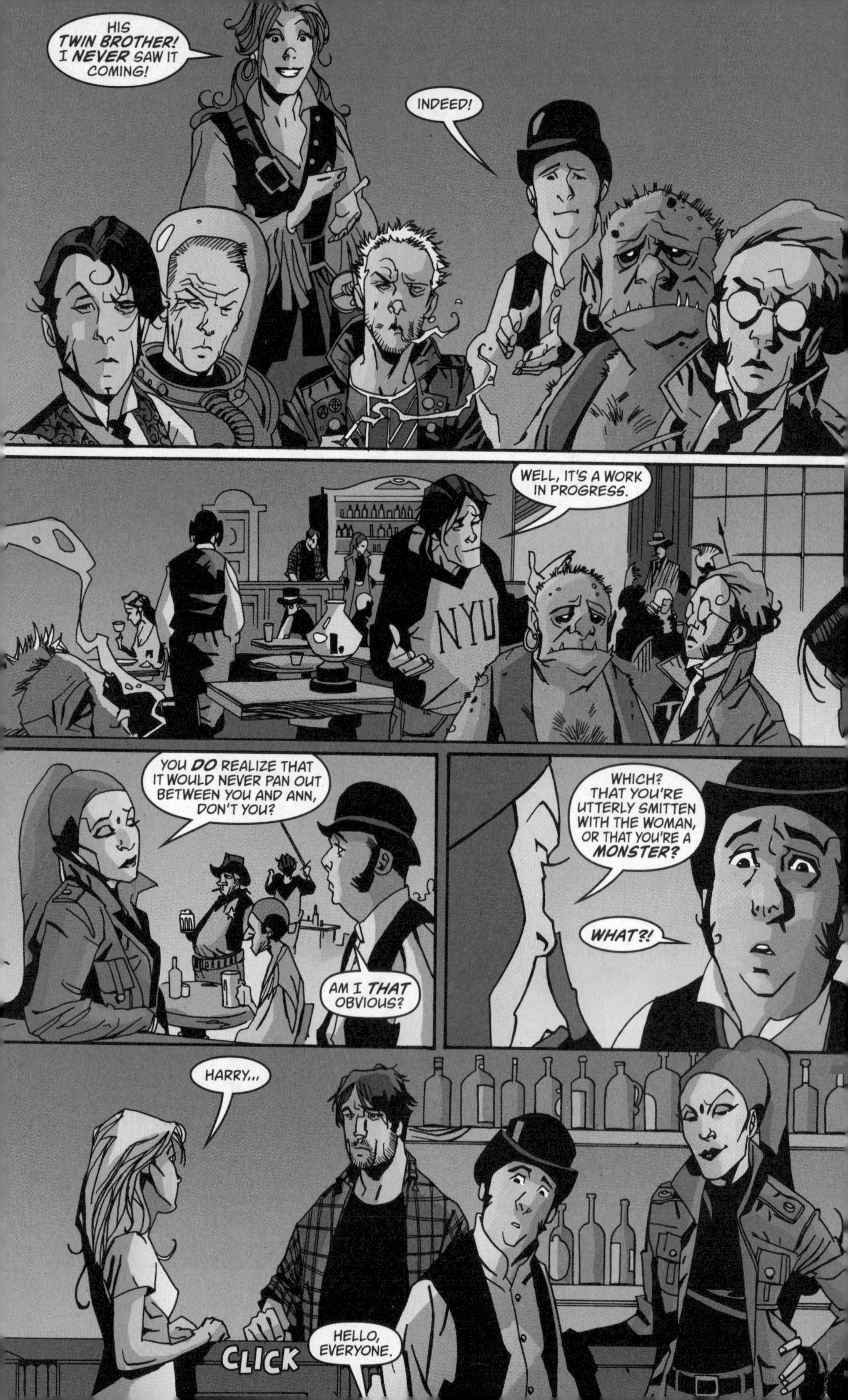
HIS TWIN BROTHER! I NEVER SAW IT COMING!
INDEED!
WELL, IT'S A WORK IN PROGRESS.
NYU
YOU DO REALIZE THAT IT WOULD NEVER PAN OUT BETWEEN YOU AND ANN, DON'T YOU?
AM I THAT OBVIOUS?
WHICH? THAT YOU'RE UTTERLY SMITTEN WITH THE WOMAN, OR THAT YOU'RE A MONSTER?
WHAT?!
HARRY...
CLICK
HELLO, EVERYONE.

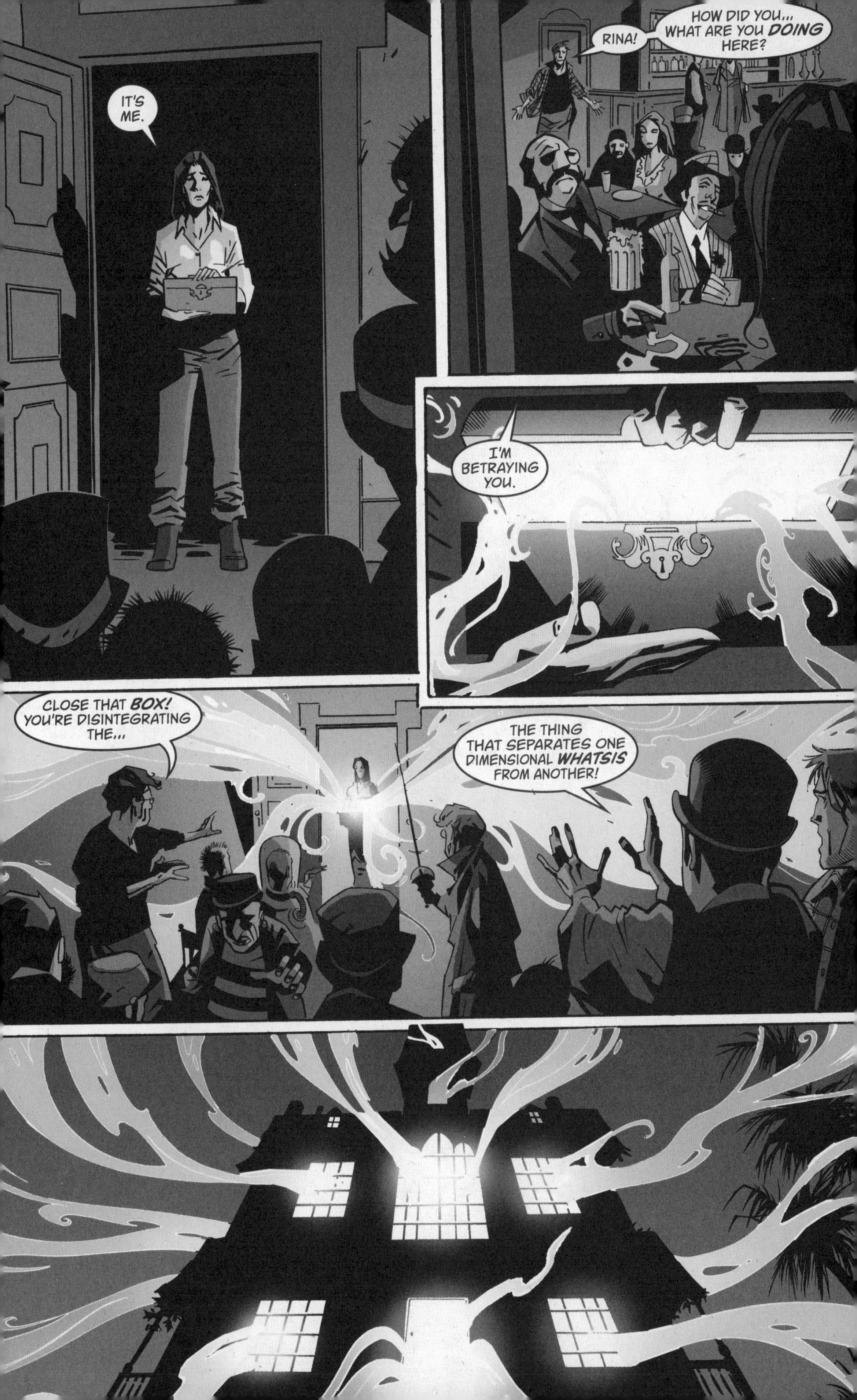
IT'S ME.
RINA!
HOW DID YOU... WHAT ARE YOU DOING HERE?
I'M BETRAYING YOU.
CLOSE THAT BOX! YOU'RE DISINTEGRATING THE...
THE THING THAT SEPARATES ONE DIMENSIONAL WHATSIS FROM ANOTHER!

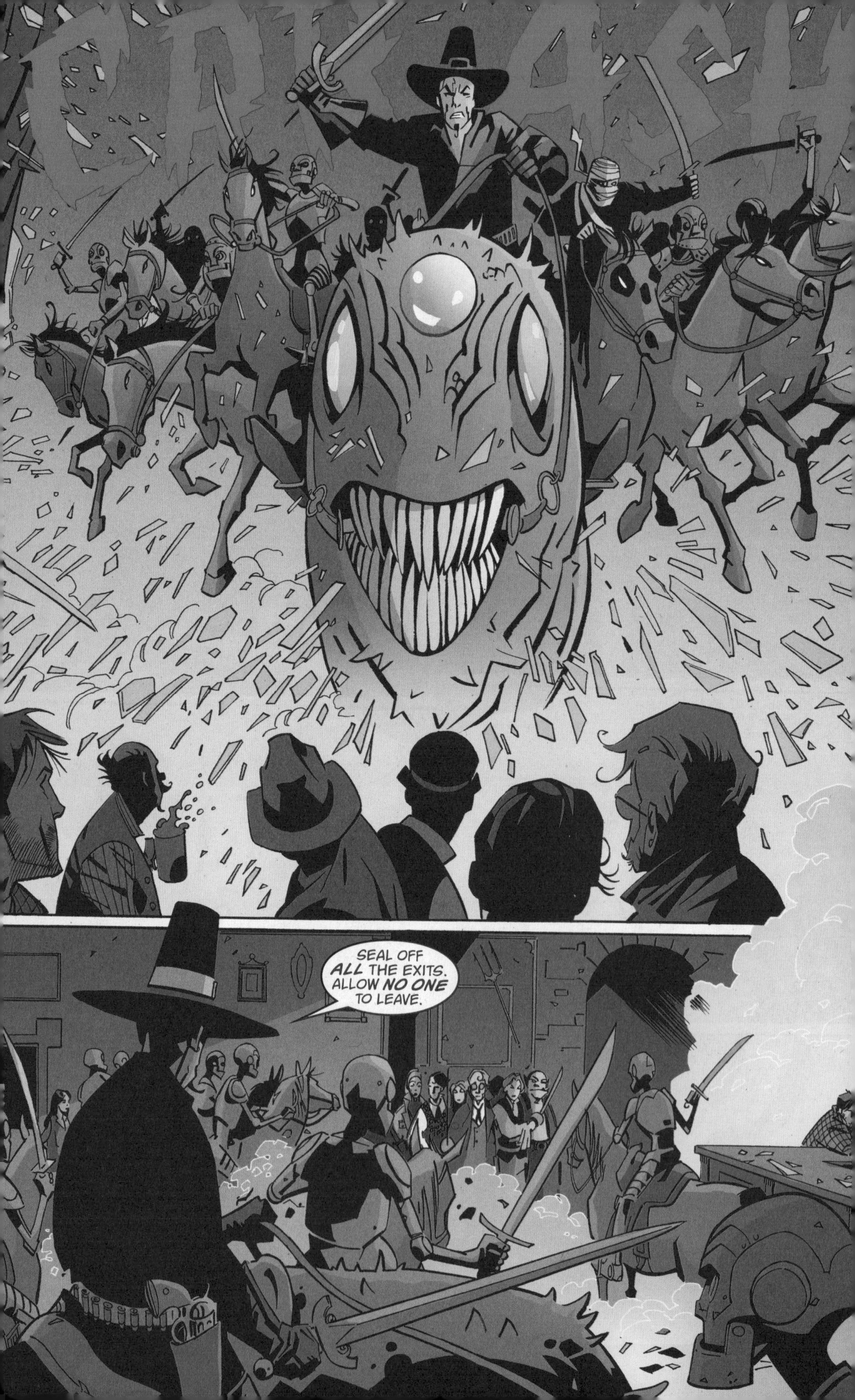
SEAL OFF ALL THE EXITS. ALLOW NO ONE TO LEAVE.

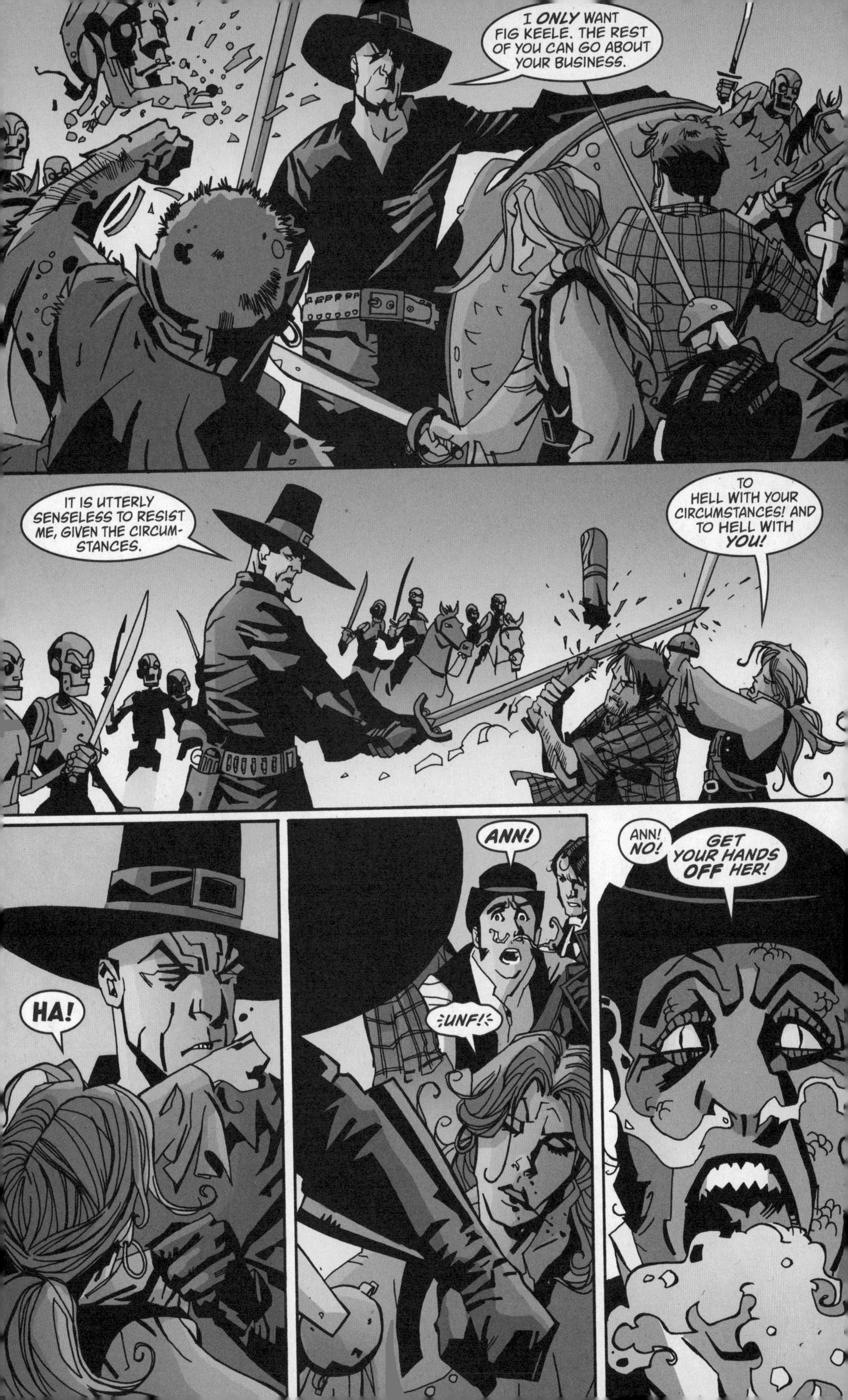
I ONLY WANT FIG KEELE. THE REST OF YOU CAN GO ABOUT YOUR BUSINESS.
IT IS UTTERLY SENSELESS TO RESIST ME, GIVEN THE CIRCUMSTANCES.
TO HELL WITH YOUR CIRCUMSTANCES! AND TO HELL WITH YOU!
HA!
ANN!
UNF!
ANN! NO!
GET YOUR HANDS OFF HER!

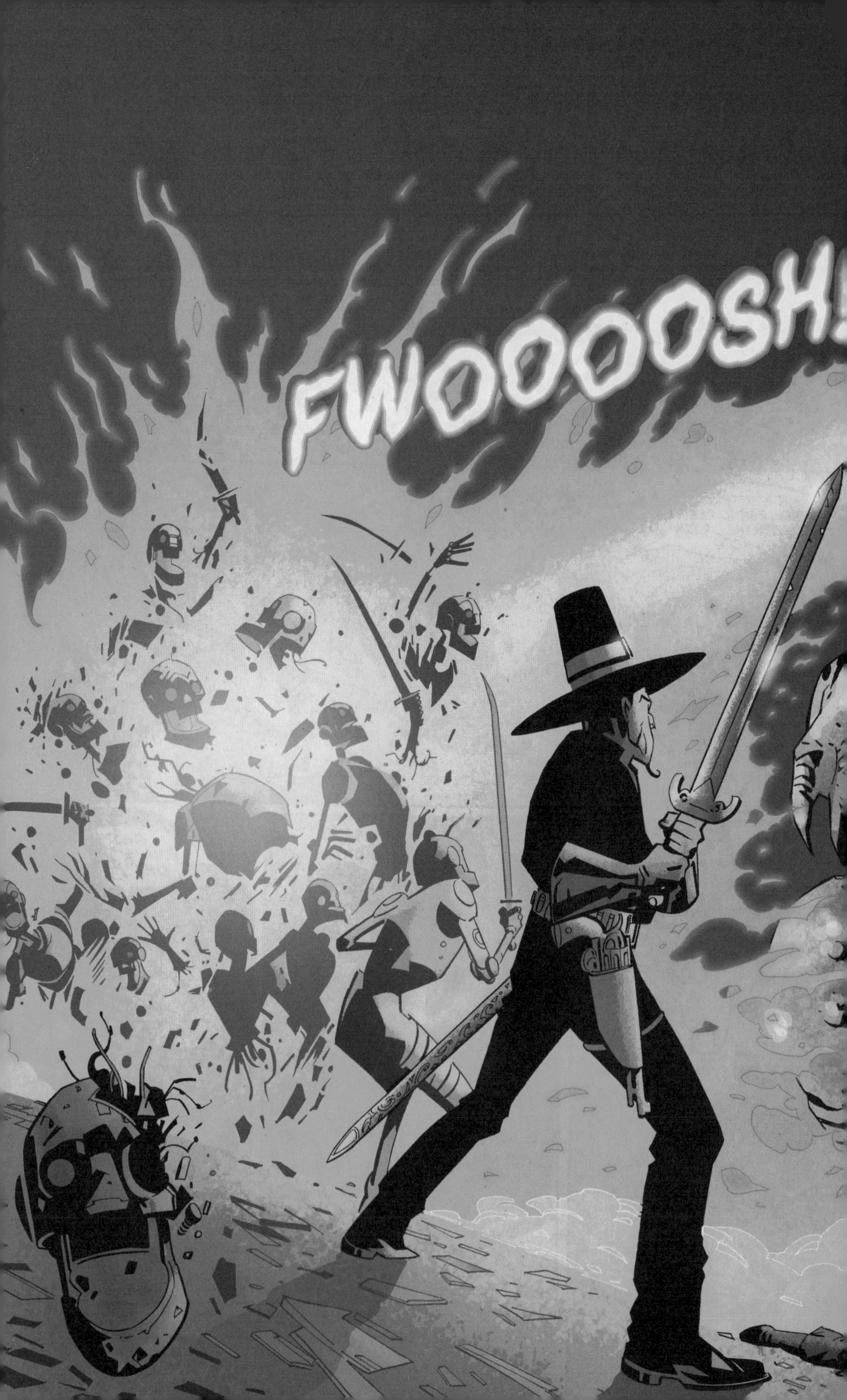
FWOOOOSH!

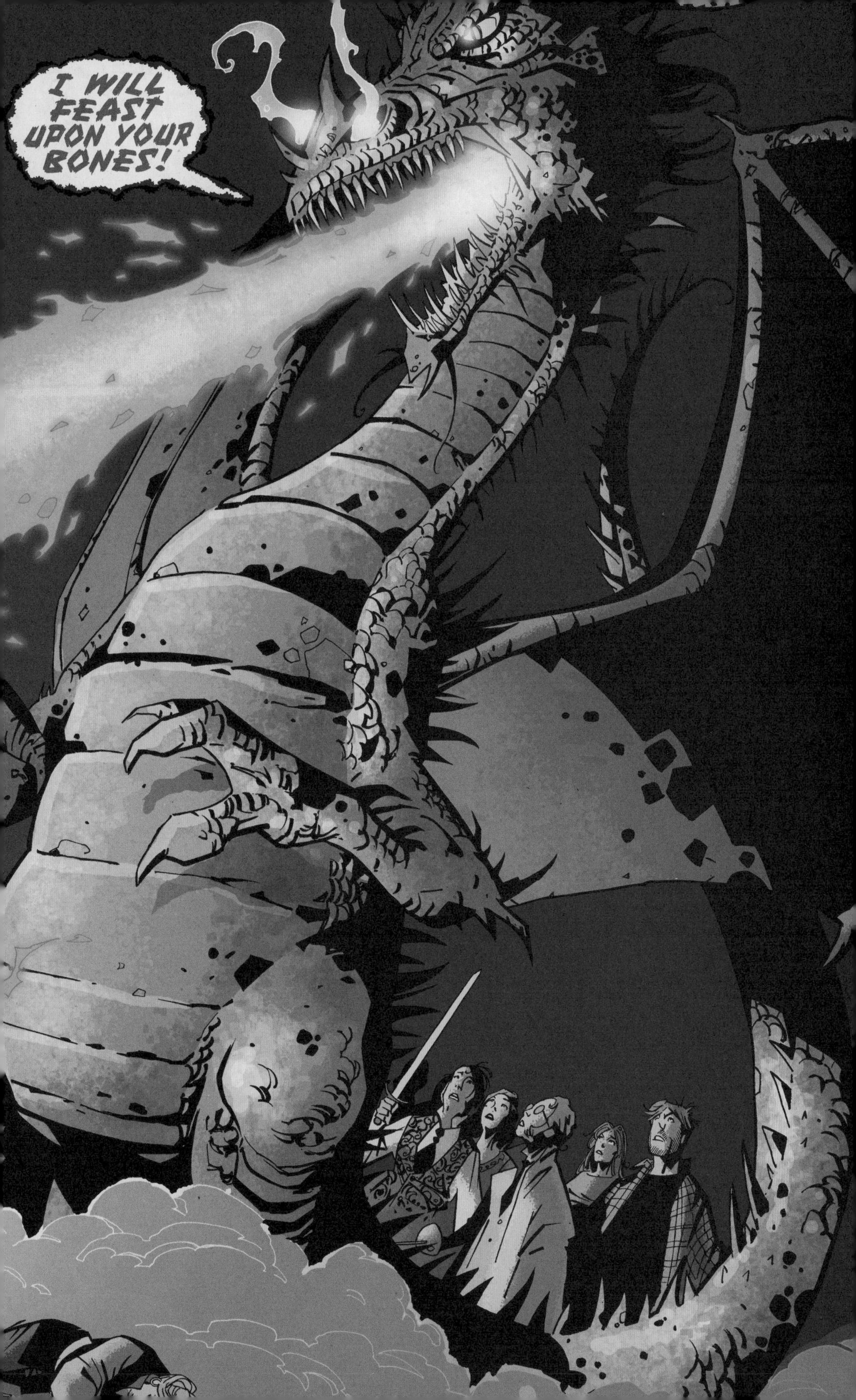
I WILL FEAST UPON YOUR BONES!

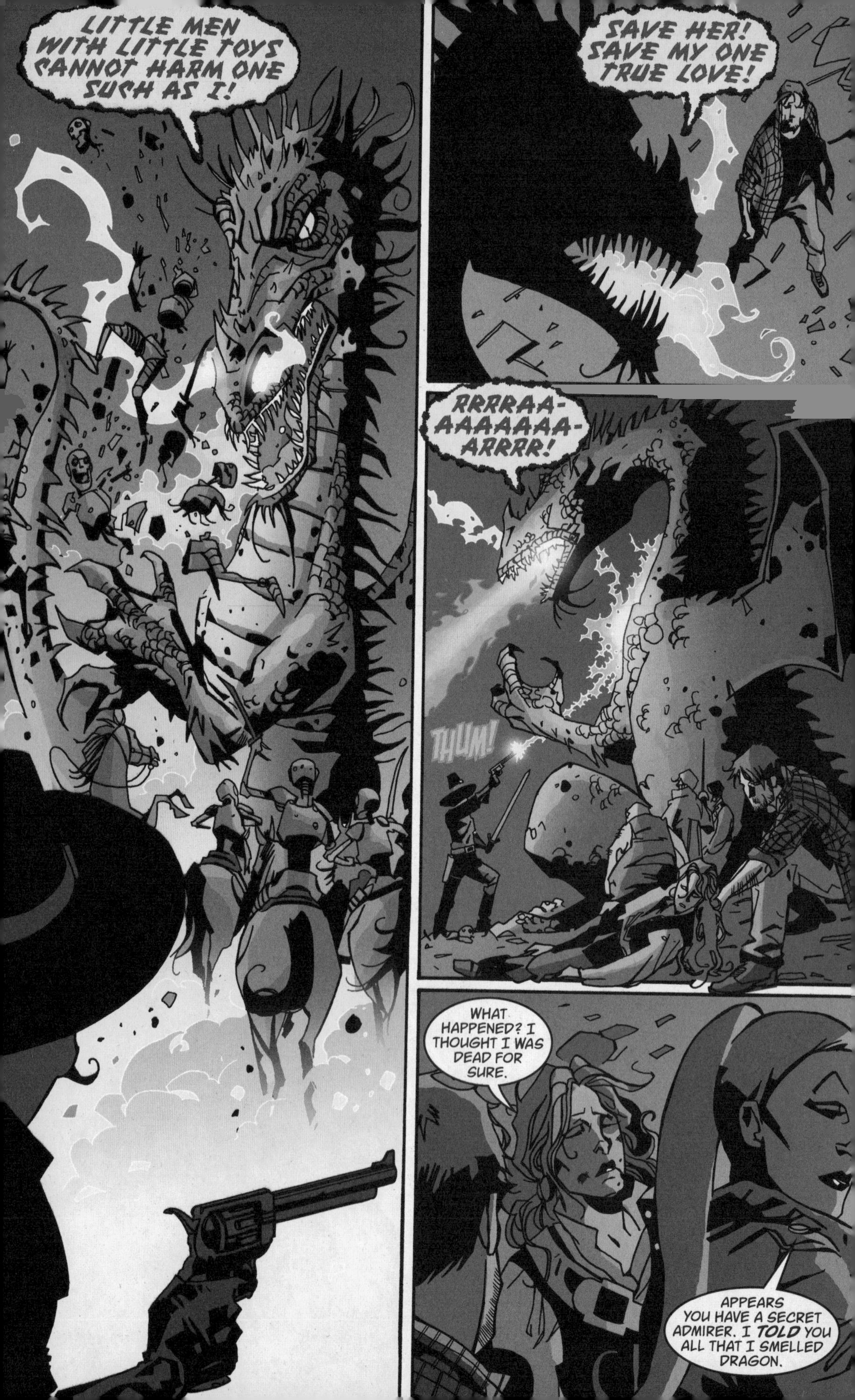
LITTLE MEN WITH LITTLE TOYS CANNOT HARM ONE SUCH AS I!
SAVE HER! SAVE MY ONE TRUE LOVE!
RRRRAA-AAAAAAA-ARRRR!
THUM!
WHAT HAPPENED? I THOUGHT I WAS DEAD FOR SURE.
APPEARS YOU HAVE A SECRET ADMIRER. I *TOLD* YOU ALL THAT I SMELLED DRAGON.

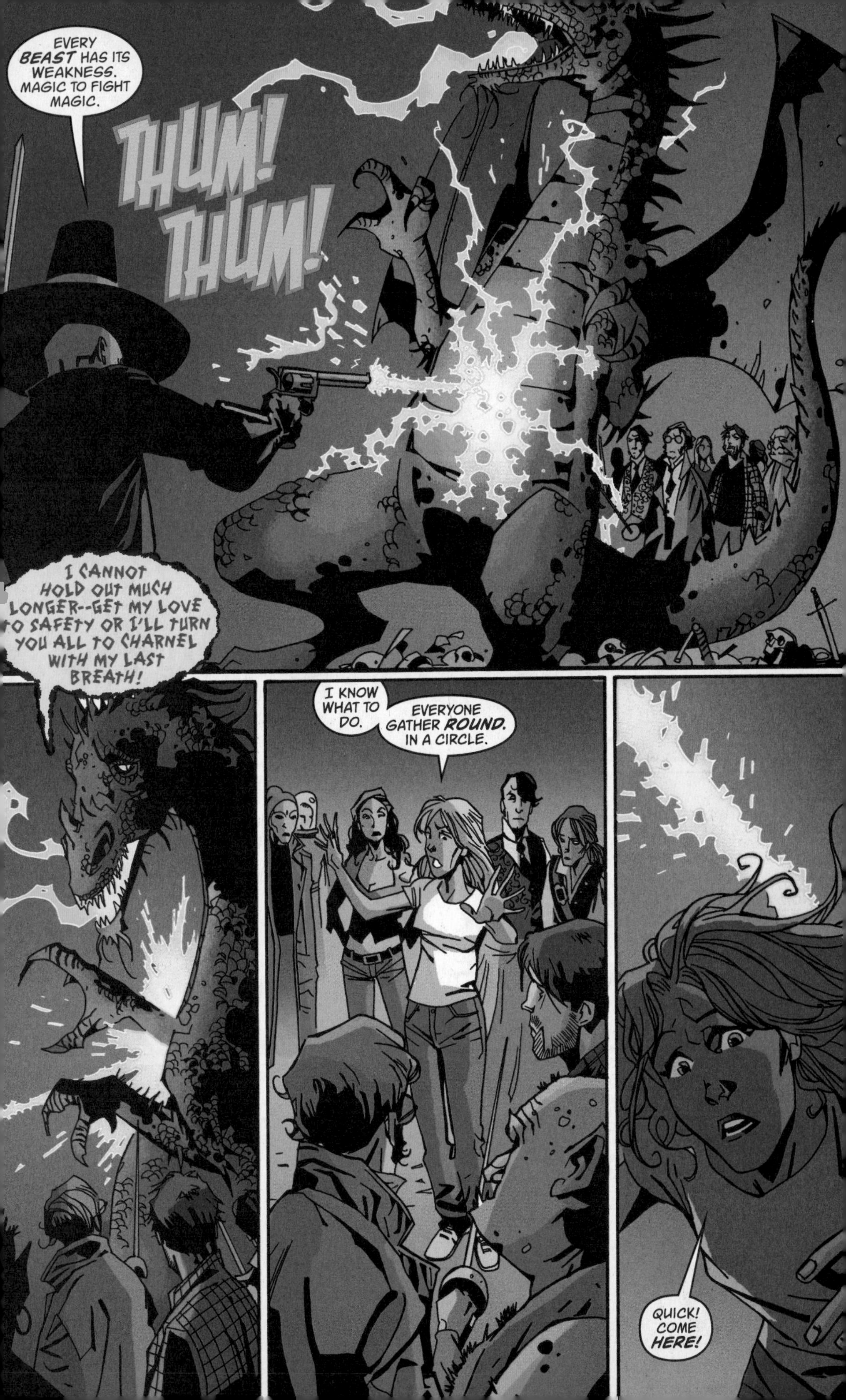
EVERY BEAST HAS ITS WEAKNESS. MAGIC TO FIGHT MAGIC.
THUM! THUM!
I CANNOT HOLD OUT MUCH LONGER--GET MY LOVE TO SAFETY OR I'LL TURN YOU ALL TO CHARNEL WITH MY LAST BREATH!
I KNOW WHAT TO DO.
EVERYONE GATHER ROUND. IN A CIRCLE.
QUICK! COME HERE!

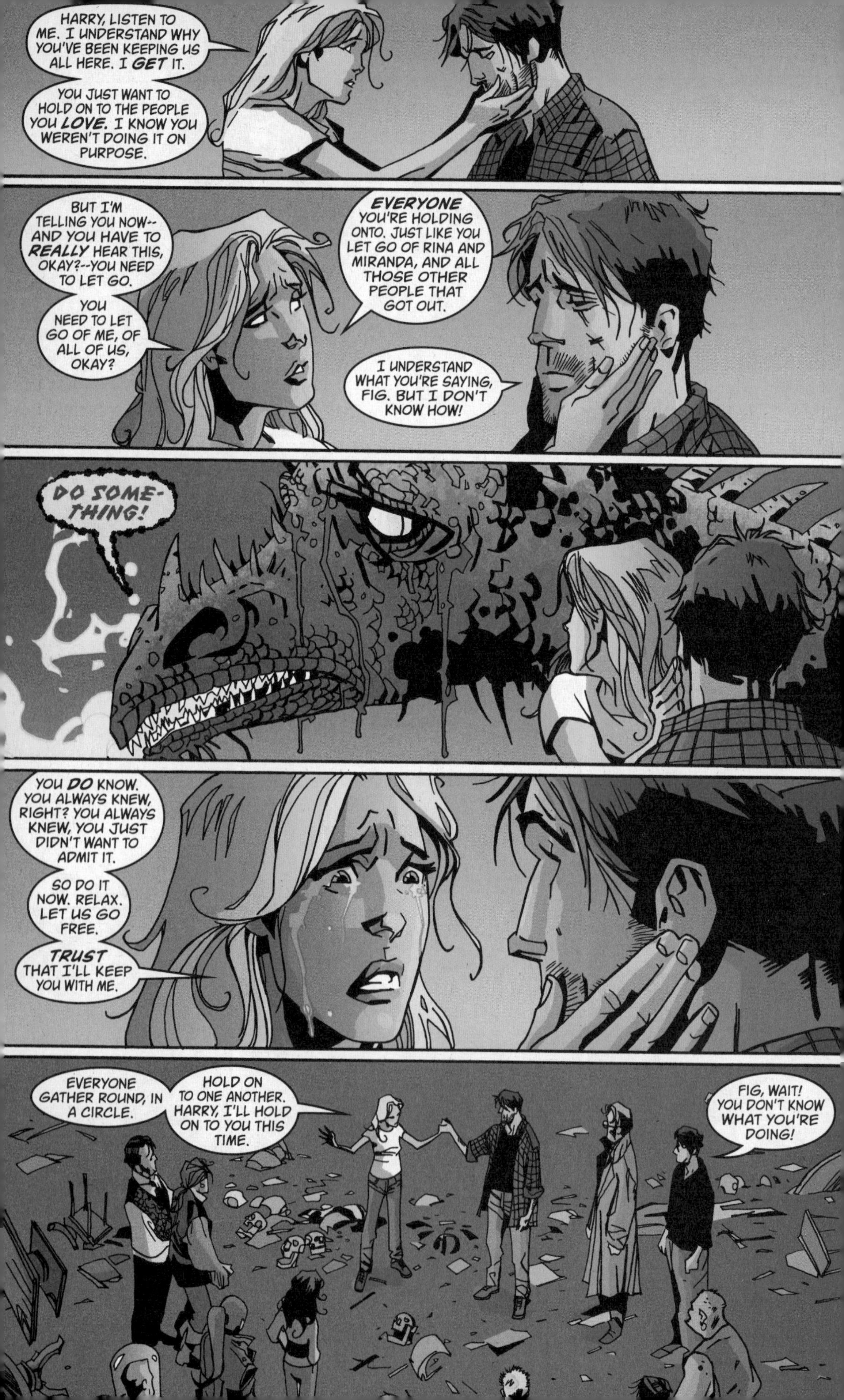
HARRY, LISTEN TO ME. I UNDERSTAND WHY YOU'VE BEEN KEEPING US ALL HERE. I GET IT.
YOU JUST WANT TO HOLD ON TO THE PEOPLE YOU LOVE. I KNOW YOU WEREN'T DOING IT ON PURPOSE.
BUT I'M TELLING YOU NOW-- AND YOU HAVE TO REALLY HEAR THIS, OKAY?--YOU NEED TO LET GO.
YOU NEED TO LET GO OF ME, OF ALL OF US, OKAY?
EVERYONE YOU'RE HOLDING ONTO. JUST LIKE YOU LET GO OF RINA AND MIRANDA, AND ALL THOSE OTHER PEOPLE THAT GOT OUT.
I UNDERSTAND WHAT YOU'RE SAYING, FIG. BUT I DON'T KNOW HOW!
DO SOME-THING!
YOU DO KNOW. YOU ALWAYS KNEW, RIGHT? YOU ALWAYS KNEW, YOU JUST DIDN'T WANT TO ADMIT IT.
SO DO IT NOW. RELAX. LET US GO FREE.
TRUST THAT I'LL KEEP YOU WITH ME.
EVERYONE GATHER ROUND, IN A CIRCLE.
HOLD ON TO ONE ANOTHER. HARRY, I'LL HOLD ON TO YOU THIS TIME.
FIG, WAIT! YOU DON'T KNOW WHAT YOU'RE DOING!

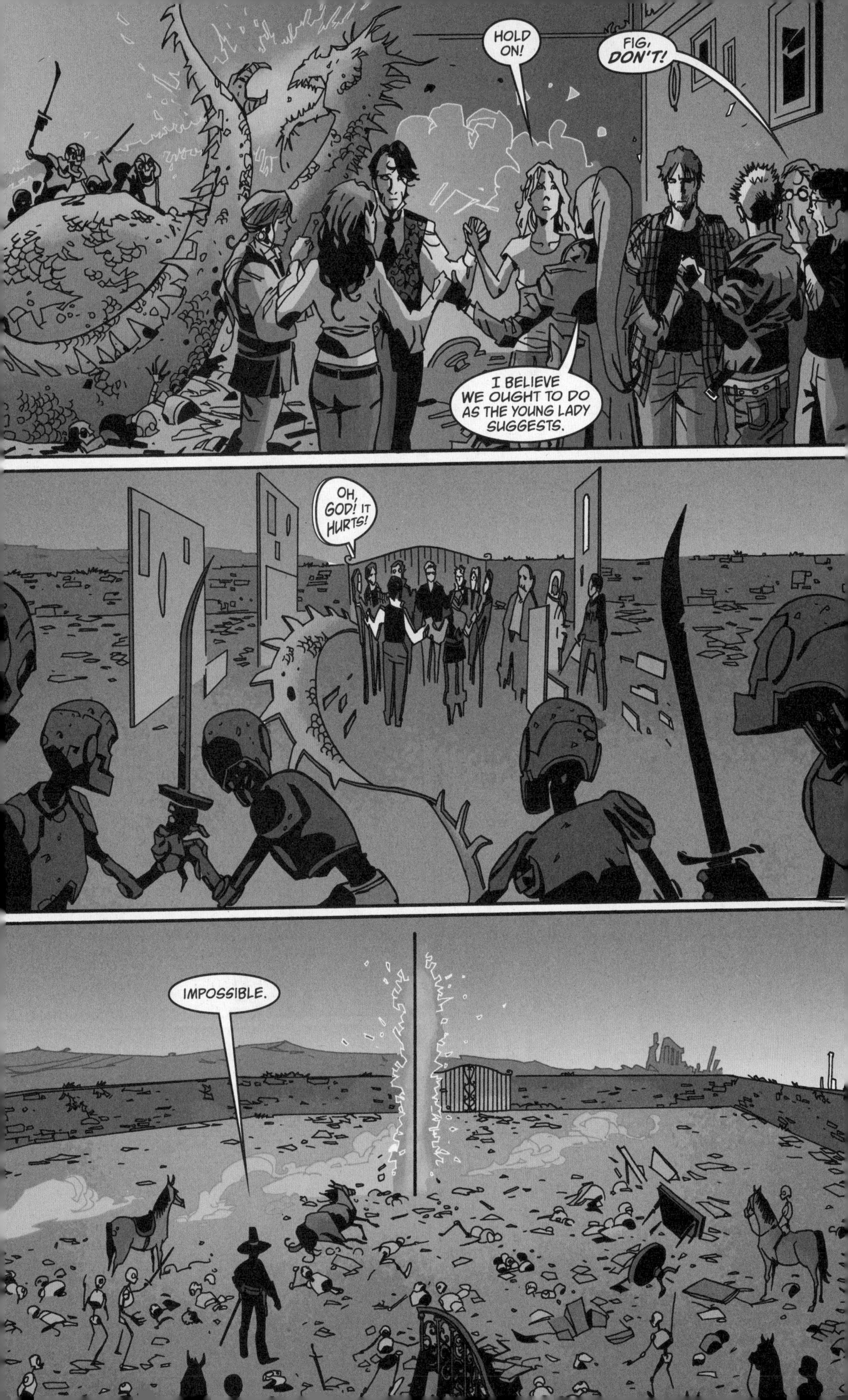
HOLD ON!
FIG, DON'T!
I BELIEVE WE OUGHT TO DO AS THE YOUNG LADY SUGGESTS.
OH, GOD! IT HURTS!
IMPOSSIBLE.

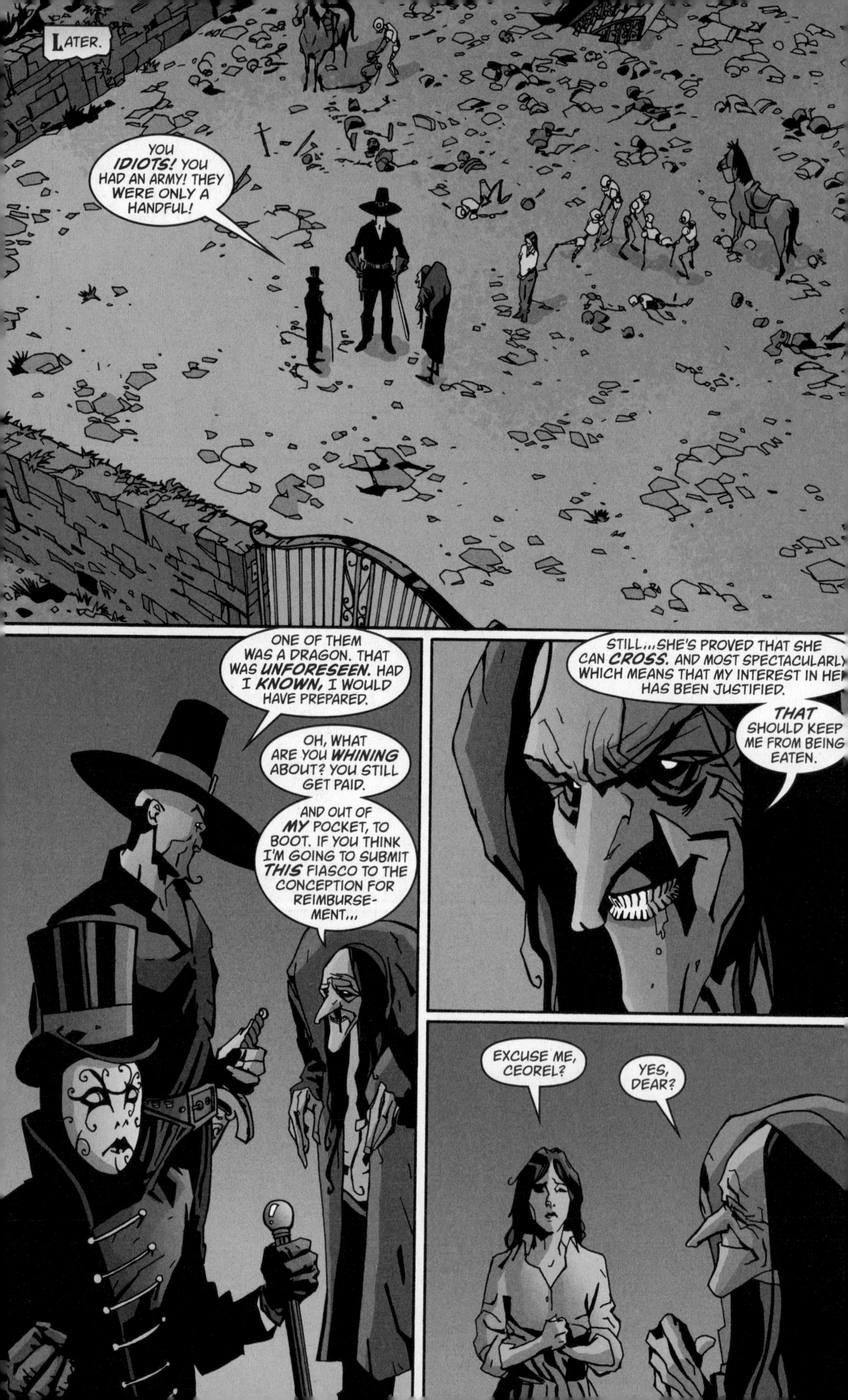
LATER.
YOU IDIOTS! YOU HAD AN ARMY! THEY WERE ONLY A HANDFUL!
ONE OF THEM WAS A DRAGON. THAT WAS UNFORESEEN. HAD I KNOWN, I WOULD HAVE PREPARED.
OH, WHAT ARE YOU WHINING ABOUT? YOU STILL GET PAID.
AND OUT OF MY POCKET, TO BOOT. IF YOU THINK I'M GOING TO SUBMIT THIS FIASCO TO THE CONCEPTION FOR REIMBURSE-MENT...
STILL...SHE'S PROVED THAT SHE CAN CROSS. AND MOST SPECTACULARLY
WHICH MEANS THAT MY INTEREST IN HE
HAS BEEN JUSTIFIED.
THAT SHOULD KEEP ME FROM BEING EATEN.
EXCUSE ME, CEOREL?
YES, DEAR?

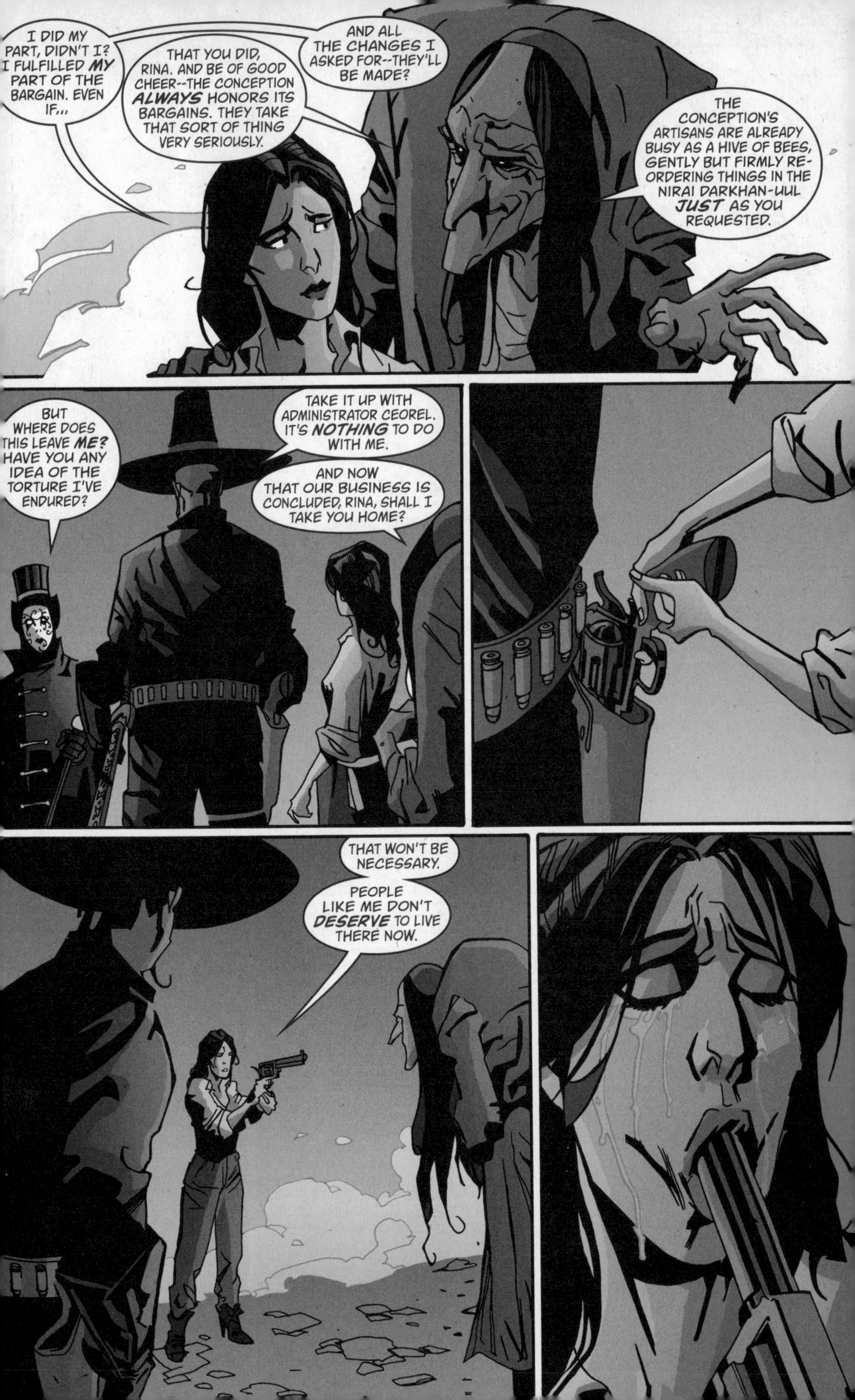

I DID MY PART, DIDN'T I? I FULFILLED MY PART OF THE BARGAIN. EVEN IF...
THAT YOU DID, RINA. AND BE OF GOOD CHEER--THE CONCEPTION ALWAYS HONORS ITS BARGAINS. THEY TAKE THAT SORT OF THING VERY SERIOUSLY.
AND ALL THE CHANGES I ASKED FOR--THEY'LL BE MADE?
THE CONCEPTION'S ARTISANS ARE ALREADY BUSY AS A HIVE OF BEES, GENTLY BUT FIRMLY RE-ORDERING THINGS IN THE NIRAI DARKHAN-UUL JUST AS YOU REQUESTED.
BUT WHERE DOES THIS LEAVE ME? HAVE YOU ANY IDEA OF THE TORTURE I'VE ENDURED?
TAKE IT UP WITH ADMINISTRATOR CEOREL. IT'S NOTHING TO DO WITH ME.
AND NOW THAT OUR BUSINESS IS CONCLUDED, RINA, SHALL I TAKE YOU HOME?
THAT WON'T BE NECESSARY.
PEOPLE LIKE ME DON'T DESERVE TO LIVE THERE NOW.

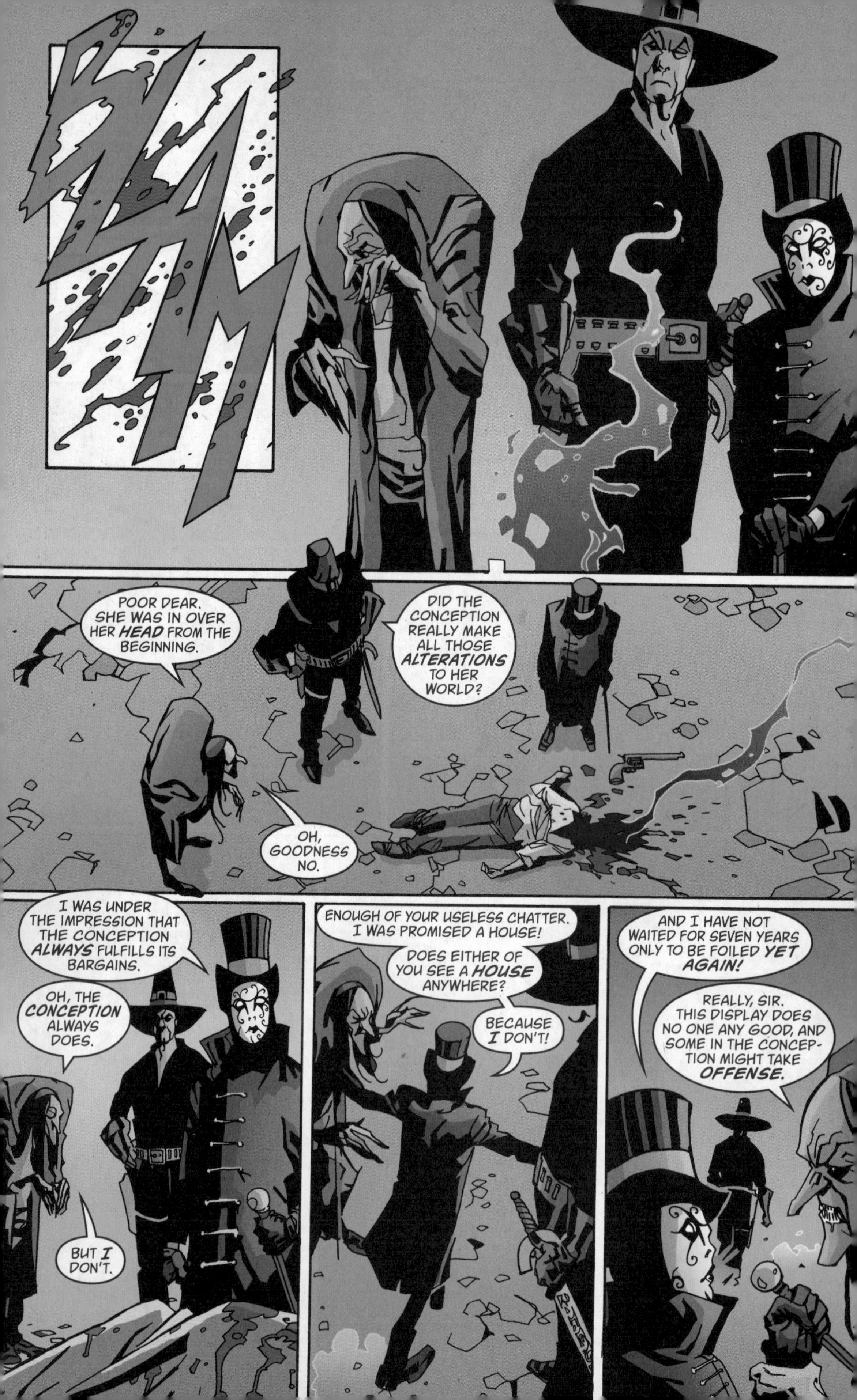
BLAM
POOR DEAR. SHE WAS IN OVER HER HEAD FROM THE BEGINNING.
DID THE CONCEPTION REALLY MAKE ALL THOSE ALTERATIONS TO HER WORLD?
OH, GOODNESS NO.
I WAS UNDER THE IMPRESSION THAT THE CONCEPTION ALWAYS FULFILLS ITS BARGAINS.
OH, THE CONCEPTION ALWAYS DOES.
BUT I DON'T.
ENOUGH OF YOUR USELESS CHATTER. I WAS PROMISED A HOUSE!
DOES EITHER OF YOU SEE A HOUSE ANYWHERE?
BECAUSE I DON'T!
AND I HAVE NOT WAITED FOR SEVEN YEARS ONLY TO BE FOILED YET AGAIN!
REALLY, SIR. THIS DISPLAY DOES NO ONE ANY GOOD, AND SOME IN THE CONCEPTION MIGHT TAKE OFFENSE.

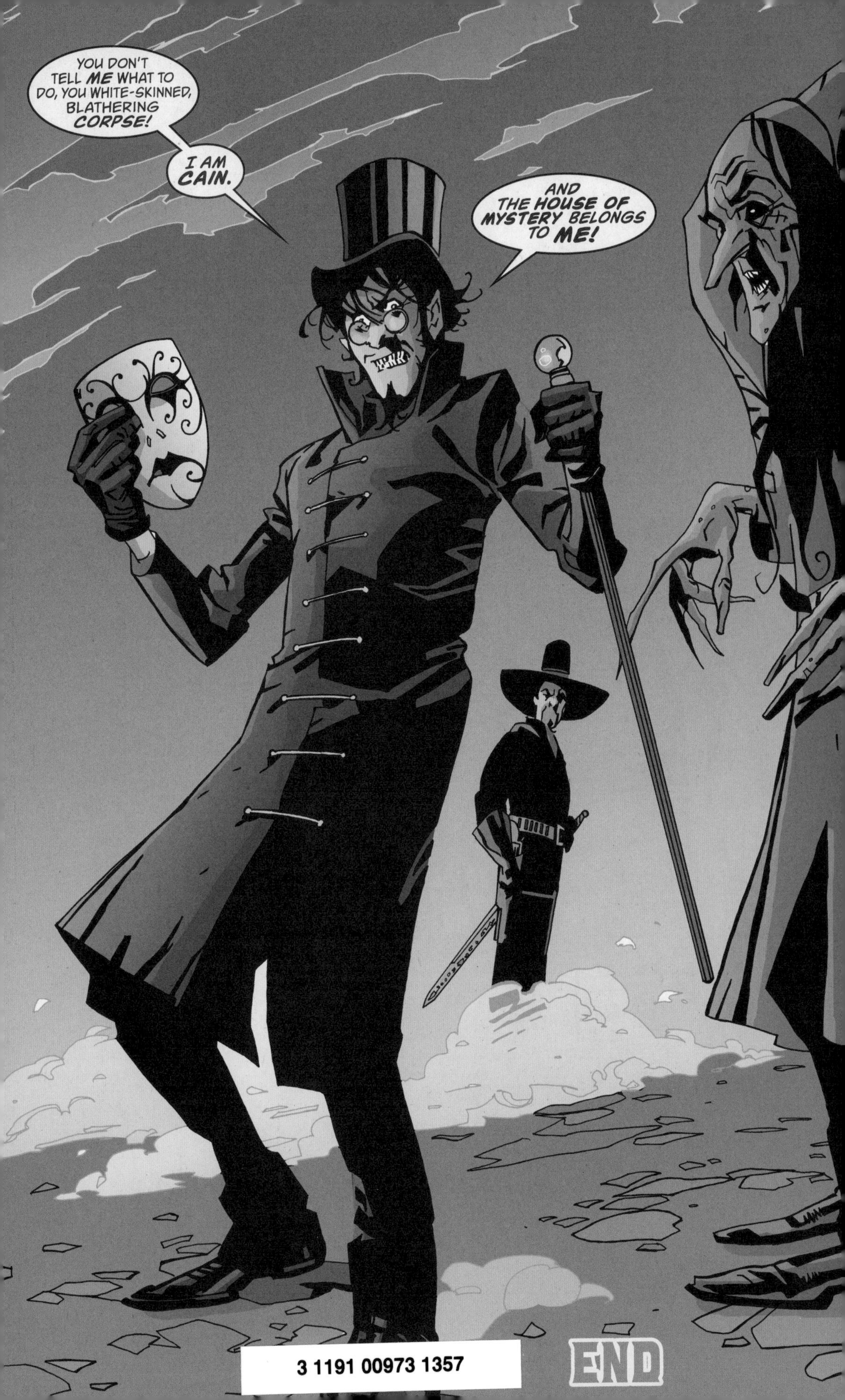
YOU DON'T TELL ME WHAT TO DO, YOU WHITE-SKINNED, BLATHERING CORPSE!
I AM CAIN.
AND THE HOUSE OF MYSTERY BELONGS TO ME!
END

The Space Before

Character sketches by Luca Rossi

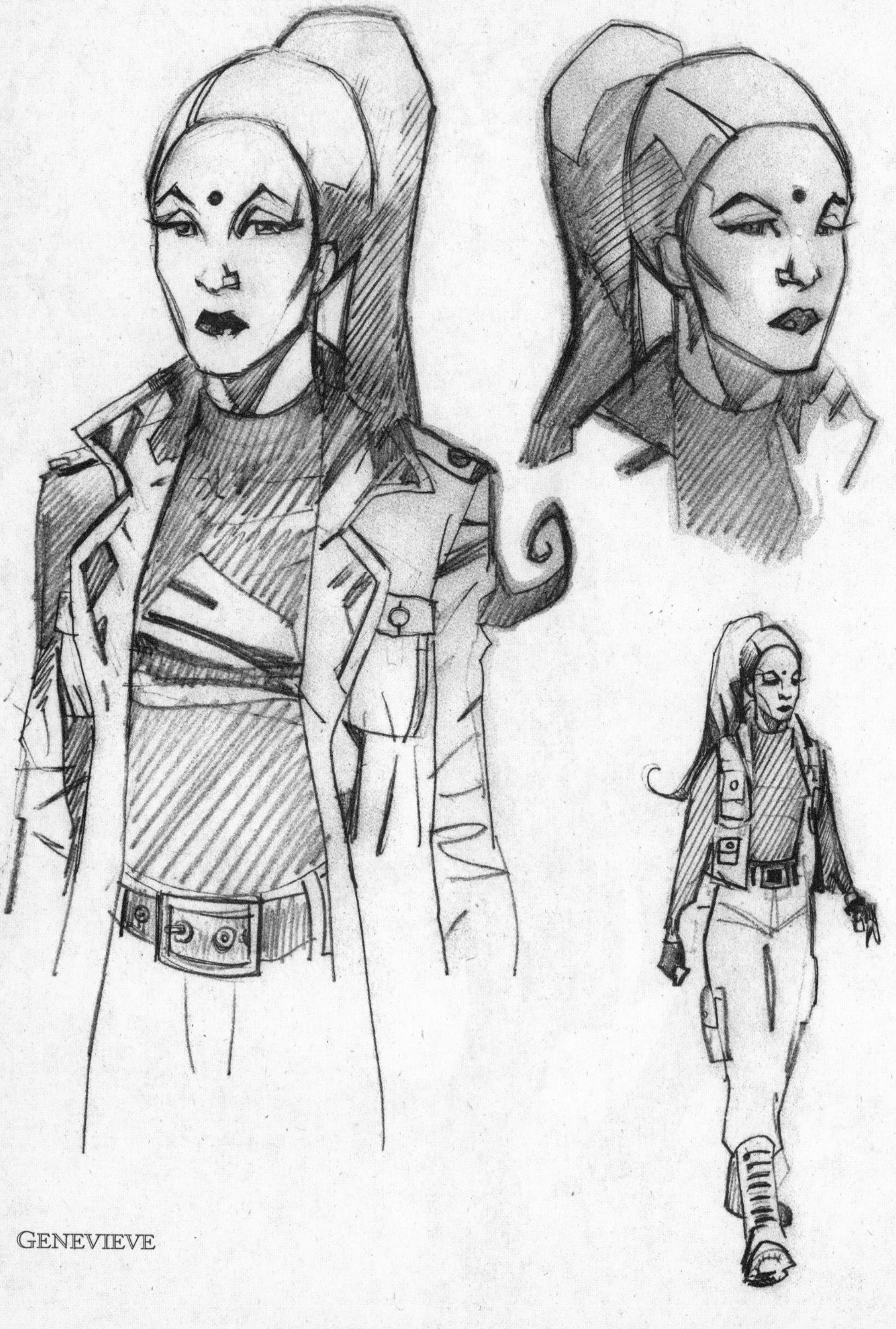

Genevieve

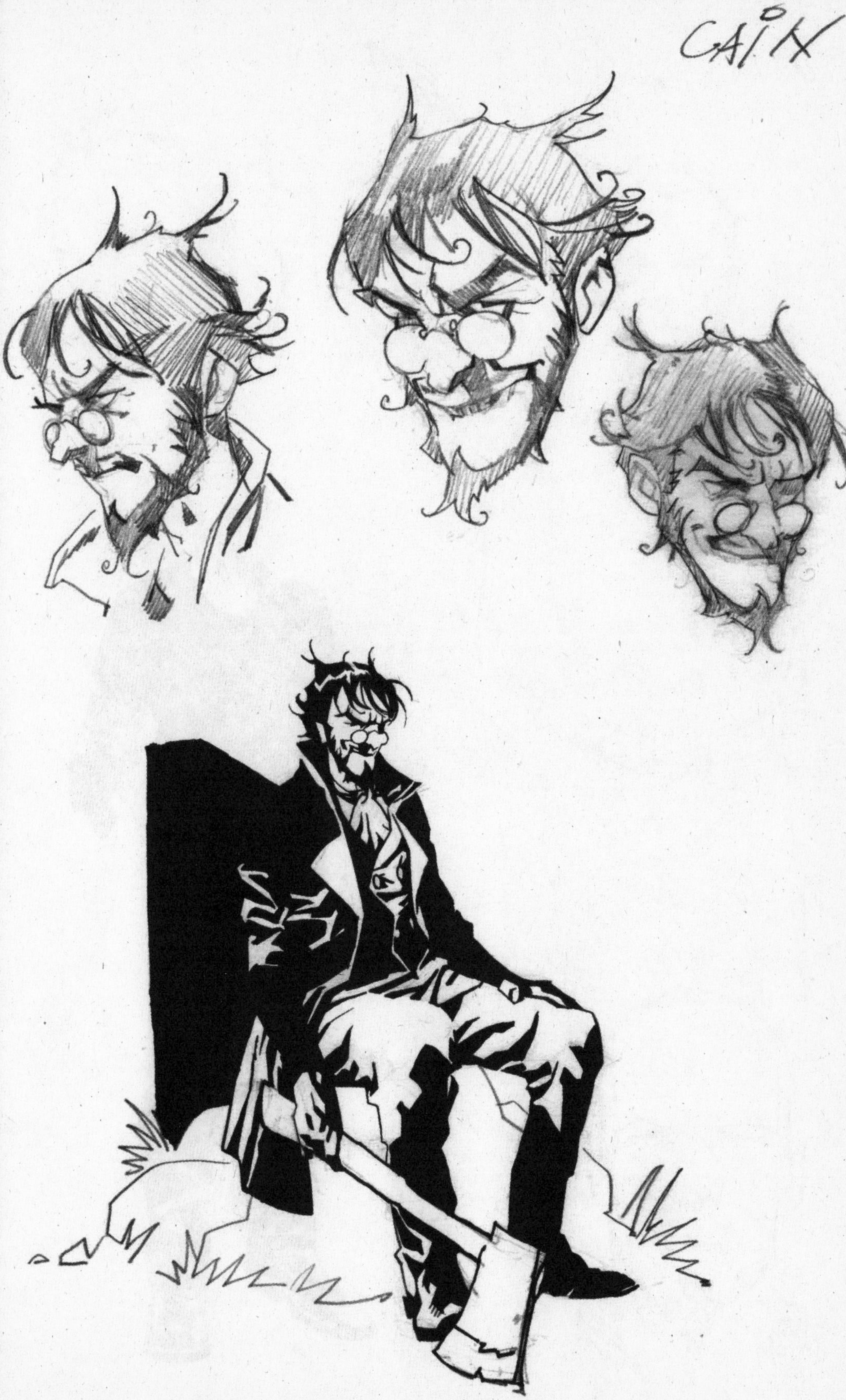
CAIN

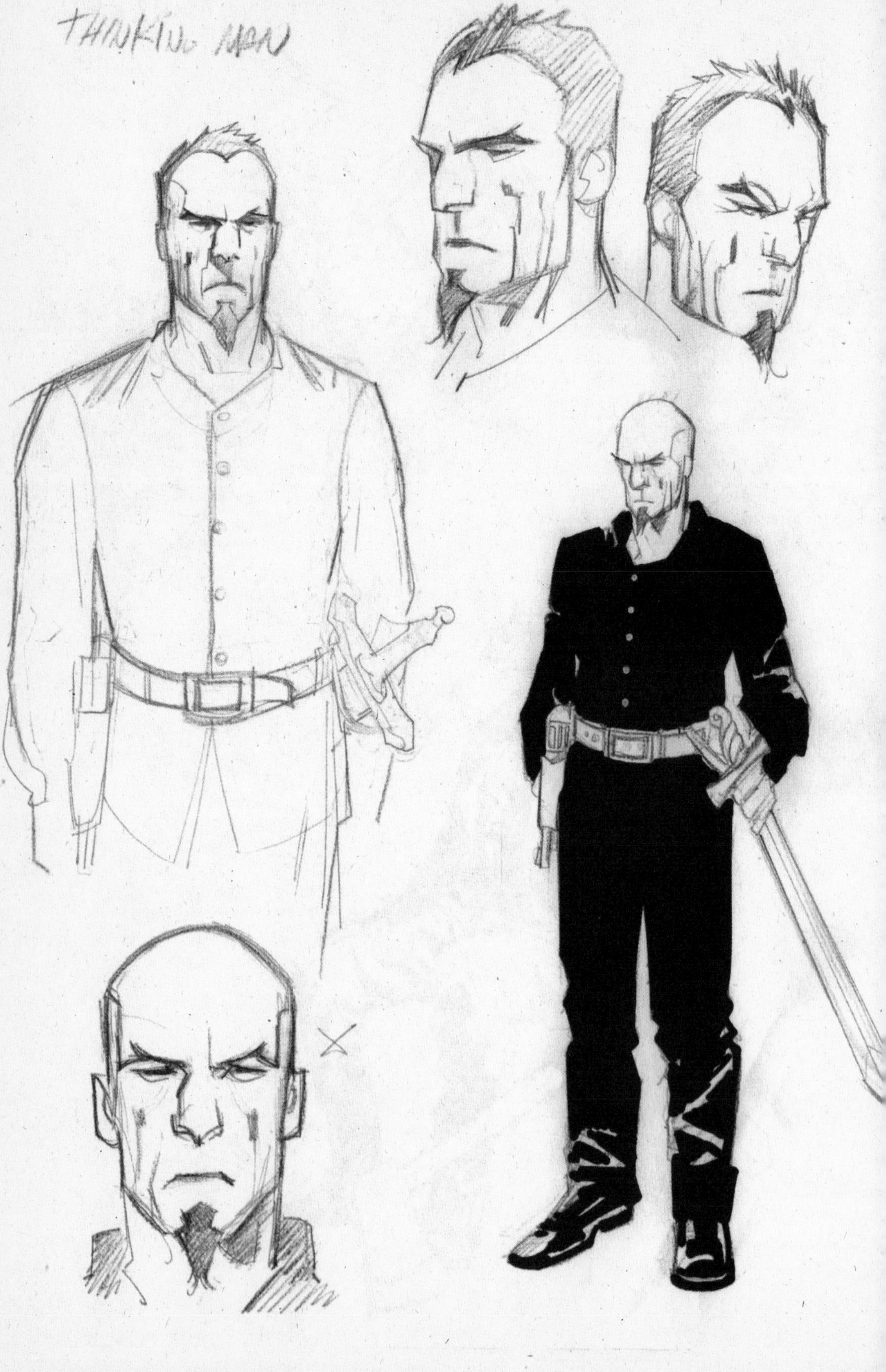
THINKING MAN

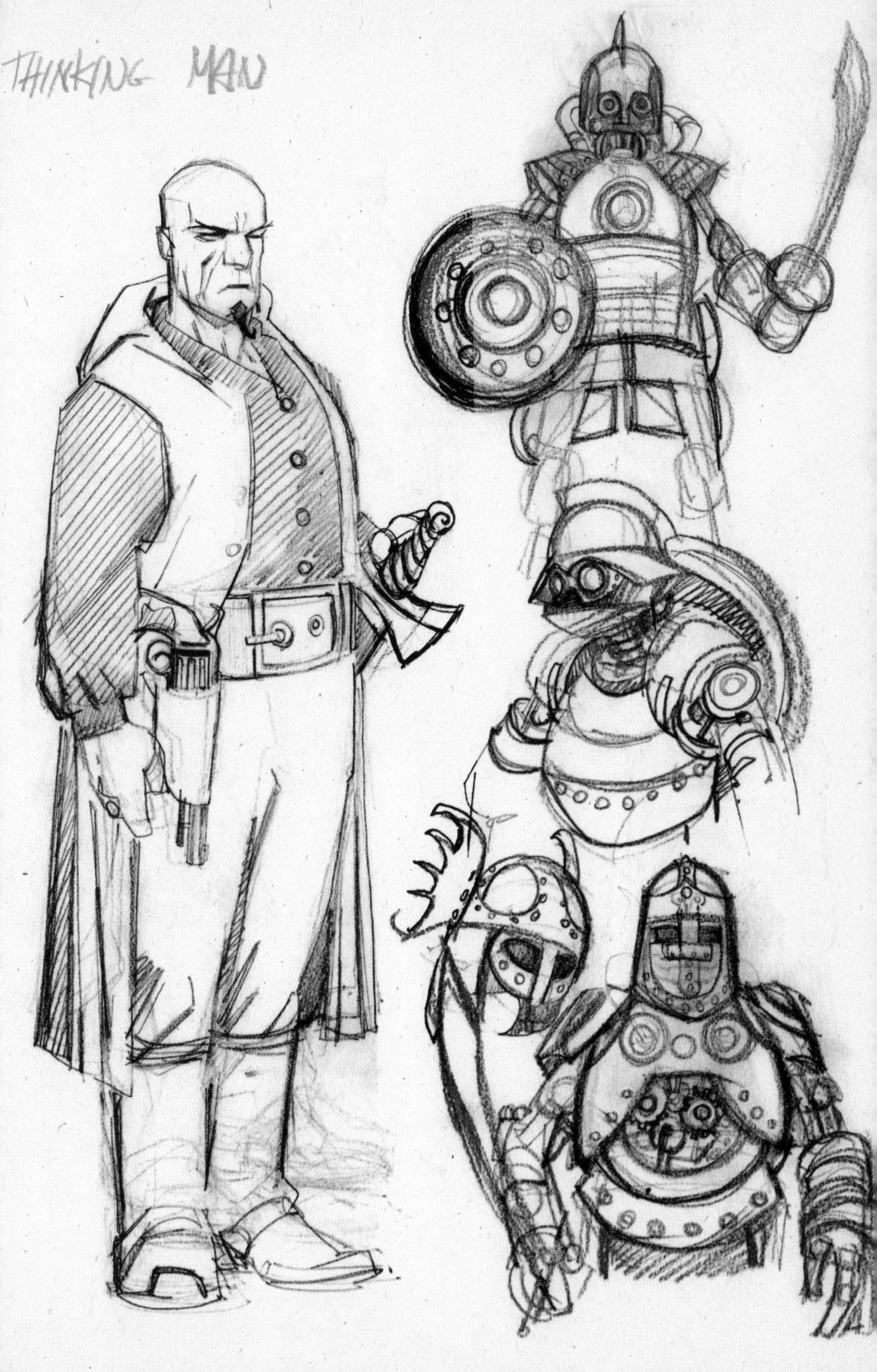
THINKING MAN

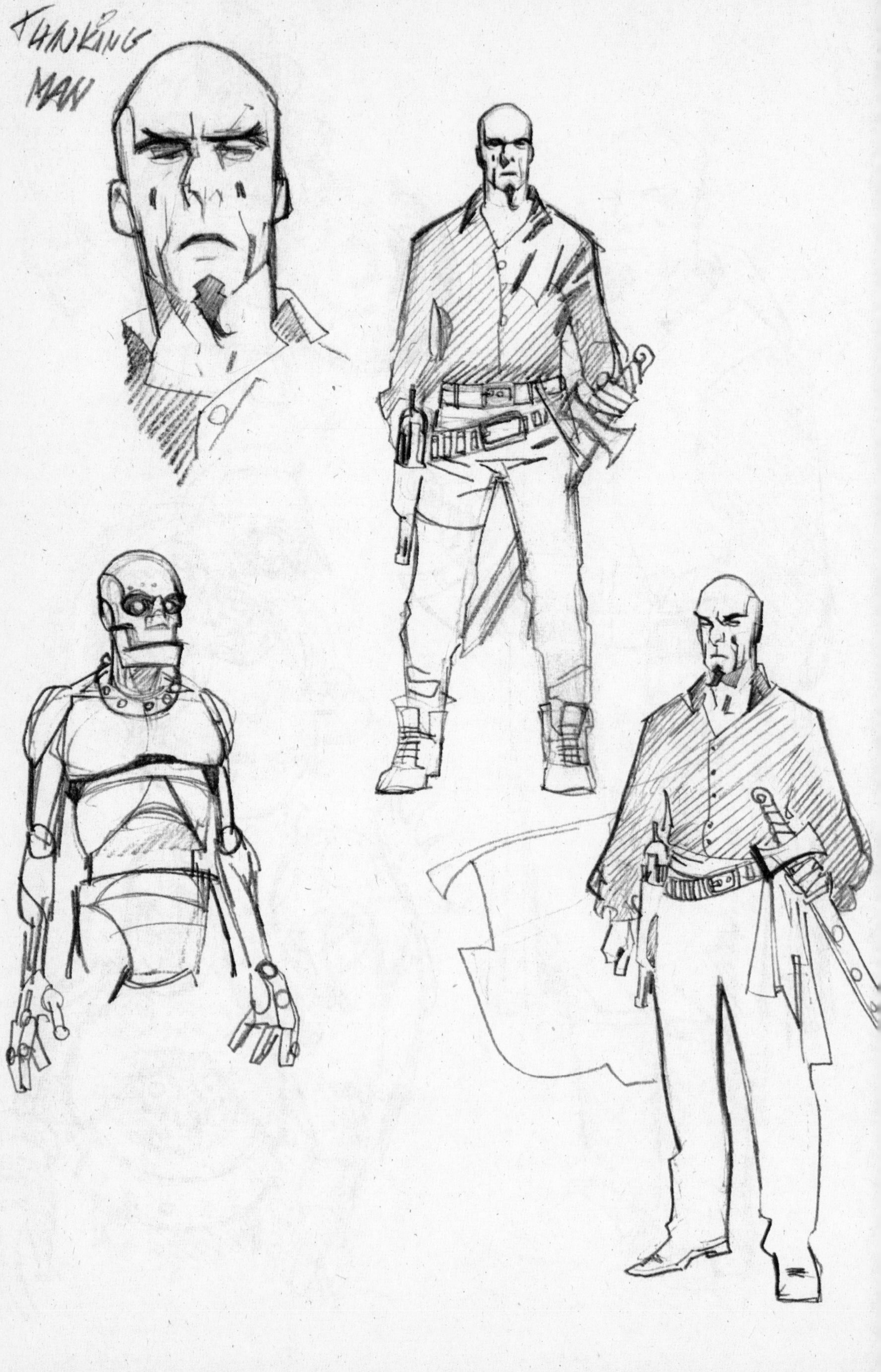
THINKING MAN

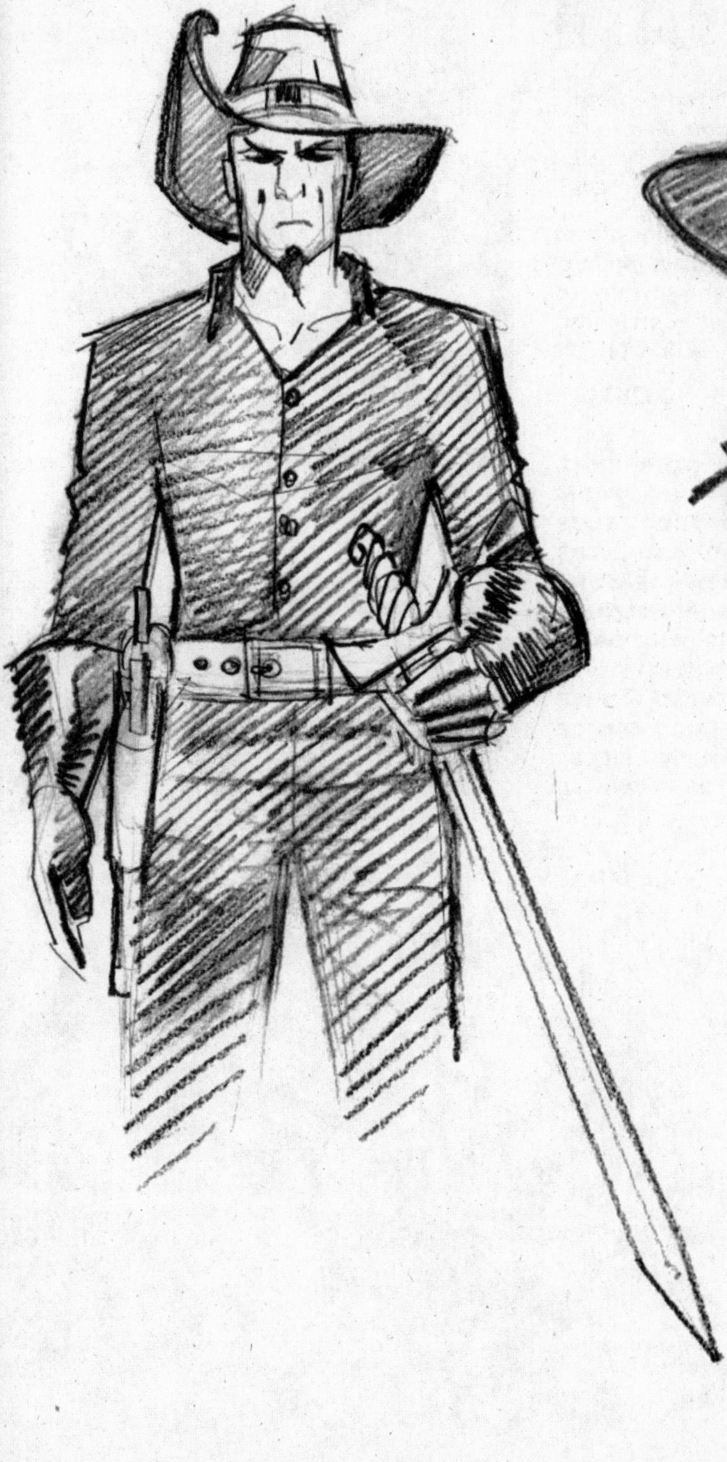
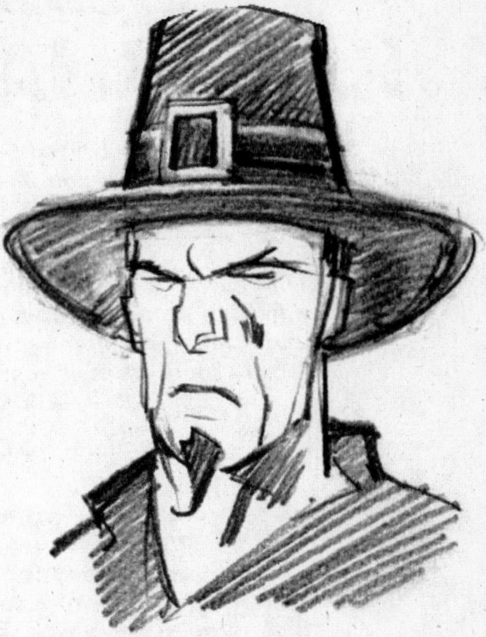

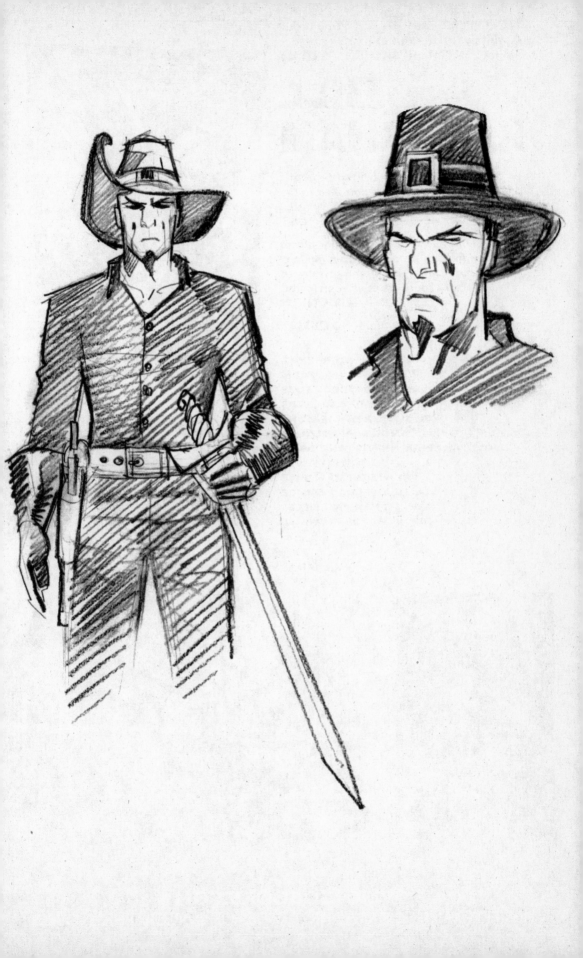

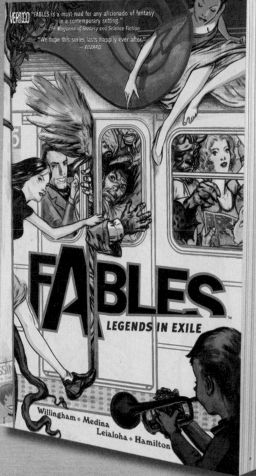